Longman

Guardian NEW WORDS

*

Edited by

SIMON MORT

Longman Group UK Limited,
Longman House, Burnt Mill, Harlow,
Essex CM20 2JE, England
and Associated Companies throughout the world

British Library Cataloguing in Publication Data

Longman Guardian new words.
1. English language—Dictionaries
I. Mort, Simon
423 PE1625

ISBN 0-582-89327-5

Set in Hell Digiset Times New Roman
Printed in Great Britain
by J. W. Arrowsmith Ltd., Bristol

INTRODUCTION

OF THE VARIOUS TRENDS in publishing in the last decade and a half, one of the most pronounced has been an increasing interest in publications on words. As the competition in the dictionary market has become keener, so the number and variety of publications in related fields has burgeoned. Etymology, confusion of similar words, usage, borrowing of words, technical vocabulary, teenage vocabulary, sporting vocabulary, and ethnic patois have all generated prolific publications, scholarly and popular.

So, what is the point of another book on the subject? Of the plethora of works produced by the Partridges, the Quirks, the Vallinses, the Howards, the Greens, the Cottles, the Hudsons, the Rooms, the Aitchisons and the rest, no single document produces a time-capsule of a year's words. Addenda to general dictionaries do so to a degree, but they normally cover more than a single year, reflecting the irregular intervals at which dictionaries are revised, and the entries are limited perforce to simple definitions.

This book has three purposes. Firstly, it seeks to entertain. We trust that it will generate discussion. It will probably give rise to surprise or astonishment. We have no doubt that it will occasion argument and, sometimes, strong disagreement. Secondly, we hope that it will constitute a work of record, so that, in some years from now, the patterns, logic, and fashion of word formation of 1986 may be found conveniently packaged for reference. (And naturally this linguistic record also forms an indirect historical record of events and trends during the year.) Thirdly - and of more immediate relevance - we see the book as a companion for someone reading a newspaper and encountering unfamiliar vocabulary, not covered by a general dictionary.

Of course, this has had its problems, since the task was virtually without precedent. As in Samuel Johnson's greater undertaking, 'choice was to be made out of boundless variety, without any established principle of selection; adulterations were to be detected, without a settled test of purity'.

The most obvious illustrations of the uncertainties which we faced were those of time, of durability, and of newness. Broadly, this is a book of 1986. However, the year has had to be adapted somewhat in order to permit publication by Christmas; so traces of autumn 1985 (and very occasionally of earlier times) may be found lurking on some pages. There may even be a case for a *lexicographical year* (defined: a year artificially contrived to permit a lexicographical work to feature in the Christmas market; analogous with *financial year, academic year,* etc). Yet even when scrutiny of sources is limited in this way, a further complication arises with technical words. A decade or two may elapse between invention of a term and its emergence from the laboratory or workshop into the public glare of a national or local newspaper. For example, the wealth of computer vocabulary which appeared in the principal dictionaries in the later 1960s (and is now in extremely common usage) was largely coined towards the end of the 1940s. We have used the criterion that a term novel to the average layman – itself a woefully nebulous concept – deserves inclusion.

On the matter of durability, this book can be judged only by the reader of the 1990s. Of course, some words are probably nonce. Some will just be the fashion of a particular season or a particular phase of topicality. Others, perhaps imaginative inventions of *Private Eye,* may catch the public attention and take up permanent residence in the language. Many will undoubtedly achieve the respectability of a place in the *Longman Dictionary of the English Language* and its peers.

Our thinking in the face of these dilemmas is best explained by illustrations. For example, we have avoided tedious lists of feminisms which demonstrate no novelty and could be applied to almost any noun and a number of adjectives, such as a description of Sarah Ferguson as 'a *directrice* of a West End graphic arts company' or the *-woman* suffix (as in *roadswoman*). We have also omitted the virtually limitless sexual neutralizations: *barperson, bookperson, craftsperson, houseperson, superperson.* The *Private Eye* suffix *-ette* – normally jocular, but being taken increasingly seriously – (as in the 11 July 1986 edition a *pupilette*) seemed an unnecessary entry. There are several other suffixes whereby nouns are coined from verbs and adjectives are derived from nouns. These have mostly been omitted likewise and only included by significant exception: *-style, -esque,* and *-ee* produced the most examples of this kind of formation. *Private Eye,* master of the nonce, again demonstrates this kind of innovation ('Street of Shame', 2 May 1986): 'He is none other than George G Ale, Thatcher-lover extraordinaire, life-long Tory and £100,000 *redundee* from the Daily Getsworse.' On the same basis we tried to resist the over-versatile *-gate* ending (the *Watergate* analogy), as in *Brittangate* (in reference to Leon Brittan), but we were overwhelmed by *Westlandgate* citations and it has earned its place. *Yuppiegate* has gone in just for fun. The *non-* prefix, as in *non-handicap* (of racing) and *non-weapon* (as in certain weapon-systems being so categorized for purposes of international bargaining), was also judged unsuitable.

This is a book of words and, although short phrases are considered as words for lexicographical purposes, there is no place for idiomatic clauses, however fashionable or however durable they may seem. Such expressions as *There you go* have therefore been eschewed. This vogue saying was the subject of a slightly clumsy series of letters in *The Times*, attempting to trace its origins. Strangely, the many possibilities explored did not include Dublin English, aficionados of which will have been familiar with the saying for many years.

Some types of candidate for inclusion have been considered more critically. Regionalisms (such as *youse*) which happened to crop up in a review of someone's memoirs did not seem to deserve inclusion; nor did whimsical and trendy pronunciations, although they may have been dignified by print, such as *seeyer* (= see you), *meeja* (= media) and its variants *meejah* and *meeja.*

Words which made their debut some time ago, but which have been dormant in the intervening period, produced particular problems. *Chunnel* has made occasional appearances since the 1920s and although there have been quite long periods when it was unseen, the pattern only reflects the waves of enthusiasm for the project. *Villagization*, however, although an old word, has been revived in a very particular sense relevant to government policy in Ethiopia. *Ultra-orthodox* was noted in 1877 (in a noun formation), but it related to first-century practices and the 1986 revival of the term is an indication of its topicality in Israel (in the form of objections to public posters showing women in swimwear). Some familiar words seem to have developed a specific new sense. The metaphorical use of *banana skin* is amply documented in newsprint and fiction since the turn of the century, but the sometimes inept defensive tactics of the present government have given it a specific new meaning. This is sufficiently frequently used to give it a place in these pages.

Several expressions are shown to have been current in North America for some years and to have been introduced recently to the British Isles. This traffic is far from new. In the earlier part of the century the eminence of Britain in world affairs and in literature meant that more words travelled westwards. Since the Second World War, US films and TV programmes, coupled with American propensity for Old World travel, have ensured that more words followed *teenager* and *commuter* in the opposite direction. This has been particularly true in fields of technology and of management techniques in which the United States have been pre-eminent. Selection of American words has therefore produced special problems. We have endeavoured to choose words which seem to have come to live comfortably in British writing and which, on the whole, no longer seem incongruous or alien. Sometimes they are very specialized or esoteric words but they serve a purpose which no existing British English term can manage. Sometimes it has been felt helpful to quote American newspapers to provide the best illustrations of these uses, but in every case they are words which are catching on here.

Some terms, although recently prominent, are so directly related to a particular event or an identifiable vogue before 1986 that they have been left out: *AIDS*, *break-dancing*, *dioxin*, *dungeons and dragons*, *in vitro* (medically commonplace but brought to public attention by the Warnock report in 1984), *massaging* (of statistics), *mole* (popularized by the televising of John le Carré's novel *Tinker, Tailor, Soldier, Spy*), *rate-cap*, *sell-off*, *SERPS*, *SDI* (and its crassly inaccurate popularization *star wars*).

We have frequently gambled on the potential durability of nonce words, but exceptional uses of straightforward words have been left out, however notorious they may have been. So there is no place for *undue* as a euphemism. Kenneth Baker caused speculation bordering on panic by suggesting after Chernobyl that there was no cause for *undue* alarm. *Flaky* (or *flakey*), used by President Reagan of Colonel Gadaffi in January 1986, survives because it stimulated a short vogue for the word.

We disagreed for some time about *Rambo*. The film of that name on general release in 1985 gave rise to a great deal of vocabulary. However, it is still a virile source of new words and so *Ramboesque* and *Ramboism* have been shown to illustrate this.

The style and structure of the book seek to combine readability with ease of reference, with entries typically offering a three-part structure of definition, quotation, and commentary.

Each entry begins with a formal definition. While these have been made as accurate and informative as possible, here again the newness of our material sometimes poses particular difficulties. The meaning of a word is developed by a consensus of users over a period of time, but some words which have been only briefly or infrequently in use can be defined only in provisional terms. It is quite possible that their accepted meaning will change in the course of time.

In most cases, a definition is followed by at least one quotation. These have been selected from the Longman citations database not only as evidence of the use of the word, but to show the kind of context in which it appears, and often to add some useful or amusing extra information about it.

Where it seems useful, we have added a commentary to amplify the definition and provide background and comparison. These observations (prefixed by the symbol ►) are inevitably a bit subjective. Any comment on a subject as personal and thus as emotive as language, and the events and situations which it mirrors, must be. Sometimes points are made which seem obvious to every 1986 reader, such as the occupation of pop-singers or the specialization of athletes or the office held by government ministers. These have been included for the benefit of readers in years to come, bearing in mind the role of the book as a historical document.

Etymologies are included only where they are not obvious. Showing them automatically every time for such entries as simple blends would be superfluous and irritating to the browsing reader.

Some trends have been detected. The semantic developments of any period will show some. The *mini-* prefix which was fashionable in the more austere period of the first Wilson government is virtually absent from the 1986 crop. Instead, we are almost drowned in *mega-* and *super-* combinations. The European Community's vocabulary is well represented. Analysts of the government's policy will be pleased to see medical terminology and military language almost equally demonstrated. Apart from computers and related technology, the field to have yielded most words is the protection of the environment. Certain bizarre and unusual preponderances have arisen, such as a wealth of obscure and exotic fruits which have recently appeared in shops.

As is always the case, particular events have generated collections of words. Chernobyl and events in South Africa have initiated wordage proportionate to the interest which they have prompted. The City is represented topically by the *Big Bang* and a whole dynasty of its progeny. The continuing proliferation of communications technology yields a good crop, sometimes boring, sometimes amusing, and frequently inelegant, but profuse nevertheless.

Some cross-references are an inescapable and fascinating part of the semantic jigsaw. Cross-references to other entries in the book are shown in SMALL CAPITALS. References to other words which are of interest qua words are shown in *italics.*

In casting our net for sources we have endeavoured to reflect general usage. Daily, weekly, and periodic journals have been examined along with semi-technical publications which may be considered a bridge between esoteric specialist argots and general commonplace use. Those cited are:

Best of Health
Blitz
Bookseller
Business
Business Success
Cardigan & Tivy-Side Advertiser
City Limits
Company
Cosmopolitan
Daily Express
Daily Mail
Daily Mirror
Daily Telegraph
Datalink
Eastern Daily Press
Economist
English Today
Financial Times
Glasgow Herald
Green Cuisine
Guardian
Hampstead and Highgate Express
Harlow Extra
Here's Health
Herts & Essex Observer
Hitchin Express
i-D
Illustrated London News
Inter City
International Herald Tribune
Investors Chronicle
Listener
Living
Majorcan Daily Bulletin
Marxism Today
Modern Railways
Nature
New Health
New Internationalist
New Scientist
New Socialist
New Society
New Statesman
New York Times
News of the World
Newsweek
North Herts Mirror on Sunday
Observer
Options
Over 21
Oxford Star
Oxford Times
Personal Computer World
Practical Computing
Private Eye
Publishers Weekly
Punch
Saffron Walden Weekly News
Scientific American
Scotsman
She
Spare Rib
Spectator
Star
Sun
Sunday Express
Sunday Telegraph
Sunday Times
Taste
TES
Time
The Times
TLS
Today
UK Press Gazette
USA Today
Which
Which Computer
Woman
Woman's Own
Woman's World

In a work of semi-anthology there must be many bouquets for assistance. Those who gave help as providers of citations, expert comments, and validation are too numerous to make it feasible to list them. However, special thanks must go to Vernon Porter for continuing his computer-related explanations well into the night and Lieutenant-Colonel Nigel Williams for assiduous help by correspondence on military affairs.

Many of our earlier ideas ended up in culs-de-sac. Some of the dead ends were disguised in such exhaustive and helpful explanations that it greatly eased the disappointment. Ten out of ten go to the chartered surveyor who substantiated his distressing claim about the word *lotting* (defined: the division of a large estate into lots for resale), 'I have come across the term which is in general use and has been used by me for at least 32 years, so I can hardly describe it as new' with an informative and entertaining essay on the subject. Nought out of ten goes to the publisher who, asked to comment on two words well within his field of expertise, replied 'I am a broken reed on both these', giving instead a hype for his forthcoming autobiography, which we forbear to reproduce here.

Particular thanks go to Nikolai Dejevsky for his courteous but firm discipline and loyal support. His eye on the calendar reminded us that while language is dynamic, publication timetables do not wait for its development.

The whole project would have foundered hopelessly without the wit and encyclopaedic knowledge of Brian O'Kill, of the Longman Dictionaries and Reference Division. His enthusiasm, and the work of his colleagues Heather Gay, Elizabeth Walter, and Katherine Seed, have ensured that we overcame various hazards along the way and avoided the temptations of being distracted into an unbalanced and unrepresentative approach.

Simon Mort

Guardian Business Services Ltd
(a subsidiary company of the Guardian
and Manchester Evening News plc)

adaptive suspension vehicle *noun* (*abbreviation* **ASV**) a walking robotic vehicle designed to carry sensitive devices over rough ground and equipped with radar, lasers, computers, etc which coordinate movement, read commands, and relay information

> The most impressive piece of hardware at the International Conference on Advanced Robotics in Tokyo last week was a walking robot. It is known as the adaptive suspension vehicle (ASV) and was developed with $5 million from the Defence Advanced Research Project Agency in the US. - *New Scientist*, 26 Sept. 1985

► This has particular value in a military context where the terrain may be hazardous through enemy fire or mines.
It is part of a tradition of robotic vehicles which has been developed since the late 1960s (largely prompted by the revival of Irish disorders) to spare endangering men unnecessarily.

---

adaptogen *noun* any of a group of substances (eg ginseng and royal jelly) that are used as tonics and natural remedies to revitalize the body

> Health and beauty expert Leslie Kenton ... claims - and her views are supported by researchers such as Soviet scientist I.I. Brekhman ... that adaptogens such as Royal Jelly are rich in 'structural information' in that they possess a 'high-quality health-supporting energy' which cannot be measured in chemical terms alone. - *Guardian*, 26 March 1986

---

advertorial *noun* a newspaper feature which appears to be an editorial but which has been paid for by an advertiser (who has usually also supplied the material on which it is based)

> How well is the concept of advertorial established in the public's mind? ... There is no law to make periodicals flag the advertising. - *UK Press Gazette*, 2 June 1986

► These frequently occur in the trade or advertising press.
They may be written round a fluent press release on a new product, with little change to the original.
A specific form of the medium, relating to a foreign (or commonwealth) country and promotion of its companies, is the supplement which appears from time to time in broadsheet newspapers.

Aerobie *trademark* - used for a plastic ring, approximately the size of an LP, which is aerodynamically designed to travel a long way when thrown

> The Aerobie boasts a place in the *Guinness Book of Records* as the one man-made object thrown further than any other - 1,114 ft 6 in. - *New Health*, June 1986

► It is very much on the lines of the Frisbee, which was extremely popular in the early 1970s. However, it is distinguished from its antecedent not only by being larger. It incorporates a metal ring, is hollow like a polo-mint, and in cross-section has an aerodynamic shaping. Thus it travels further than a Frisbee. It retails at about £6.

---

aerospaceplane *noun* SPACE PLANE

> The US Congress has voted £425 million for research into a Mach 25 aerospaceplane ... capable of flying between New York and Tokyo in two hours. - *Airport*, April 1986

Africar *trademark* - used for a lightweight all-terrain motor vehicle which has a plywood chassis and bodywork and is designed for use in Africa

> With few alterations, Africars can become mini-buses, ambulances, jeeps, military vehicles, vans or pick-ups. - *Guardian*, 23 June 1986

► This unusual vehicle was developed by the British inventor Tony Howarth. Production in Britain is scheduled to start in Autumn 1986, and later in Australia and Bangladesh. Many versions of the basic vehicle are planned.

---

ageism *or* **agism** *noun* discrimination against a person on the grounds of age, especially of advanced age

> Mrs Ann Clwyd, the Labour MP for Cynon Valley, will introduce a backbench bill today against 'ageism'. The bill will seek to secure a guaranteed minimum retirement age for men and women of 60 years. It follows an attempt by the management of the Japanese company, Hitachi, in her constituency to secure early retirement for those aged 35 and over within their high technology factory. - *Guardian*, 21 Jan. 1986

> Agism is bad for men but worse for women. An older woman - unless she has made the top - is invisible. No longer desirable, she is expected to be even more deferential and servile. - *Guardian*, 13 May 1986

---

ageist *adjective* of or showing AGEISM

---

agricultural disarmament *noun* the dismantling of protectionist agricultural policies, such as subsidizing exports and allowing surpluses to accumulate

> The calls for agricultural disarmament are getting louder

– and better informed. The summiteers in Tokyo in May ... 'agreed that when there are surpluses, action is needed to redirect policies and adjust structures of agricultural production in the light of world demand'. – *Economist*, 21 June 1986

---

airbag *noun* a safety device in cars, consisting of a bag stored in the front part of the passenger compartment and designed to inflate automatically in the event of an impact, cushioning the occupants against injury

> Mercedes are introducing improvements to their impressive range of big 'S' class saloons and coupes. ... But if you want their new airbag safety device, now optional on all models, it will cost you another £955.60p. – *Daily Telegraph*, 19 March 1986

► Airbags have, in fact, been available since the early 1970s, but are still fitted to few cars. Research into car safety continues to focus on seatbelts.

---

airgate *noun* the part of an airport gate that links the aeroplane to the building

> So far, reaction to the hi-tech steel rectangle with the daffodil yellow 'arms' ('airgates' linking aeroplane to building) has been mixed. – *Financial Times*, 10 April 1986

---

airside *noun* the area of an airport beyond the passport control – compare LANDSIDE

> The terminal [at Heathrow] is designed to filter people through to the airside, where the main attractions are, as quickly as possible. – *Daily Telegraph*, 11 March 1986

Alpha man *noun* a fantasy male who is held to be superior to any ordinary male

> He is, of course, that well-known fantasy male, the Romantic Hero, or as psychologists refer to him, the Alpha Man. He is better, more attractive, more interesting, richer and more powerful than any ordinary man. Unfortunately, this paragon is met only through the pages of a romantic novel, and never in real life. The Alpha Man has had many incarnations over the years. He has been Mr Darcy in *Pride and Prejudice*, Mr Rochester in *Jane Eyre*, Rhett Butler in *Gone with the Wind*, and Max de Winter in *Rebecca*. – *Over 21*, April 1986

---

alpinodrome *noun* a place in which climbing contests are held on artificial cliffs

> For the traditionalists, the new climbers are circus acrobats, not mountaineers. ... So far, only the French Alpine Club has

> formally split with the new tendency, which is also in favour of pay-to-enter 'alpinodromes'. - *Economist*, 9 Aug. 1986

---

alternative therapist *noun* a practitioner in any of the alternative forms of medical treatment or therapy (eg osteopathy or IRIDOLOGY)

> The number of alternative therapists registered each year in the UK is increasing five times as fast as the number of doctors, according to the EEC's European health committee - *Family Circle*, 19 March 1986

Altracurium *trademark* - used for a muscle relaxant drug that has applications in a wide range of surgical procedures, especially those requiring controlled ventilation of the patient

> Strathclyde University's pharmacy department has won the Queen's Award for Technological Achievement for discovering a muscle relaxant which has helped more than three million people in 30 countries of the world. The research was carried out by professor John Stenlake, professor of pharmacy at the university and a team of post-graduate students over a period of 10 years. The university's patent was financed and developed by the Wellcome research laboratories at Beckenham in Kent, and the relaxant drug, Altracurium, introduced to the medical world in 1982. - *Glasgow Herald*, 21 April 1986

Ambisonics *noun* a system of broadcasting high-fidelity surround-sound that uses four loudspeakers to give the effect of sounds coming from spatially distinguishable sources

> Professor Peter Fellgett of Reading University has a special interest in recorded natural sound. He is co-inventor of the Ambisonics surround-sound system, which many engineers believe is the best way to record and reproduce natural sound. - *New Scientist*, 19 Dec. 1985

---

animal-free *adjective* containing or using no product derived from animals

> Being forced into tight mental corners thinking up explanations of her animal-free way of life was certainly the case for Kath Clements, who has written a highly personal interpretation in Why Vegan (GMP Publishers, £2.95). - *Green Cuisine*, Spring 1986

► Vegans, who favour totally animal-free diets, are vegetarians who take the discipline to extreme lengths. They avoid any food which has been produced even as an indirect result of stockbreeding, for example cows' milk (because of its connection with the slaughter of bull calves and bullocks). Other items avoided by those following an animal-free way of life include honey, jellies and other foods made with gelatine, leather goods, certain soaps containing animal fats, and any toiletries or cosmetics which are tested on animals.

---

animalist *noun* someone who is concerned with animal rights

> A movement is coalescing as the sheer growth of vegetarianism and the militancy of its young supporters rocks the meat industry. Devout animalist Stephen Pope sees its insularity from the rest of left politics as the reason for its success. - *New Socialist*, July 1985

► This new sense has nothing to do with the philosophy of animalism. The traditions of interest in animal affairs which have been concerned with mistreatment of domestic pets and with protest against field sports are well established. They trace their origins back to the early decades of the century and periodically enjoy vogue revivals.
The animal rights interest which has emerged in recent years takes the matter further by wishing to extend to animals various human rights.

---

animatronics *noun* a branch of theatre and film technology that combines the techniques of traditional puppetry with modern electronics to create special effects in the field of animation

> An object like a giant Easter egg appears high at the centre of the stage and opens to reveal a three-dimensional, moving image of Olivier's face. ... The image relies on an established technology called Animatronics. - *New Scientist*, 17 April 1986

► Blend of *anima*tion and elec*tronics*.
The technique has been particularly important in puppetry, especially with the use of marionettes which depend on electrical effects to make them less wooden and stilted.

---

anti-chic *noun* the concept of dressing and grooming oneself with deliberate disregard for smartness or fashion

> Offstage, she almost makes a feature of anti-chic, she wears no make-up and prefers comfortable old clothes, probably a reaction to the habitual dressing up of an actor's life. - *Living*, March 1986

► Every period has a group which chooses to counter smart haute couture through lack of money, absence of desire to compete, or a wish to outrage. Sometimes it is motivated by a desire to emphasize practicality as opposed to elegance.
The Angry Young Men of the late 1950s with their uniform of beards and heavy shapeless jerseys dressed in such a style. The sloppy-joe, a girls' loose jumper or cardigan of recent years, is in the same tradition. It is now taken to extreme lengths involving bicycle chains and other mechanical artefacts not hitherto associated with dress.

---

anti-chub *adjective* of weight control; fat-reducing

> The real problem is that, scientifically, we are still in the dark

> ages of weight control. And the reason is that anti-chub science has never been given the same political priority as anti-missile science. – *New Scientist*, 10 Oct. 1985

► This is a jocular term, probably nonce, which represents the current fashion for reducing weight. The serious medical effects of being overweight have been recognized and given much publicity during the last decade and a half. The passion for losing weight takes the form of slimming, jogging, aerobics, and JARMING. Those who pursue such a philosophy may wish to climb onto the BRANWAGON.

---

anti-life *adjective* not PRO-LIFE

Anton Piller application *noun* a legal application, (eg for an order to search premises for documents) of which the defendants are not notified if the judge considers that there is reason to believe that they might tamper with evidence

> Lawyers instructed to sue the Minister of Law and Order, Mr Louis Le Grange ... mounted what is known in legal circles as an 'Anton Piller' application in their search for further evidence. – *Guardian*, 9 Jan. 1986

► The judgment in *Anton Piller v Manufacturing Processes and others* is, in fact, a decade old. It was handed down by three Law Lords, including Lord Denning.
Anton Piller were a German firm which wanted to bring a copyright action against their London agents. They heard that documents vital to the case were likely to disappear, conveniently to Piller's antagonists. Counsel for Anton Piller made a secret application to the court to allow his client to search the premises.
The approach infringed several principles, eg that which provides that the defendants have the right to be heard before prejudicial action is taken against them. However, the Law Lords allowed these exceptional steps on the overriding need for justice to be done.
Its current prominence is the result of its invocation by South African courts.

---

aquatube *noun* a long tubular water slide which bends and twists, eventually depositing the user in a pool

> The Harlow Pool ... is expected to be as popular as ever, especially with the added attraction of ... two giant aquatubes, which were opened in March. ... Aquatubes or slides have been popular on the Continent for several years, but have only recently been introduced in British pools. – *Herts & Essex Observer*, 24 July 1986

---

arb *noun, informal* an arbitrage(u)r; someone who engages in the near-simultaneous purchase and sale of the same or equivalent security in different markets in order to profit from price discrepancies

> Stock index contracts due to expire at the end of June ...

> suddenly looked 'cheap' against their equivalent options contracts traded on the stock exchange, which were several points higher. So the 'arbs' (as they are commonly known) switched out of the options into the futures. - *Investors Chronicle*, 13 June 1986

► The concept of arbitrageur, while not new, is currently fashionable because of the rash of takeovers. As an extension of their usual practices, arbitrageurs now buy large blocks of shares in companies under takeover. They then resell these - after a suitably suspenseful interval - to the highest bidder.

Their interest is purely financial and selfish. An anecdote has it that a banker needing a heart-transplant requested: 'Give me an arbitrageur's heart. It will never have been used.'

---

architecture *noun* the design and specification of the physical arrangement and interconnections of the various parts of a microprocessor and the computer system it controls

> Considering the dazzling speed of change in their industry, computer manufacturers can be remarkably conservative about some aspects of their business. ... Most have long tended to be cautious about altering the architecture, or set of basic designs, at the heart of the their machines. However, Hewlett-Packard ... has broken boldly with tradition by announcing that it is switching over to a radically new type of architecture which will be used as the basis for virtually its entire product range in future. - *Financial Times*, 26 Feb. 1986

---

architecture study *noun* a theoretical research study of EUROPEAN ARCHITECTURE

> Britain secured the first plum contracts for international picking from America's multi-billion-dollar Strategic Defence Initiative yesterday. Though small at $14,300,000 (£9,530,000) compared with American research efforts Mr George Younger, Defence Secretary, called them 'significant.' A so-called 'architecture study' contract of $10 million (£6,660,000) to examine defending Europe against intermediate and short-range missiles, bomber and cruise missiles, goes to the Ministry of Defence. - *Daily Telegraph*, 25 June 1986

Asian pear *noun* a juicy New Zealand pear which resembles a golden apple

> A fruit treat ... called the Asian pear is about to appear on the British market. According to Mr Brian Aitken, European manager of the New Zealand Apple and Pear Marketing Board, it is 'so moist and juicy you need to wear a wet suit to eat it'. - *Daily Telegraph*, 24 March 1986

Asian tiger mosquito *noun* any of a species (*Aedes albopictus*) of mosquitoes that have a vicious bite and can transmit serious viral infections to humans

> A dangerous breed of mosquito capable of causing paralysis, brain damage and death has invaded the United States to the growing alarm of public health authorities. The Asian tiger mosquito, *Aedes albopictus*, has spread from its original habitat in northern Japan and the tropical zones of south east Asia to Latin America, the Caribbean and now the southern states of America. - *Daily Telegraph*, 23 June 1986

► This mosquito is thought to have carried out its migration by way of cargoes of used tyres.
It causes inconvenience by its bites, which leave welts and result in itching. However, its serious dangers are from carrying viral diseases. It is a carrier of encephalitis, which is likely to paralyse the victim and may be fatal, and dengue fever.

A/S Level *noun* an examination for secondary schoolchildren in Britain, due to begin in 1989, which will be the equivalent of half an A Level and is designed to allow post-O-level pupils to study a wider range of subjects than at present

> It is envisaged that students will take two A levels and two A/S levels, preferably in contrasting areas, so that they study science and technology as well as arts subjects. - *The Times*, 7 July 1986

► The initials stand for Advanced Supplementary. It is intended that courses should begin in 1987 and that exams will be sat in 1989. The pattern should be 2 'A' Levels taken with 2 'A/S' Levels.
It is felt that this will encourage a breadth of study such as is the case in most continental and North American schools. To this end, combinations of technical and non-technical subjects will be recommended.

---

astrodome *noun* an indoor stadium with a translucent domed roof

> The designer, George Williamson, the Welshman who built the National Stadium at Cardiff Arms Park, has already put together astrodomes in Bahrain and places in the Far East. - *Guardian*, 5 Feb. 1986

► The first building of this type, the *Astrodome* in Houston, Texas, opened in 1965. An earlier sense of *astrodome*, dating from the 1940s, is 'a transparent dome in the upper surface of an aeroplane for making observations'.

ASV *noun* ADAPTIVE SUSPENSION VEHICLE

A-team *noun* a group of highly trained and resourceful people brought together to tackle a difficult assignment

> Mr Kinnock has persuaded colleagues that the burden of Labour's campaigning in the coming General Election must

be shared between himself, Mr Hattersley and an 'A-Team' of six leading front-benchers. – *Daily Telegraph*, 17 March 1986
The Conservative party is to go into the General Election with an 'A-team' of ministers ... who will share the burden of major campaign appearances with Mrs Thatcher. – *Daily Telegraph*, 26 Aug. 1986

► As the first letter of the alphabet, the *A* denotes superlative on the same lines as the vogue phrase *numero uno.*
The phrase probably originated in the sports sense of the best team (as opposed to the B-team). However, it has been popularized by the ITV (MCA) television series. This describes a group of Vietnam War heroes who have – needless to say (cf *Rambo*) – been wrongly convicted at a court martial and who break free to fight injustice.
Their principal attraction lies in their personification of all the more obvious fantasies with extreme success, enormous strength (BA Baracus), the impertinence of a comic (Murdock), and cool laid-back decision-making coupled with dressing up in improbable disguise (Col Smith). There are parallels in the series' appeal with the film *The Magnificent Seven*, which filled cinemas at the beginning of the 1960s.

-athon *or* **-thon** *suffix* a contest or feat of endurance, often one organized for charitable fund-raising

► This suffix, derived from *marathon*, was first used in the USA in the 1930s in *walkathon* and *talkathon.* Later words formed from it include *danceathon*, *telethon*, and *workathon.* As the citations show, it continues to produce bizarre and facetious words.

Bikeathon Television personalities ... awaiting the start in Hyde Park yesterday of the Bikeathon, a 20-mile cycle ride in aid of handicapped and underprivileged children. – *Daily Telegraph*, 9 June 1986
Duckathon Hundreds of plastic ducks will take part in a fund-raising charity 'Duckathon' in September. ... The ducks will be driven across the lake at the Lodge by a giant wind machine and each duck will be sponsored at a pound each, with six races during the afternoon. – *Saffron Walden Weekly News*, 5 June 1986
pedalathon 70,000-odd commuters ... wheel into work every day in London alone. ... Amid the early morning pedalathon, it is the ensemble which distinguishes the individual. – *Daily Telegraph*, 18 Aug. 1986
readathon The Puffin Readathon 4–11 October: A unique sponsored reading promotion in aid of the Malcolm Sargent Cancer Fund for Children. – *Bookseller*, 26 July 1986
Swimathon Hundreds of people are already preparing to take the plunge in the charity swimming marathon 'Swim for Essex'. ... Chief organiser Trevor Watson said 20 pools were being used ... for the Swimathon. – *Harlow Extra*, 9 Sept. 1986

---

atomic vapour laser isotope separation *noun* (*abbreviation* **AVLIS**) a technique for separating one isotope from a mixture (eg for the enrichment of uranium 235, the isotope used in nuclear reactors), in which a laser, tuned to a precise frequency, is used to knock an electron off atoms of the desired isotope, thus giving the atoms a positive charge and enabling them to be separated in an electric field

> The emergence of AVLIS, an effective separation and enrichment technique for one isotope, means, categorically, that it can in principle be used for any isotope. - *Guardian*, 11 July 1985

---

audience-friendly *adjective* see -FRIENDLY

---

autocrime *noun* theft of a motor car or its contents

> Last year, there were nearly 800,000 recorded instances of 'autocrime' ... in England and Wales, the Home Office tells me. Car crime and domestic burglary now account for about 40 per cent of crime against property and people. - *Daily Telegraph*, 20 Nov. 1985

► Such criminal activity has probably attracted more attention of late as the number of car-owners increases.
Strangely, however, there has been no increase in the number of convictions, which are roughly proportionate to the number of offences. During the last 10 years the number of convicted offenders in England and Wales hovered around the 37,000 mark per annum. The highest was 43,928 (1978) and in 1984 it fell to 31,120.
It is a continuing and prevalent form of offence as it is easy to execute without advance planning and in some people's views not so morally reprehensible as many other forms of theft which involve breaking into property.

AVLIS *noun* ATOMIC VAPOUR LASER ISOTOPE SEPARATION

Back Country Action *noun* the invasion of a nuclear testing site by anti-nuclear activists shortly before a test is to be conducted, with the intention of delaying that test and drawing public attention to it

> Autonomous groups, with the support of the American Peace Test, plan further site invasions - referred to as 'Back Country

Actions' – to delay and to dramatise the dangers of each of these future tests. – *New Statesman*, 11 July 1986

► This kind of protest, a parallel to the rather less dramatic lying down in front of bulldozers (literally and figuratively) in the case of motorway routes, is particularly popular at sea. The ecological organization Greenpeace has engaged in it in the Pacific ocean.
It probably owes its name to the back country areas of Nevada and so on where land testing is carried out in the USA. Thus the protest is in the back country of the Far West, as opposed to the White House, the Pentagon, and other urban targets.

---

back-in *noun* a POISON PILL that gives shareholders of a company threatened by takeover the right to sell their shares back to the company at a price agreed by its board – compare FLIP-OVER, FLIP-IN

Douglas V. Brown, [Wall Street investment bankers] Kidder Peabody's vice president ... explains: 'There are three basic versions of poison pill defences as they have evolved. There are various bells and whistles that can be added on but basically the three types include the 'flip-over' ... the 'flip-in' ... the 'back-in'. ... The two most prevalent are the flip-over and flip-in.' – *Daily Telegraph*, 4 Aug. 1986

---

backplane *noun* a connector system plugged into a computer to extend its capabilities (eg by connecting it to peripherals such as printers or extra memory units). For a microcomputer, a backplane usually consists of a printed circuit board into which other circuit boards can be plugged.

To the left of the power supply at the back of the machine is the back-plane databus. This consists of eight slots, six of which are of the two-socket kind capable of taking standard PC/XT cards and PC/AT cards, with their expanded address lines. – *Personal Computer World*, Feb. 1986

► It is the means whereby the circuit boards are connected. Its role is broadly that of a junction. It may crudely be described as the backbone of the system, and this indicates its vital importance.

---

bag lady *noun* a female vagrant, typically one who carries all her belongings in shopping bags

Katharine Hepburn turned out to get the Lifetime Achievement Award from the Council of Fashion Designers of America. ... Said Miss Hepburn: 'Imagine – that the original bag lady should get an award for the way she dresses.' – *Daily Mail*, 22 Jan. 1986

Half the 'bag ladies' and 37 per cent of homeless men are mentally ill. – *The Times*, 3 March 1986

This summer is not going to be a season for going brief or

> bra-less. That went out with the bag lady look with its shapeless tops and bottoms, in both fabric and flesh. – *Daily Telegraph*, 1 May 1986

► The term *bag lady*, originally a shorter form of *shopping bag lady*, has been known in American English since the late 1970s. Its introduction to the fringe of British English owes more to a vogue enthusiasm for quasi-sociological terms than to the concept itself being new.
Its transatlantic passage can first be seen through two novels (both published 1984). The Anglophile Alison Lurie (*Foreign Affairs*) describes the disappointed Chuck Mumpson, who is looking for his titled ancestors in Wiltshire, finding only a hermit 'with scraggy beard and long hair and a droopy straw hat like some old bag lady'. Martin Amis (*Money*) has John Self, who is half-American and half-English, discovering a hotel drinks cabinet. He believes that this 'must have started up in direct response to the many bagladies [sic; one word], bums and dipsoes who hang out in this part of town'.

---

balloon angioplasty *noun* a technique for treating blood vessels (especially coronary arteries) that have become blocked by cholesterol plaque, in which a tiny balloon manoeuvred to within the blockage is inflated and squeezes the plaque back into the walls of the vessel

> Balloon angioplasty is already routine in the US, and increasingly practised in Britain in hospitals such as Guy's and the National Heart in London, and university medical centres in Birmingham and Leeds. – *Guardian*, 30 May 1985

► The technique is proving to be an increasingly good way of treating angina. Although the procedure is very tricky and demands daring as well as skill, it is favoured by doctors and patients alike as it avoids the need for major heart surgery.

---

banana skin *noun* something that causes a humiliating accident or misadventure – used especially in political contexts

> Let's assume that the Tories get support consistent with their opinion-poll performance over the past eight months – around a third of the total vote. In this case, we may begin to see a pattern which, barring the banana-skin factor, could last for some time. – *Today*, 6 May 1986

> Senior politicians are nothing if not good presenters, and it is not until there is a really bad slip on a political banana-skin that we begin to realise how diffuse is the system for co-ordinating even the most major public policies. – *Listener*, 30 Jan. 1986

> The government has done nothing for unemployment, and has just skidded on Westland, Land Rover, Libya and Sunday trading: four banana skins in as many months. – *Economist*, 17 May 1986

► The surely rare, but undoubtedly spectacular, misadventure of a

pompous man slipping on a banana skin gave rise to figurative uses as early as 1907. P.G. Wodehouse used it in 1934.
These have all been general uses, however. Since the election of the second Thatcher government in 1983 a much more specific secondary sense has formed. The over-confidence of a large parliamentary majority and almost religious confidence in the principles on which the government was returned have produced some unhappy oversights.
As a result of careless handling - the image of the pompous man not noticing the banana skin is valid - one embarrassment after another has flawed the government's record. The Westland affair, the abolition of the metropolitan county councils, and pay rises for senior civil servants at a time of restrained public spending have all caused problems less by their substance than by their presentation and their timing.

---

bank switching *noun* a technique for memory management, used in microcomputer systems that require more memory than the microprocessor can directly address, in which different banks or pages of memory can be selected at different times, or for different applications

> One way of beating the 640K limit is to use a technique called bank switching or paged memory. On the IBM PC under PC-DOS, this involves using some of the spare address space between 640K and one megabyte to act as a 'window' into more memory beyond a megabyte. Software swaps lumps of the expanded memory into that window as required.
> - *Guardian*, 3 July 1986

---

barker card *noun* an eye-catching card which advertises a product in a shop and is placed on the shelf which the product occupies - called also SHELF TALKER

> Once people are in the store they are tempted to buy the new products partly through 'barker cards' or 'shelf talkers'.
> - *Taste*, May/June 1986

► The term is derived from *barker* in the sense of one who touts for a shop or on a market barrow. It dates from the early nineteenth century. Yet it has always been more common in American English, where it is applied not only to shops but also to entertainments. The hero of Rodgers and Hammerstein's musical *Carousel* (20th-Century Fox film, 1956) was a barker at a fairground.

---

barn egg *noun* (the EEC term for) an egg produced by hens kept uncaged in sheds at a high density - compare SEMI-INTENSIVE EGG, DEEP LITTER EGG

---

basemat *noun* a dense platform made usually of concrete, that forms the foundations of a nuclear reactor site and acts as an impenetrable layer to prevent the core burning through the earth in the event of a MELTDOWN

> According to what Hollywood terms the China Syndrome, if this heat is not removed, then the reactor core will melt and

> burn its way through the earth. In fact there was never any possibility of the Chernobyl reactor's core melting its way through the bottom concrete basemat, much less into the earth. – *New Scientist*, 15 May 1986

---

becquerel *noun* (*symbol* **Bq**) the SI unit of radiation activity equal to 1 reciprocal second

> As if the measurement of radiation was not already complicated enough, like other units of measure it has recently been converted into new standard units. The basic measure of radiation activity is now called a becquerel, which is immensely smaller than the old measure called a curie. One becquerel represents one count per second of radioactivity and is the unit which measures the amount of radiation in substances like milk and water. The basic measure of absorption of radioactivity – the amount that has actually gone into the body – is now called a gray, which is 100 times larger than the old measure, the rad. The measure of the effect of that dose of radiation – which depends on how big the body is, how much has been absorbed and where – is now called a sievert, but still tends to be known by the previous unit's name, the rem. One sievert equals 100 rems. – *Daily Telegraph*, 8 May 1986

> The results ... confirmed that five of the lambs had more than the 'action level' of 1,000 becquerels per kilo. In Arran, a lamb was found with 1,145 becquerels per kilo and in Easter Ross on the east coast, one was found just over the limit at 1,017 becquerels, on a farm at Capel Curig in Snowdonia. – *Guardian*, 25 June 1986

> The primary purpose of introducing the becquerel was to help turn public opinion here, in the USA and in Germany against nuclear power, since higher figures sound more impressive if the units are not understood, and to provide the Department of Environment with an excuse for demanding safety precautions. – *Farmers Weekly*, 4 July 1986

► It is very much smaller than the *curie* and is useful for measuring radiation in, say, milk or water.

It is named after Antoine-Henri Becquerel (1852-1908), the French discoverer of radioactivity. It is alleged that this name was chosen out of courtesy to the French now that the *curie* (to which they might lay a proprietorial claim) has been superseded. Becquerel had co-operated with Pierre and Marie Curie, and in 1903 received the Nobel Prize for Physics jointly with them.

The measurement was the subject of a vigorous and acrimonious correspondence on the letters pages of *Farmers Weekly* during the summer of 1986. One correspondent went so far as to describe it as 'the fraudulent unit, the becquerel', claiming that it had been introduced to mislead the public.

Either in jest or in error, the word is sometimes transformed into *bugger-all.*

---

bed-hop *verb, informal* to be sexually promiscuous; sleep around

> Glamorous Joanna, who plays bed-hopping Linda Cochran in the series, was married to dashing Poldark star Ralph Bates. - *Sun*, 8 Feb. 1986

> I would have had to read 'Goldilocks' under the bed-covers if they'd realised it was a story about 'A little girl who goes bed-hopping and gets her oats.' - *Observer*, 19 Jan. 1986

► The term attempts to trivialize through jocularity the sustained fashion for brief, but sometimes pleasant sexual liaisons which has existed since the early 1960s.
The normalizing of this taste for variety is often said to date from a number of socio-political events. Ready availability of female contraception, the mini-skirt, the 1964 Socialist government are amongst those most regularly held responsible. Philip Larkin, in his poem 'Annus Mirabilis', is more specific:
Sexual intercourse began
In nineteen sixty-three
(Which was rather late for me) -
Between the end of the *Chatterley* ban
And the Beatles' first LP.

---

belonger *noun* a member of a large stable middle-class social group having basically conservative values, upholding the status quo, and interested in security and material comforts

> Young & Rubicam says the Tories can win only if they can attract full support from the 40% of the electorate whom they call 'belongers'. - *Economist*, 9 Aug. 1986

> Market research ... has caused fierce arguments in the Conservative Party. Is the new American 'psychographic' technique for delineating segments of the electorate to be used in fighting the next general election? Are we to stop talking about ABs, DEs and C1s and hunt out instead the 'belongers'? - *The Times*, 25 Aug. 1986

► A great deal of the success of the Conservative party at the 1979 General Election, and (to a degree) that of 1983, is attributed to the advertising efforts and imagination of Saatchi & Saatchi.
Their undisputed position as the party's advisers was challenged during the summer of 1986 by Young & Rubicam. They used a system of social classification involving rather twee terminology. It was devised by Arnold Mitchell, a Californian market researcher. It divides the population into nine categories based on their VALS (values and lifestyles).
The *belongers* are the largest group. They are basically middle-class but

cannot be considered identical to yuppies and their companion groups (GUPPIES, RUMPIES, and so on), as belongers embrace all age-groups and are not socially or morally very adventurous.
Other Mitchell categories include *survivors* and *sustainers*, which are the two bottom categories. *Sustainers* are those who are not well-off but are not impoverished. At the top of the tree are *achievers*, en route to which they will have been *emulators*.

---

benefit shop *noun* WELFARE SHOP

---

benzotrithiadiazepine *noun* a TRITHIADIAZEPINE derivative that acts as a nonmetallic conductor

> See quotation at TRITHIADIAZEPINE

Big Bang *noun* a fundamental or far-reaching change in organization; *specifically* the deregulation of the London Stock Exchange in 1986 that allows foreign institutions to become full members of the Stock Exchange, abolishes fixed commissions on stock and bond deals, and abandons rigid distinctions between banking, broking, and jobbing

> As big bang looms closer the large financial service companies are straining harder at the leash. At the same time the wave of mega-mergers is producing new practices which the regulators must also keep up with. – *The Times*, 6 March 1986

> Behind the great City scramble is the imminent arrival of 'Big Bang', otherwise known as the October Revolution when London's guarded money markets will be thrown open to the world. – *Daily Mail*, 28 March 1986

► This adds a new and important sense to the two which have existed for some time. The first is a theory as to the creation of the universe, and the second is a colloquial reference to a nuclear explosion.
This removal in October 1986 of all the restrictive practices which protected the London Stock Exchange is an important feature of the Conservative government's efforts to produce a free market wherever possible. It was the result of an original initiative by Cecil Parkinson when Secretary of State for Trade & Industry (June–October 1983).
The USA liberated their Exchange similarly on 1 May 1975, in a process codenamed *Mayday*.
For related terms, see POST-BANG; SEAQ, TAURUS; SHARE SHOP; SINGLE CAPACITY, DUAL CAPACITY; GOLDEN HANDCUFFS, GOLDEN HELLO, and GOLDEN PARACHUTE.

---

big splash theory *noun* a theory in cosmology: the moon was formed by the condensation of debris splashed out by the impact of a large meteorite on the Earth

> The latest theory of our Moon's origin – 'the Big Splash' – says that the Moon formed ... from debris splashed out by the

impact of a large meteorite on the Earth. - *Guardian*, 31 Jan. 1986

► The origin of the moon has remained a matter of frustrating uncertainty even in the years since its first visit by man.
There were broadly four theories before the development of this currently fashionable notion. The first was the *captive hypothesis* which suggested that the moon was formed in another part of the solar system and was captured by the Earth. The chances of achieving such a capture are remote and make this particularly unlikely. Another long-standing concept is the *fission hypothesis* which provides for a chunk of crust flying off the Earth's surface and leaving, in effect, the Pacific Ocean. The *precipitation hypothesis* sees the moon as being an accretion of bits and pieces which were circling the Earth as planetesimals. The *binary planet hypothesis* considers that the Earth and the moon are sister planets, which were formed, as it were, in parallel.
However, none of these theories, including the big splash theory, accounts for the fact that the Earth is made of different material from the moon, except possibly the *captive hypothesis.*

Bikeathon *noun* see -ATHON

---

binary weapon *or* **binary** *noun* a chemical weapon consisting of two substances which are non-toxic when separate but combine to form nerve gas after a shell containing them has been fired

> The new generation of American binary chemical weapons will never be deployed in Britain in peacetime, Mr Stanley, Minister of State for Defence, said. - *Daily Telegraph*, 29 April 1986

> The US Congress recently gave qualified approval to the development of a new generation of 'binary' weapons. ... NATO's Supreme Commander in Europe, Bernard Rogers, has said that there is 'no question of stocking binaries anywhere except in the US'. - *New Scientist*, 11 July 1985

► The two components involved are independently harmless. They are loaded into a carrier munition. The chemicals then mix together during the period of flight, before being released at the target as a toxic chemical agent.

---

bio *adjective* biotechnology

> THE BIO-BOMBSHELL : The growth of the bio industry is told in this video story of the latest and most far-reaching revolution in science. - *New Scientist*, 22 May 1986

► The colloquial abbreviation includes a wide range of genetic engineering interests; for example food, vaccines and drugs, fuels, agriculture, and pollution control.
It has been coined as a direct product of the vogue anxiety regarding any kind of tampering with the natural environment.

---

biocomputer *noun* a SIXTH-GENERATION computer

---

biocomputing *noun* the use of BIOCOMPUTERS

> A sequence for the entire human genome, while itself a goal, is only a tool for a better understanding of human genetics, points out Eric Lander of the Whitehead Institute in Cambridge, Massachusetts. Just knowing the sequence tells you almost nothing, argues Lander; it will be useful only when coupled with a better understanding of the structure and function of proteins. Toward that end, Tooze says the European Molecular Biology Laboratory will be putting more of its resources into biocomputing and crystallography. – *Nature*, 31 July 1986

---

biohazardous *adjective* of or involving a biohazard (biological agent or condition that constitutes a hazard to humans or their environment)

> The scientists point to the need to find an internationally acceptable symbol for biohazardous waste. The skull and crossbones was rejected because of its piracy connotations. – *Guardian*, 20 May 1986

---

bioholonics *noun* the science or study of the cooperative interaction between individual elements (holons) which make up a biological system

> The buzzword among the blue-sky researchers of Japan now is bioholonics. ... The end-point ... is a sixth-generation computer that thinks for itself. – *Guardian*, 7 March 1986

---

biologue *noun* a biographical radio programme

> The blonde queen of hearts was the subject of Anyone Can See I Love You ... with Hetty Baynes putting in a marathon performance of the radio equivalent of what in films is called a bio-pic, a biologue in other words, with Marilyn telling all from the early Norma Jean days. – *Daily Telegraph*, 4 June 1986

---

biomotor *noun* a computer-controlled device that mimics the action of (a set of) muscles

> Another Tokyo team has already produced a biomotor which ... [is] claimed to be 90 per cent efficient and could drive an artificial hand. – *Guardian*, 7 March 1986

---

bioreactor *noun* a vessel, apparatus, or piece of equipment used industrially for biochemical reactions (eg fermentation) or for processing biological materials

> A long-established soya sauce maker in Singapore, Chuen Cheong Food Industries, will soon install its own new process, which its inventor, Dr Leslie Young, a biochemist at

the National University of Singapore claims is as good as Kikkoman's. After the first three days, the bean mash goes into a 'bioreactor' - a fermenter equipped with sophisticated process controls. - *Financial Times*, 17 Jan. 1986

---

biotech *noun or adjective* (of or using) biotechnology

The Government is now backing biotech. Two companies have been set up, one for the chemical, one for the agricultural side. Both were initially launched on a mixture of private and government money. ... But just compare this with what ICI is putting into its biotech plant venture - £15 million for the lab., £100 million for research alone. ICI also bought a large seed company in the United States to provide sales outlets. On the scale they're working now, I can't see either company providing the foundation for a major biotech industry. - *Listener*, 20 Feb. 1986

---

birthroom *noun* a room attached to the maternity department of a hospital, providing a more relaxed and comfortable environment for giving birth than a normal delivery room

The birthroom, a new concept in the management of labour, is discussed in a leading article in the current issue of The Lancet. ... The birthroom offers women comfortable and homelike surroundings close to the labour suite. They could come there with their own community midwife under the supervision of their own general practitioner obstetrician. If all went well they could return home in hours. - *Daily Telegraph*, 2 Sept. 1986

---

black tar *noun, US slang* a very potent refined form of heroin

Black tar, also known as bugger, candy, dogfood, gumball, Mexican mud, peanut butter and tootsie roll ... started in Los Angeles and has since spread to 27 states, but has yet to find a market niche in New York. What makes black tar heroin unique is that it has a single, foreign source - Mexico - and finds its way into Mexican-American distribution networks, often via illegal immigrants. - *Economist*, 7 June 1986

► There is a variety of synonyms for this kind of heroin, as demonstrated by the citation. Most are based on its appearance. *Candy* is an old term. The others are apparently new.

---

blitter *noun* a chip, designed especially for animated graphics, which can transform long strings of bits and move them between different memory locations

Hot on most people's list is a version of the ST with a 'blitter' chip for high-speed graphics, to give the ST hardware facilities more comparable with the Amiga. - *Guardian*, 21 Aug. 1986

---

blue-sky *adjective* having no specific practical aim; pure, theoretical

The buzzword among the blue-sky researchers of Japan now is bioholonics. - *Guardian*, 7 March 1986

[Sir Clive] Sinclair says he hopes to float a new company and to continue researching 'blue sky' projects, ideally for other companies. - *New Scientist*, 10 April 1986

► The term was originally (1906) applied to speculative or worthless securities. Later, it was applied to visionary or unrealistic thought. In the current sense, it is a vogueish term: some high-technology companies employ people for blue-sky research, in addition to those concerned with specific project development.

---

boatlift *noun* the transport of cargo or passengers by boat, especially from an inaccessible place or an area of danger or hardship

The United States authorities on the receiving end of the boatlift, in Key West, intercepted many of the Mariel criminals and put them immediately in jail. - *Economist*, 7 June 1986

► Formed by analogy with *airlift.*
An enormous number of boatpeople, as they become called, left Vietnam by various flimsy craft at the end of the war in 1975. Refugees from what they saw as the likely repressions of the Communist regime, they were frequently subjected to robbery and rape by the pirates who roam the SE Asia seas.
The most spectacular incident of this type of exodus in 1986 featured two lifeboats containing a total of 152 Tamil (Sri Lankan) refugees who arrived on the Newfoundland coast in mid-August. They proffered initial well-rehearsed protestations that they had travelled directly from Sri Lanka. This stretched the imagination as their clothes were dry and their chattels were wrapped in German newspapers, which they claimed had heavy circulations in Sri Lanka. They eventually admitted to having come from Hamburg and explained that they had been cut adrift a suitable distance from the Canadian coast. For this service they seem to have paid the equivalent of £1,400 each.

---

body *noun* a type of top or blouse, shaped like a leotard and fastened with poppers under the crotch

A blouse transformed into a body has the added advantage of looking neat all day without your once having to rearrange or tuck it in. The body is one of the subtlest ways of emphasising the waist without restricting it, and also liberates women to move more freely in slit skirts and sarongs, confident that no underwear is showing. - *Observer*, 24 Aug. 1986

---

boiler-room *or* **boiler shop** *or* **boiler house** *noun, informal* a company using high-pressure salesmanship to sell new shares of dubious value or authenticity to private investors

> The boiler-rooms, most of them based in the Netherlands and Belgium ... have been going after the British investor with great enthusiasm since 1985. - *Daily Telegraph*, 14 June 1986

> The Dutch authorities are finally acting to close down the 'boiler shop' share-pushing operations based in Amsterdam. ... Many of the boiler house firms are linked to convicted fraudsters. - *Daily Telegraph*, 30 Aug. 1986

---

bomb-driven laser *noun* an X-ray laser in which the energy source is the explosion of a small nuclear bomb and which is designed as a space-based DIRECTED-ENERGY WEAPON

> The most controversial element of the star wars programme is one which is being pursued primarily by the Department of Energy independently of SDI - X-ray lasers in which the energy source is the explosion of a small nuclear bomb. The bomb-driven X-ray laser relies in principle on an intense burst of X-rays that strips away the inner electrons from the atoms of the X-ray laser material. - *New Scientist*, 20 June 1985

---

bottom-hop *verb* to practise BOTTOM-HOPPING

> Although world leaders still seem to prefer lighthouse-climbing and chasing dogs along beaches, the Maharishi's men are optimistic about getting the square root of 1 per cent of the world's population to bottom-hop - the necessary quota for world peace. - *Guardian*, 16 Aug. 1986

---

bottom-hopping *noun* the yogic practice of jumping while in the lotus position using the buttock muscles, described by followers of the Maharishi Mahesh Yogi as 'flying'

► The rather undignified journalistic nickname for what is also known as *yogic flying.*
Exponents of transcendental meditation have long stressed the value and the ease of levitation. It drew wider attention in August 1986 through the Transcendental Meditation Games held in London. Hurdles, long jump, high jump, and speed racing events were held in imitation of conventional athletics meetings.
The activity consists of apparently effortless rising (and forward movement) in the lotus position.
The principal aim of the activity has nothing to do with recreation. It is believed that world peace can be maintained for as long as 7,000 people are suspended in the air simultaneously; a feat which presumably it would be almost impossible to orchestrate, apart from any difficulties imposed by faith or athletic competence.
(The facetious references to lighthouses and dogs in the quotation at BOTTOM-HOP relate to stories of the Queen climbing a Scottish lighthouse

and the Prime Minister walking her host's King Charles spaniel on the beach during a Cornish holiday. These events had received immoderate silly season coverage.)

---

bought deal *noun* a financial practice in which the whole of an issue of new equity is underwritten by a single broker or investment bank, which distributes it to clients at a price agreed with the issuer

> Many British companies will be tempted by bought deals: they are quicker to organise than rights issues and also cheaper. - *Economist*, 6 Sept. 1986

► This American practice is likely to become common in Britain after BIG BANG. In contrast, the traditional British technique is to have the issue underwritten by a syndicate and offered as a rights issue to existing shareholders.

---

box-shifter *noun, derogatory* a firm which merely sells goods, such as electrical equipment, and is not involved in the production, repair, or any other aspect of those products

> This week's bad news from the loss-making Commodore company is that 70 more staff have been laid off ... including the sales and servicing back-up teams. Repairs will now be done by an outside company. ... This takes the UK operation further towards being just another box-shifter for imported goods it can't even repair itself. - *Guardian*, 5 June 1986

---

branwagon *noun, humorous* the increasing trend towards eating foods considered healthy (eg bran and fresh vegetables)

> Britain's eating habits have changed and the healthy eating 'branwagon' is here to stay. More than half the population now thinks carefully about its diet and is consciously eating healthier foods. - *Financial Times*, 17 Jan. 1986

► Jocular formation on the *bandwagon* analogy.
The present passion for health (as in ANTI-CHUB) expresses itself not only in fanatical (and occasionally fatal) exercise, but also in eating healthy (and frequently disgusting) food.
The impetus of this kind of diet, which built up steadily during the late 1970s and early 1980s, has faltered somewhat as now it has been suggested that a restriction of this kind may be bad for the eater. (See MUESLI BELT MALNUTRITION.)

---

brittle bone syndrome *noun* a condition in foetuses and newly born babies whereby the bones are so brittle that they are extremely easily and frequently broken, often with crippling and permanent consequences

> Brittle Bone Syndrome, one of the cruellest genetic disorders, is responsible for thousands of deaths in infancy around the world. It can also result in youngsters being crippled from

birth with victims suffering the agony of multiple bone fractures throughout their lives. – *Oxford Times*, 18 July 1986

► The condition affects nearly 4,000 people in Britain and is evident in many other parts of the world. Many children are crippled in this way from birth and remain so for the rest of their lives.
It attracted public interest in mid-1986 when Dr Bryan Sykes of the Nuffield Department of Pathology at the John Radcliffe Hospital, Oxford, achieved an important breakthrough. His newly devised techniques, which are the result of ten years' work, mean that doctors can carry out antenatal tests to predict whether a foetus will be affected or not. This will relieve many pregnant women of anxiety and will allow those so disposed to terminate the pregnancy if appropriate.

---

bugger *noun, US slang* BLACK TAR

---

bulldog bond *or* **bulldog** *noun* a fixed-interest sterling security issued in Britain by a foreign borrower

> From Monday gilts will face stronger competition from the so-called Bulldogs. ... They are already exempt from stamp duty and, from today, capital gains tax. – *The Times*, 2 July 1986
>
> Dual-capacity trading in the bulldog bond market got off to an encouraging start yesterday ... with turnover higher than many had expected. – *Daily Telegraph*, 8 July 1986

---

burrito *noun* a tortilla filled (eg with chilli con carne or ham and cheese) and baked

► A Mexican dish – or range of dishes – whereby hot wheat tortilla is filled with something delicious and baked. The result of this preparation is then passed around the room. Everyone eats a bit and makes a considerable mess.
Among the many specific fillings are melted cheese (producing *queso fundido*), scrambled egg and sausage (*huevos revueltos con chorizo*), and beef (*mozhomos*).

---

burundanga *noun* hyoscine (depressive and sedative drug, also called scopolamine)

> Bogota's perpetually strained police chiefs [are] currently reeling under what is being billed here as the 'burundanga' crime wave. ... Each week at least 20 cases are reported of sane and law-abiding citizens dutifully handing over their wallets, credit cards and car keys to ruthless criminals who ... are not pointing a gun at them. Others write out cheques for their entire savings for the criminals to cash. Wealthy, elderly women toddle into banks to withdraw their jewellery from safe deposit boxes and then deliver the gems to the crooks waiting outside. These are perfect, as well as bizarre, crimes,

> as the victims can later no more describe the thieves than recall what happened during the preceding hours or days. - *The Times*, 7 July 1986

► The drug is produced from the fruit of certain shrub species grown in the Andes. A couple of drops have dramatic effects when dropped in the victim's drink.

---

bustier *noun* a bodice-like article of clothing worn as a top

> Other designers, too, have been producing denim lines - notably Katharine Hamnett, whose jeans, bustiers, shorts and jackets, trimmed with diamante, give nice well-off girls the chance to sleaze with the Rockers. - *Guardian*, 10 April 1986

► The garment is an all-purpose item. Normally sleeveless and frequently producing a formidable hiatus between itself and the skirt or trousers, it does not seem to provide any purpose other than decoration and emphasis of the bust.

It is the most recent in a sequence of treatments of female breasts. In the seventeenth century, they were sometimes left completely or partially naked. From 1913 they were emphasized by the brassiere. Around 1918 they were felt to be rather embarrassing and were suppressed for nearly two decades in straight dresses. Their liberation and re-emphasis in 1935 reached its apotheosis in the falsies of the New Look, 1947-48.

The bustier follows this lineage in being favoured by prostitutes in New York and other cities of the USA to entice customers. It is now worn equally easily in evening dress and in office and other working environments.

---

buyout *noun* the purchase of the entire interest in a business, especially by its managers

> The brands being sold [by Cadbury Schweppes] to a management buyout team include Typhoo tea. - *Guardian*, 14 Jan. 1986

> With a deal agreed at the Vickers warship yard and proposed at Land Rover, management buy-outs are Britain's business flavour of the month. - *Economist*, 15 March 1986

> An offer to the public to buy shares in Land Rover forms part of the plans of managers wanting to buy the company from British Leyland, it emerged yesterday. ... The managers' buy-out plan was the first of the rival offers to be presented to Hill Samuel, the merchant bankers co-ordinating the sale. - *Daily Telegraph*, 3 March 1986

► As part of the government's encouragement of self-supporting entrepreneurial activity, bids for divisions of companies or entire companies now usually include one from the management.

This may be in response to a government privatization venture. For example, in August 1986 a group of five senior managers bought the

Devon General section of the National Bus Company. Their example has been followed in other parts of the group.

cajun *noun* the syncopated dance music of the Louisianian Cajuns (descendants of French-speaking immigrants from Acadia) which usually consists of French vocals with steel guitar, fiddle, and accordion accompaniment

> Neither Louisiana nor San Antonio, but an international celebration of Tex Mex & Cajun at sun kissed Clapham Common. The Balham Alligators' inebriated cajun boogie is guaranteed to add froth to any event. – *City Limits*, 14 Aug. 1986

► Cajuns are the descendants of French Canadians driven by the British in the eighteenth century from the French colony of Acadia (now Nova Scotia, New Brunswick, and Prince Edward Island). They settled in the state of Louisiana, where they formed self-contained enclaves. Here they became easily identified and somewhat segregated – like many communities – by their language. Theirs is basically French with elements of English, Spanish, and German.
The word *Cajun* is a phonetic approximation of *Acadian*, perhaps altered by a basically derogatory and unfounded association with *Injun* (= Indian).
Cajun music – usually lively, foot-tapping stuff – is increasingly heard in Britain. Apart from its musical sense, the word is commonly used to describe a style of cooking (with particular reference to sauce). For example, on the menu of the Rock Garden, Covent Garden, *Cajun Wings* are described as being 'Chicken Wings coated in our own secret Louisiana blend of hot spices, slowly roasted and served with a bowl of barbecue sauce for dunking'. The same menu offers *Cajun Chicken* (drumsticks with New Orleans hot spices) and *Louisiana Cajun Blackened Steak*.

calmodulin *noun* a calcium-binding protein that regulates many cellular functions (eg the release of hormones) and affects cell shape and division

> Calmodulin can, for example, trigger the breakdown of microtubules when other regulatory proteins are present. Since cancer cells differ from normal ones primarily in their shape and rate of division, calcium-activated calmodulin may play a role in the biochemistry of the disease. – *Scientific American*, Nov. 1985

camcorder *noun* a piece of photographic equipment which comprises a video camera and a recorder in one portable unit

> Built into the Canovision 8, our latest 8mmm camcorder, is a well-earned reputation for body design and lens quality. - *Observer*, 4 May 1986

---

canvas

– on canvas *slang* held in solitary confinement, with only a canvas mattress and a canvas smock, as a form of punishment in prisons

> Eleven days into his sentence Harris was told that his father had died. He was put on Strict Security Observation ... under which inmates are held 'on canvas'. - *New Statesman*, 19 April 1985

► An unsubtle formation on the analogy of *in solitary* (confinement) and indirectly *on-the-blanket.*
This latter was evident in Northern Ireland (especially in The Maze - formerly Long Kesh - Prison). Hunger stikes around 1972 were followed by on-the-blanket protests by both Orange and IRA special category prisoners between 1976 and 1980. This involved breaking beds, fouling cells, and pouring excreta and urine into the passages. Such prisoners were also said to be *on protest.*

---

carambola *noun* a greenish-yellow tropical fruit, usually 7–12 cm long with a distinctive lobed appearance and a sweet-sour taste

> Other exotic fruits now becoming available in Britain include the carambola, from Indonesia. - *Daily Telegraph*, 3 April 1986

► The fruit comes from Brazil, Israel, and Indonesia. Not only does it have a bizarre elongated shape but also a star cross-section and a glossy skin. General preference is to serve it sliced, and it has been known to make appearances in fruit salad. Some relegate it to jams and jellies, thus losing its principal attraction which is its intriguing appearance.
Also known as STAR FRUIT.

---

carcerand *ncun* any of a group of chemicals characterized by being composed of molecules whose shape (eg a hollow sphere) allows them to trap smaller molecules (the guests) within themselves (the hosts)

> Donald J. Cram and his co-workers, at the University of California at Los Angles, have designed a new class of chemical Alcatraz - a spherical molecule which can trap smaller molecules permanently within it. The chemists named the new class of compounds 'carcerands' after the Latin word for prison. - *New Scientist*, 22 Aug. 1985

► Carcerands have a number of applications, especially as industrial catalysts and biochemical enzymes.

Caridex *trademark* - used for a technique in dentistry in which tooth decay is removed by means of a chemical solution, thus preventing or greatly reducing the need for drilling

> Keith Stoneback, one of the inventors of the sytem, called Caridex, says 95 per cent. of patients prefer his painless method. - *Daily Telegraph*, 4 July 1986

> People whose teeth start to chatter in terror at the thought of the dentist's drill may be able to smile if a method of removing decay chemically catches on. Caridex ... uses a harmless acid solution, monochloroaminobutyric acid, which is warmed and applied to patches of decay by an instrument that looks like a fine-tipped pen. - *Sunday Times*, 1 June 1986

---

cash cow *noun, informal* a business from which liquid assets can be easily and consistently derived

> A takeover, by which Hanson Trust obtains what is known in the city as a Cash Cow, is really just like a visit from a kindly vet, the James Herriot of capitalism. - *Guardian*, 28 July 1986

> He had called Dairy Farm the company's 'cash cow' and its steady turnover had sustained the group's cash flow through Hong Kong's property slump from 1981 to 1983. - *Economist*, 13 Sept. 1986

---

casual *noun, British informal* a young person who dresses in expensive casual clothing (eg designer knitwear and sportswear); *especially* a person who adheres to a youth subculture characterized by such clothing and associated with violent behaviour, especially premeditated and organized violence at football matches

> '14-24' - British Youth Culture - Communications Through Commodities' is the last exhibition at The Boilerhouse's present site (it's moving to the east of London in the autumn), and it looks at the emergence of youth as a distinct economic category, from the great surge in mass culture which took place in the aftermath of the Second World War to the eclecticism of 1986. From the Teddy Boys to the Casual Boys - from I.D. tags to i-D Magazine. - *i-D*, Aug. 1986

> A new breed of football hooligan known sometimes as 'casuals' who are 'bent on fighting the opposition in order to enhance their own prestige' are described by the [Popplewell] report. - *Guardian*, 17 Jan. 1986

► The two (interim and final) Popplewell reports and numerous other studies have identified a variety of specific and highly organized types of football hooligan. These are sometimes based on particular teams. Sometimes they are more localized and relate to specific housing estates. Since several catastrophes, notoriously that at the Heysel Stadium in Brussels on 29 May 1985, the government has sought to clamp down on football-spectator violence, with a certain amount of success. The problem

has been reduced by the banning of English teams from continental matches as a result of the Brussels incident.
However, a series of friendly (sic) matches in Amsterdam in August 1986 gave rise to several disagreeable incidents. One of these appeared to result from deliberate provocation by casuals. On the ferry *Koningen Beatrix* between Harwich and the Hook of Holland, West Ham's *Inter-City Firm*, a typical casual group, are believed to have stirred up the fans of Manchester United by taunts about the now historically remote 1958 Munich air disaster which killed most of the United team.

---

catalogue-speak *noun* see -SPEAK

---

cavitand *noun* any of a group of chemicals whose large basin-shaped molecules act as hosts to accommodate smaller, especially linear, molecules as guests. Such host-guest interactions cease after a time as the two molecules are not chemically bonded and hence cavitands can serve as catalysts in a number of reactions.

> The second paper reports on the construction of an enormous molecule from two cavitands, rather like sticking two coconut shells together. When this type of molecule is formed, up to six molecules of solvent may be trapped inside. – *New Scientist*, 22 Aug. 1985

CCD *noun* CHARGE-COUPLED DEVICE

---

cellphone *noun* a CELLULAR RADIO telephone

---

cellular radio *or* **cell radio** *noun* a reliable and fast computer-controlled communications system for users of portable radio telephones (eg in-car telephones)

> The research team has pieced together meticulously a neat picture of world chaos. They cover not just cellular radio, but all other aspects of mobile radio, radio paging and the technology of mobile telephones. Most of the old services are wasteful of the radio frequency spectrum. Nothing can generate more frequencies. The only solution to overcrowding and interference is more efficient use of existing frequencies. This is what cellular radio achieves, by dividing the service area into a honeycomb of small cells each served by separate low-power transmissions. In this way the same frequencies can be used over and over again across the area covered. – *New Scientist*, 3 July 1986

> Cell radio ... is now changing the lifestyle of UK users. It is not a toy, like an upmarket CB radio. Cell radio is a business tool, like a telephone, an answering machine or a typewriter. – *Listener*, 3 April 1986

► Areas of a city, town, or region are divided into radio transmission zones known as cells. Each cell has its own transmitter/receiver, usually on a high building. A cluster of cells is controlled by a central computer so that calls from a car are fed to the public telephone system or to another group of cells. A scanning system keeps track of the signal level from a vehicle and the computer automatically transfers to a transmitter/receiver in another cell so that the user does not notice the passage from one cell to another. Cellular radio can easily handle 50,000 calls per hour, compared with 1,500 calls using conventional shortwave radio.

CELV *noun* COMPLEMENTARY EXPENDABLE LAUNCH VEHICLE

CH *noun* CORPORATE HOSPITALITY

---

challenged *adjective, chiefly US* suffering from a disability that makes achievement unusually difficult; handicapped

> This bestselling author [Richard Simmons] of The Never Say Diet Book creates a comprehensive fitness program for the physically challenged. - *Publishers Weekly*, 10 Jan. 1986

► Part of the trend to find new euphemisms for disabilities.
Some management philosophies encourage a parallel use of this word. They require managers to speak of *challenges* as opposed to *problems*, as in 'I had a challenge on the way in to the office this morning'.

---

charge-coupled device *noun* (*abbreviation* **CCD**) a data storage device consisting of an array of metal-oxide semiconductor cells on a silicon chip, that is used chiefly in imaging systems

> Sony and Pioneer have replaced the traditional tube in cameras with a new type of microchip. Acccording to some experts this charge-coupled device (CCD) provides a better picture and less distortion. - *Observer*, 4 May 1986

► CCDs are being increasingly used in television cameras for storing images, especially in the field of robotics, since they can recognize not just black and white but also a range of grey tones. The CCD is about 30 times more sensitive than a photographic plate so it is also used in astronomy for taking pictures of faint celestial objects in minutes rather than in hours.

---

chayote *noun* a pale-green pear-shaped gourd, originating in tropical America, which can be smooth-skinned or ridged and covered in prickly hairs, and which is typically eaten sliced and fried in batter - called also CHOCHO, CHRISTOPHENE

Ch/Ch syndrome *noun* Chernobyl/Challenger Syndrome: a set of disasters involving high technology which have resulted from pressures put upon those in charge of that technology to progress faster than is expedient

> Challenger and Chernobyl were not 'accidents'. Both were disasters waiting to happen. ... The Ch/Ch Syndrome affects more than post-war mega-technology; the very place of

> science and technology in our civilization is put into question. – *Guardian*, 19 May 1986

► Stunning blows to the technological confidence of the First and Second Worlds were dealt by the disasters of the explosion of the American *Ch*allenger space-shuttle shortly after take-off (January 1986) and the series of explosions at *Ch*ernobyl nuclear power-station (May 1986). Despite a reasonable number of hiccups along the way, but nothing immoderate, the USA space enterprise and the USSR nuclear power generating programme had developed well. These very public catastrophes dealt grave damage to national and the relevant professional confidences. The consequent woe was exacerbated by the swingeing criticisms of the inquiries. For example, the NASA inquiry blamed management incompetence, internal feuding, and disregard for safety.

Chernobyl factor *noun* the repercussions of the Chernobyl nuclear reactor disaster

> The Chernobyl factor appears to have cast its shadow over not just British lamb, but the homes of those unfortunate enough to live near the four areas shortlisted for the NIREX nuclear dumping site. – *Daily Telegraph*, 3 July 1986

> The 'Chernobyl Factor' brought a steep fall in lamb prices at the country's livestock markets yesterday. It was the first market day since the Government imposed a 21-day ban last Friday on the movement and slaughter of sheep in parts of Cumbria and North Wales, after testing showed higher than permitted radiation levels in some sheep. – *Daily Telegraph*, 24 June 1986

► The use of the term ... *factor* has been a popular phrase formation to describe human reactions to major events since the *Falklands Factor*, whereby an aggressive posture and military success in the Falklands revived flagging Conservative spirits and fortunes in 1982.
The emissions of radioactivity from the Chernobyl nuclear reactor at the beginning of May 1986 spread across Scandinavia, a substantial part of England and Wales (particularly the northern areas), and some parts of Scotland.
The immediate effect was a fall in lamb prices. A Ministry of Agriculture ban on movement of sheep in Cumbria and North Wales followed. This restriction affected 8,000 farmers. There was some criticism of the Ministry of Agriculture for scaremongering. In fact only 16 sheep were found to have eaten grass over 1,000 BECQUERELS, and the highest reading was a lamb in North Wales at 4,000.
Longer term results took the form of a temporary hiccup in house prices in areas which had achieved particular adverse press coverage in this way.
In August 1986, the general nervousness took a more practical form with formidable and well-orchestrated obstructive demonstrations against the exploration of sites for dumping nuclear-contaminated artefacts (an expression of the NIMBY syndrome). Doubtless there would have been earlier opposition to this enterprise, but equally certainly its ferocity and the breadth of support for the demonstrations was the result of the breadth

breadth of support for the demonstrations was the result of the Chernobyl disaster.

Chicken American syndrome *noun* a condition among Americans of reluctance to visit Europe for fear of terrorist activities

> Britain and Europe are said to be growing daily more furious with America precisely because Americans are *not* behaving like citizens of an imperialist power - travelling abroad in droves on business trips or holiday sprees, spending lavishly and invigorating the national economies of the Old World. ... There is already a catchy name for this phenomenon - The Chicken American Syndrome. - *Daily Telegraph*, 4 June 1986

> The London offices of American banks and newspapers are to become fortresses. As Russell Baker told his readers in the *New York Times*, the ugly American has been usurped in European demonology by the 'Chicken American'. - *Spectator*, 24 May 1986

► In the American bombing of Libya, the United Kingdom's role appeared to many as that of an accomplice. In no way did the British Government initiate the operation. Yet widespread disapprobation attached itself to this subordinate role. This came from sources as diverse as the British public, American liberals, the Arab nations, and - it was alleged - even the Queen. As a result of the whole episode it was felt that Britain would become a target for reprisals by Arab terrorists.
Consequently, American tourists changed their holiday plans. A £249 million tourist trade surplus in April 1985 was replaced by a £50 million deficit in April 1986. The problem was not limited to the UK. Sylvester Stallone, the macho hero of *Rambo* (see RAMBOISM) and the *Rocky* series, refused to attend the Cannes Film Festival as part of this abstention. In fairness to the visitors, unfavourable $-£ exchange rates and the emissions of the Chernobyl nuclear plant also contributed to the syndrome.
By July, signs of improvement in the tourist trade were evident and by August things were almost back to normal. Nevertheless, on 3 August some substance was given to the anxieties by machine-gun and rocket attacks by a pro-Libyan group on RAF Akrotiri in Cyprus.

---

chiller *noun* a terrifying or eerie tale, usually dealing with the supernatural

► Combination of *chill* and thr*iller*. It is a descendant of the traditional ghost story. More recently this has been succeeded by horror stories of unnecessary carnage. The chiller genre includes such monstrous entertainments. Chillers may appear on TV, cinema, radio, or in book form.

---

chiller cupboard *noun* a cupboard or cabinet which is kept at a low temperature in order to preserve food, but which is not as cold as a fridge

> There are ventilated cupboards, where dry groceries can be stashed away ... and chiller cupboards for keeping wine and

cheese, cooked meat and eggs at their best. – *Taste*, May/June 1986

Chinese wall *noun* **1** a code of practice prohibiting the exchange of sensitive information among different departments (e g the corporate finance and fund management departments) of a financial institution, in order to avoid conflicts of interest and insider dealing **2** a similar restriction within a business organization

> A dozen leading Japanese commercial banks asked the government to knock holes in the Chinese wall between banking and securities business. – *Economist*, 12 April 1986

> Neither Boeing nor Airbus can keep a Chinese wall between their government-funded military work and their civil activities. – *Economist*, 3 May 1986

---

chlamydia *noun* any of a genus (*Chlamydia*, especially *Chlamydia trachomatis*) of microorganisms that are intracellular parasites causing infections of the eye and of the urinogenital system

> Only recently has the true severity of chlamydial infection come home to doctors. *Chlamydia trachomatis*, a major cause of blindness in the Third World, is now known to be responsible for some 40 per cent of cases of pelvic inflammatory disease in Britain. – *New Scientist*, 7 Nov. 1985

---

chocho *or* **chow-chow** *noun* CHAYOTE

---

chorionic villus sampling *or* **chorion villus sampling** *noun* (*abbreviation* **CVS**) a technique for the prenatal diagnosis of congenital defects in foetuses, in which cells from the chorionic villi (finger-like projections of the placenta) are removed and examined for abnormalities

> A pioneering technique for identifying the fatal inherited disease cystic fibrosis has brought hope to hundreds of mothers who might otherwise not risk giving birth, the British Association heard yesterday. ... The test, called Chorion Villus sampling, involves taking a minute piece of genetic material, DNA, from the tiny stems, the villi, surrounding the 8–9 week old fetus. – *Guardian*, 6 Sept. 1986

> A new way of detecting genetic disorders early in pregnancy is 'acceptably safe and reliable', according to researchers in San Francisco. The test will allow earlier detection of abnormalities than provided by amniocentesis, the technique currently offered to pregnant women. The new technique is called chorionic villus sampling (CVS). – *New Scientist*, 3 July 1986

► This method of detecting disorders in pregnancy originated in the Prenatal Diagnosis Programme at the University of California. A canula is

passed through the mother's cervix and tiny samples of tissues are taken from the chorionic villi.
It has several advantages over amniocentesis, the conventional technique. CVS is performed during the third month of pregnancy (a month earlier). Results are available in one or two weeks (half the time). It is less emotionally distressing.

CHP *noun* COMBINED HEAT AND POWER

---

christophene *noun* CHAYOTE

---

chronobioengineering *noun* the application, especially to medical science, of CHRONOBIOLOGY and bioengineering

> Dr Douglas Wilson, Chairman of the British Society of Chronobiology ... (who recently attended the first NATO meeting on chronobioengineering) thinks that in the future, patients will be able to rely less on hospital staff, as implanted pumps will dispense chemotherapy such as morphine or insulin at the right time. For example, hospitals spend a lot of money buying heparin, a drug used as an anti-coagulant agent to prevent thrombosis. When too much is given at night there is a risk of bleeding, whereas in the early morning there is a risk of thrombosis. So, by using regulated pumps, doctors can improve the drug's effectiveness dramatically. – *Listener*, 10 April 1986

---

chronobiology *noun* the study of the body's internal biological rhythms

> Chronobiology has many other applications. Not only does it dictate when we should receive drugs, and sleep and work, it tells us when it's best to learn. Apparently we're at our most receptive in the afternoons. It can also be used to manipulate our environment. – *Listener*, 10 April 1986

> Recently an eminent American biologist published a programme that, he promises, will revolutionise air travel. Charles F Ehret, a 62-year-old biologist, is senior scientist at the Argonne Illinois National Laboratory, and a world authority in the field of chronobiology. ... Thirty years of study have shown that our entire body chemistry changes through the day. Dr Ehret calls this 'being a redhead at dawn and a blonde at midnight'. His programme sets out to control jet lag by manipulating those factors – telling our body to move forward if travelling eastwards, or backward if travelling westward. – *Airport*, April 1986

---

circotherm oven *noun* an oven which contains a fan to circulate the heat, thus cutting down on cooking time and removing the need to preheat the oven

---

classist *adjective* of or showing discrimination against a person on the grounds of his/her social status

> The sex, race, social station and general circumstances of a criminal are normally held to come into this category. I disagree. Any information about anybody is bound to be sexist, racist, classist, ageist or something. – *Private Eye*, 17 May 1985

► The noun *classism*, meaning distinction of social class, dates back to the mid-nineteenth century. It is only in the period since the second world war and especially since 1964 that distinction on grounds of class has been widely considered undesirable or, indeed, unavoidable. Before that, whatever views were held on class structure, the system was generally believed to be permanent and immutable, the occasional efforts of the Levellers and other highly active pressure groups notwithstanding.
It joins other words based on the *-ist* suffix, such as *sexist* and HETEROSEXIST (both derogatory) as well as *feminist* and ANIMALIST (non-derogatory).

---

clone *noun* a microcomputer that can use software and hardware designed for another manufacturer's computer, specifically an IBM personal computer

> These days, if you hear someone referring to a clone, the odds are overwhelming that he means one thing only – a copy of the IBM personal computer. Unlike the replicated sci-fi heroines, who were invariably identically nubile, computer clones do not necessarily bear any close physical resemblance to their original. What they will do is run any program designed for the IBM P.C. – at least that is the theory. – *Daily Telegraph*, 3 March 1986

---

closed user group *noun* (*abbreviation* **CUG**) a service (eg offered by viewdata) that gives a group of people exclusive access to a body of stored information

> Teletel offers three types of service. First, there are free ones, like the phone directory. ... The second type is also free access, but you pay for it via a higher phone bill. ... It is only the third type, closed user groups (CUGs), where you have to get a password, and where the IP bills customers direct. – *Guardian*, 13 Feb. 1986

CMOS *noun* COMPLEMENTARY METAL-OXIDE SEMICONDUCTOR

---

cocktail effect *noun* the (potentially dangerous) effect of mixing two or more consumable substances together

> Bear in mind that while some additives have been tested individually for safety, no testing has been done or indeed can

satisfactorily be done on the so-called 'cocktail effect'.
- *Green Cuisine*, Spring 1986

---

cohabit *verb* to practise COHABITATION

So far, the Conservative government that France elected in March has been able to 'cohabit' with the Socialist president. - *Economist*, 28 June 1986

---

cohabitation *noun* expedient power-sharing between two differing political parties, especially when the President and the Prime Minister of a nation belong to opposing parties

Both at the Matignon and at the Elysee, officials stress that cohabitation has been going smoothly. - *Economist*, 24 May 1986

There is now a far right and a Communist left [in France], both protest parties with no prospects of governing. ... Some think the next two years could bring a further movement to the centre, with the emergence of a middle-of-the-road party from the cohabitation experiment. - *Economist*, 22 March 1986

Like France, Portugal is adjusting to the 'cohabitation' of a Socialist president and a Conservative prime minister. President Mario Soares, who took office as president on March 9th, seems to be getting on fairly well with Mr Anibal Cavaco Silva. - *Economist*, 5 April 1986

► The word is probably a loan-translation of the French word *cohabitation* rather than an extension of the existing English term.
This kind of alliance is currently demonstrated by the relationship between the socialist President François Mitterrand and the neo-Gaullist Prime Minister Jacques Chirac, and it is this pact which gave the expression currency. It gives no hint of party amalgamation and is purely the result of force of circumstances.
Yet it suggests greater affinity and co-operation than has been evident in any recent coalition in the British Isles, such as the Lib(eral)-Lab(our) Pact of 1977 in the UK or the support of the minority Labour party to Fine Gael in the Irish Republic. Mitterrand has even given way on certain foreign policy issues.
The French President prefers to describe the relationship as *co-existence.*

---

colour-enhance *verb* COLOURIZE

Last month, Walt Disney Home Video released a color-enhanced version of *The Absent-Minded Professor.*
- *Publishers Weekly*, 6 June 1986

---

colourization *noun* the process of COLOURIZING

Fred Zinnemann, who took pains in 'High Noon' to give his western the look of contemporary photographs, regards 'colourisation' as a moral outrage dictated by greed. – *Economist*, 16 Aug. 1986

► Since the 1960s audiences have been accustomed to every film (and indeed advertisement or other material shown in a cinema) being in colour. Since the mid-1970s similar attitudes have developed towards television. Thus black-and-white films in either medium are considered unacceptable to most audiences.

The colourization of 1930s films is regarded by cinema purists as a mercenary perversion.

---

colourize *or* **colourise** *verb* to add simulated colour to black-and-white film by a computerized method of matching various shades of grey on the original film to colours on the computer's PALETTE

While Roach Studios has confined its colorization activities to movies that, in their original monochrome format, are in the public domain, a number of publishers have since begun colorizing movies to which they hold or have acquired exclusive rights. – *Publishers Weekly*, 6 June 1986

---

colourizer *or* **colouriser** *noun* someone who COLOURIZES

A campaign designed only to protect a definition of 'classic' films ... and which would cast, say, Laurel and Hardy or Rogers and Astaire to the colourisers, smacks of elitism. – *Economist*, 16 Aug. 1986

---

combined heat and power *noun* (*abbreviation* **CHP**) (the technology of) a system in which energy from power stations, generators, etc, is employed as a source for both heat and electric power

Makukhin confirmed that construction would continue on nuclear plants to produce combined heat and power. Waste heat from reactors being built at Minsk and Odessa would be piped through the cities to provide heating for homes and factories. – *New Scientist*, 26 June 1986

For years, government scientists have known about a technology that would double the efficiency of Britain's power stations, provide millions of homes with cheap heating, give jobs to tens of thousands of people in inner cities, save hundreds of lives a year and produce no nasty effluents. ... The technology is called combined heat and power, usually abbreviated to CHP. – *New Scientist*, 22 May 1986

► This economical way of recycling heat attempts to counter the excessive waste of energy which is inherent in conventional power stations.

It may be seen on a large scale in pumping waste heat into houses. On a smaller scale it will take the form of a generator-installation for a single building.

Many reports over about ten years have endorsed it as a wise use of energy resources. However, only now is it being taken seriously. It could make a useful contribution to the MONERGY campaign.

---

commonhold *noun* a proposed system of joint tenure for tenants of a privately owned block of flats, whereby in cases of serious neglect or mismanagement by the owner they would have the right to form a company to buy the property and manage it

> This 'commonhold' company formed by the tenants would have power to negotiate the acquisition of owner's rights on agreed terms, and would also have the right of pre-emption in the event of an owner serving notice of his intention to sell. – *Hampstead and Highgate Express*, 1 Aug. 1986

► A Housing and Planning Bill describing such a right was published in July 1986. It is a reaction to deterioration of areas of housing in some inner city areas as a result of both vandalism and inadequate expenditure on maintenance. It is hoped that greater involvement of occupants will protect the fabric and decoration of the accommodation. In recent years many blocks of flats in inner city areas have had to be destroyed as being beyond economical repair.

---

community charge *or* **community tax** *noun* a tax of a fixed amount per person levied on adults; a poll tax

> The Minister [Nicholas Ridley] ... said he was determined to abolish the rating system and replace it with a 'community charge'. Legislation to introduce it in Scotland is planned in the next Parliamentary session. – *Daily Telegraph*, 28 June 1986

> Mr Michael Ancram, the Scottish Office Minister ... gave a slide show presentation of how the new community tax compared against the existing system or local income tax, which he rejected. – *Glasgow Herald*, 15 May 1986

► The Conservative government have a determination to resolve the undoubted anomalies in local government finance. For example, businesses pay rates but have no electoral voice. Tenants vote on the same basis as the house-owner but pay rates only indirectly.
The problem is that there is no obvious or easy alternative. An Income Tax increase across the board (to replace rates) takes no account of local circumstances. A local Income Tax runs counter to Conservative dedication to choice. Varying local levels of VAT or some other commercial tax would cause havoc with local trading patterns.
The community tax raised equally on all voters is the heir of the poll tax which has a sorry history for having sparked disorders such as the Peasants Revolt of 1381. However, it appeals to the government on the grounds of spreading the load of local finance as evenly as possible.

---

complementary *adjective* of or being medical treatment or therapy (eg osteopathy) or a system of medicine (eg homoeopathy) that falls outside the scope of orthodox medicine as practised in Britain; alternative

> The recent BMA report, commissioned by Prince Charles, the most distinguished sympathiser of 'complementary therapies',

when he was president of the BMA in 1982-3, was critical in particular of homoeopathy. - *Listener*, 3 July 1986

---

complementary expendable launch vehicle *noun* (*abbreviation* **CELV**) any of various non-reusable remotely piloted spacecraft that provide the propulsion necessary to put payloads into space

> In future, America will use a mixture of shuttles and expendable rockets. The air force has long been eager to shrug off its dependence on NASA. It is racing to build a bigger Titan, called the complementary expendable launch vehicle (CELV), that will be big enough to launch most of the heavy payloads which, in the past, have gone on the shuttle. - *Economist*, 7 June 1986

---

complementary metal-oxide semiconductor *noun* (*abbreviation* **CMOS**) a switching device used in integrated circuits, comprising a pair of complementary transistors (an n-channel and a p-channel field effect transistor) connected in series with each other on one piece of silicon. CMOS circuits are characterized by having a low power consumption, making them useful in watches and other low-power battery-operated devices.

> But chip makers are being forced to switch to CMOS because it uses less power. This means less heat, which becomes a critical factor when a million memory cells are all jammed onto a chip the size of a fingernail. - *Financial Times*, 11 March 1986

---

computer monitoring *or* **computer supervision** *noun* automatic measurement of the output of an employee who uses a computerized work-system

> More than 13 million Americans use computer terminals in their jobs, and about one-third of these people are being scrutinized as they work. ... Computer monitoring may be on its way to becoming the next big management buzz word. ... Employees, however, say that computer supervision requires machinelike performance from them that takes no account of their personal ups and downs. - *Time*, 28 July 1986

► This is becoming an important issue in the USA, where more than 20 unions have taken action against it on the grounds that it infringes privacy and places workers under undue stress.
Parallel to this, in the United Kingdom the use of VDUs has been the subject of a number of often conflicting studies. The effects on eyesight and on pregnant women have caused particular anxieties.

---

computerspeak *noun* see -SPEAK

---

computer virus *noun* an electronic code surreptitiously inserted into a computer program and designed to spread through a computer system in order to destroy or corrupt stored data or to cause the system to malfunction

> American scientists are struggling to protect computer networks ... against a potentially devastating weapon called a computer virus. Sources ... said a computer virus attack might bring a major weapons system to a standstill, throw a computer-guided missile off course or wipe out computer-stored intelligence. - *The Times*, 12 Aug. 1986

Comrade *noun* a member of a group of black radicals in South Africa

> In recent months, the opponents of revolutionary change, the so-called moderates, have been taking action of their own against the Comrades. - *Listener*, 22 May 1986

> Similar incidents occurred in Soweto all through Tuesday night. ... The radical youths known as comrades went from house to house, ordering residents to keep their lights off so that police could not see what was going on. - *Time*, 8 Sept. 1986

> Three months ago the Crossroads squatter camp was in flames as police and government-backed vigilantes routed the 'comrades'. - *Socialist Worker*, 6 Sept. 1986

---

concert party *noun* a group of people or companies acting together, especially in a financial enterprise

> Last week, the Stock Exchange published a report on share dealing in Westland which raised the possibility of a secret concert party during the bitter proxy battle fought earlier this year for a minority stake in the company. - *Financial Times*, 23 April 1986

> GT Management has rescued the Berry Trust ... by buying 6.2 million shares in concert with five other institutions. ... The other concert party members include Kleinwort Benson, Baring Brothers, the Bank of Bermuda, the US Debenture Corporation and Assurance Groupe de Paris. - *The Times*, 12 Aug. 1986

Condor *trademark* - used for a 'sniffer' machine, incorporating a mass spectrometer, which can detect hidden explosives and is intended especially for use at airports

> Condor can check a 30-ton baggage-container in three minutes. Its great disadvantage is that it is static and although there's a hand-held probe for dealing with conventional airline baggage palettes [sic], it would take an appreciable amount of time to clear each one. - *Listener*, 3 July 1986

► This machine has been developed and manufactured by British Aerospace. Trials have proved its efficiency, but its great size and expense have hindered its adoption by airlines.

containment

Always an anxiety, attacks by terrorists by way of bombs in either cabin- or hold-luggage have generated particular precautions lately. This has been especially so since the loss of an Air India aircraft in early summer 1985 with the death of all on board.
This increased attention has been heightened by the courage of fanatics from Arab and Sikh political organizations. These express a readiness to die with the passengers whom they seek to destroy. Alternatively, and less courageously, they may use KNAVES.

---

containment *noun* **1** the prevention of the release of unacceptable quantities of radioactive material beyond a controlled zone in a nuclear reactor **2** the containment system of a nuclear reactor

---

containment building *noun* a building constructed round a nuclear reactor to limit the spread of radiation, especially in the event of an accident

> Although Chernobyl, like certain western reactors, did not have a containment building, it did have impressive multiple defences. – *Economist*, 30 Aug. 1986

---

containment dome *noun* a dome-shaped CONTAINMENT BUILDING

> But major design flaws were also involved. The Russians built no containment dome over the reactor. 'A dome could have saved a lot of lives,' said Mr Potter. In addition, there were no shutdown devices capable of halting runaway nuclear reactions in the melting core. – *Observer*, 4 May 1986

---

containment zone *noun* the zone beyond which radioactivity and radioactive material are prevented from escaping by the CONTAINMENT system of a nuclear reactor

---

contrarian *noun* someone who deliberately swims against the tide of financial affairs, eg by investing heavily in a bear market or in a depressed business, in the hope of making high profits

> Mr Templeton is famed on Wall Street for his highly individual 'contrarian' approach to investment. He relies on intensive analysis, an instinct for value, and patience. – *Financial Times*, 13 Jan. 1986

> Lloyds ... wants to be a truly global commercial bank. An old market adage, quoted by other contrarians, supports its strategy: high risks bring high rewards. – *Economist*, 12 April 1986

---

convenience store *noun* a store which is designed with the convenience of the customer in mind, eg by having long opening hours, and selling a wide range of household items as well as food

> Spar, the franchised grocery chain which is Britain's biggest operator of convenience stores, has started a drive aimed at

> more than doubling its stores to about 2,000. - *The Times*, 17 March 1986

► Common in the USA since 1965, this kind of service has been growing steadily in the UK for about ten years.
The lively competition in retailing has been given impetus by the government's support of commercial free enterprise. Larger traders have also been pressurized by the innovative techniques and long opening hours offered by entrepreneurial corner shopkeepers, many of them from immigrant communities. These novel and unconventional approaches were to have been given a fillip by the Sunday Trading Bill, but this fell flat on its face and the position on Sunday commerce is now even less certain than before.
The convenience store is a response to this general competitive atmosphere.

---

cool cupboard *noun* a storage cabinet, such as a fridge or CHILLER CUPBOARD, used for storing foodstuffs at low temperatures

> With the realisation that most people now buy at least a week's food at a time ... manufacturers have come up with three different types of cool cupboard. - *Taste*, May/June 1986

---

co-processor *noun* a microprocessing device that can be attached to computers to supplement their capabilities and equip them for particular tasks (eg producing graphics or handling large numerical computations)

> The review machine was set in hardware at 8MHz and had the optional 80287 maths co-processor fitted. - *Personal Computer World*, Feb. 1986

► A main computer will perform any task within its capabilities but may do so slowly. It is therefore helpful to off-load particular functions to a co-processor if some of the work creates peculiar and awkward workloads. In this way the co-processor can work independently (on, say, floating point calculations). However, as it can only perform specialist tasks, the co-processor will inevitably be idle for fairly long periods.

---

cordon vert *adjective* typical of or being the food prepared by a person with a high degree of skill in vegetarian cookery

► Formed by analogy with *cordon bleu* (French *vert* = green); originally a jocular term but now taken seriously enough to be used as the title of a recent vegetarian cookery book by Colin Spencer and of a mark of distinction in vegetarian cookery awarded by the Vegetarian Society.

---

core *noun* a basic or fundamental model, design, or project (eg in industry) from which new models, designs, etc evolve or are developed

> Rolls has sought to shape up the company ... by both ensuring that it sells engines in all the main categories and that its huge

> £250 million a year research and development programme is efficiently and effectively spent. Rolls has gone for value for money in R&D by developing 'core' technology, from which a family of engines in different ranges are spun off. – *Guardian*, 24 April 1986

---

co-responsibility levy *noun* a tax levied on cereal farmers within the EEC in an attempt to reduce surpluses of cereals

> The European Commission appears intent on a co-responsibility levy of up to 3 per cent on all marketed grain, bar the first 25 tonnes from each farm. – *Farmers Weekly*, 29 Nov. 1985
>
> This year UK farmers will have to start helping to pay for the cost of storing surplus grain. A co-responsibility levy will be raised of about £3.40 per tonne. – *Saffron Walden Weekly News*, 21 Aug. 1986

► This measure is an attempt by the European Commission to come to terms with the considerable embarrassment and adverse publicity attracted by the Community's substantial cereal surpluses.
The problem with any agricultural controls is that the size, techniques, traditions, and sociology of farms differ throughout the Community area. Thus it is felt that this levy with a cut-off point of 25 tonnes will penalize British production. For instance, almost all British production would be liable for such a levy, as opposed to half of West Germany's.

Corporate Hospitality *noun* (*abbreviation* **CH**) hospitality extended by a business organization to favoured clients in the interests of fostering good relations, usually taking the form of a day's entertainment at a sporting event (e g Wimbledon or Henley Regatta)

> Just as PR is a refinement of advertising ... so Corporate Hospitality (CH) is its logical extension. It consists of being extremely nice all day to the people who really count. – *Daily Telegraph*, 16 June 1986

► The concept is not new but it and the related catering appear to be a growth industry. Many companies have boxes at the smarter racecourses, such as Ascot and York. This investment is often coupled with sponsoring a race in the company name.

---

corruppie *noun* a member of the YUPPIE FIVE; *broadly* a young or youngish high-flier of dubious ethical standards

> William Safire ... who now writes a doggedly independent syndicated column, the other day linked the 'corruppies' (his permutation has not yet caught on) with the recent spate of spies-for-cash, revolving door practices among Washington officials and a denigration of patriotism he alone still manages to detect. – *Guardian*, 26 Aug. 1986

► Simply a *corrupt yuppie.* It is to be hoped that this is a Safire nonce word stemming from the YUPPIEGATE scandal.

---

costly *noun* an up-market magazine lavishly produced on glossy paper, typically having a fashionable or sophisticated content, and selling at a relatively high price; an expensive glossy magazine

> The big success story in the past two or three years has come at the very top of the market, among the glossiest of the glossies - or the costlies, as they are now being called.
> - *Guardian*, 13 Aug. 1984

► Formerly, and largely still, known as *glossies.*
They tend to be among the most highly priced magazines available, for example *Harpers & Queen* at £1.80 and *Tatler* £1.50 (both monthly publications). Rising production costs inevitably mean that they contain more and more advertisements and may even make use of ADVERTORIALS.

---

couplehood *noun* the state or condition of being a couple in marriage or a similar relationship

> Suppose ... that couplehood can be divided into different and recognisable stages of growth each as distinct in its own way as adolescence is from middle age or childhood from maturity. - *Options*, May 1986

---

crack *noun, slang* a purified, potent, and highly addictive variety of cocaine, in the form of white pellets which are smoked by users - called also ROCK, JUMBO

> In the carrying basket on his bicycle, police found a plastic rubbish bag containing another handbag and a glass pipe used for smoking 'crack'. - *Daily Telegraph*, 28 May 1986
> Oxford detectives say Crack has not yet appeared in the city but there are conflicting reports that the drug has now surfaced in London. If and when it appears here it will give the drug squad and health officials sinister new problems to deal with as they struggle to warn people of Crack's fatal attraction. - *Oxford Star*, 31 July 1986

► The name probably derives from the crackling sound which the pellets make when smoked.
It is a mixture of cocaine, baking powder (or worse components, such as strychnine), and water, which has been heated. The hard pellets which result are smoked in a pipe.
Almost unknown before this year, it has rapidly swept the USA. One estimate suggests that in six months a million people have become addicted to it. The demand for it has expressed itself in increased murder and robbery in the search for the necessary funding.
Its principal dangers are that addiction is extremely quick (frequently within two weeks) and it is quick and easy to obtain. (In Oxford it can be

obtained for as little as £6 per chip). In the short term, it causes deep depression. In the long term it damages brain, liver, and lungs.

---

credit union *noun* a non-profit-making organization, usually formed of people living in the same area or attending the same workplace or club, which uses collective savings to provide funds for cheap loans

> As Britain increasingly lives on the never-never, credit unions are quietly fighting the war against consumer debt. ... There are now more than 80 credit unions and some 20 more in the pipeline. Membership totals 20,000. And they are not just popular in Britain. There are 100 million credit union members in 68 countries. - *Daily Express*, 26 Feb. 1986

---

creep-calling *noun* making a CREEP-UP CALL

► This technique is alleged to have been used by a few mischievous employees of some local authorities who remunerate their maintenance staff according to the number of calls which they make. Thus they were apparently able to call at council houses, knock on the door very softly, and tiptoe away without the occupant hearing.
The term caused a sensation when first seen, and occasioned extensive objections. It should not be used lightly.
Creep-calling, albeit not under that name, has been employed for many years in delivering unsolicited political literature in an area known to have a strong preference for the opposing party or candidate. It is hoped to avoid abuse (or physical violence). The very weak-kneed will use this approach when actually canvassing.

---

creep-up call *noun, informal* an abortive call on a council house made by a workman who, when summoned to do urgent repairs, deliberately fails to gain access to the house so that he can report that no one was at home and receive payment for making the call without doing any work

> Council workmen are making 'creep-up calls' on Council house tenants. ... The worker ... tiptoes down the path, makes a short tap on the knocker, pushes a note through the letter box saying he called while the occupant was out, and sprints back down the path. ... The practice is so widespread in some councils that it had achieved its own nick-name. - *Daily Telegraph*, 11 Sept. 1986

Creutzfeldt-Jakob disease *noun* a rare progressive disease, usually of the elderly, that is marked by dementia, muscular wasting, and spasticity

> Growth hormone is extracted from the pituitary glands of corpses and supplies have already been halted in America because of the deaths of three young Americans who received it several years ago. They died in their 20s and 30s from an extremely rare infection known as Creutzfeldt-Jakob disease which normally affects only the elderly. The only link between the three was that all had been treated with human growth

hormone when they were children in the 1960s and 1970s. - *Daily Telegraph*, 10 May 1985

► The condition is well established but has come to public notice recently. Hans Gerhard Creutzfeldt (1885–1964) and Alfons Maria Jakob (1884–1931) published important works on the central nervous system in 1920 and 1921 respectively.

---

criminalize *or* **criminalise** *verb* **1** to make (an activity) illegal; outlaw **2a** to make (a person) criminal by declaring his/her acts illegal **b** to treat as a criminal **3** to make (a place) subject to legal prohibitions or restrictions

> There are still those who would like to go ahead with another Powell-type Bill, based on the firm principle that research should be criminalised, however good its outcome. - *Today*, 17 March 1986

> The armed forces of, amongst others, France, Belgium, Holland, Sweden, Norway and Denmark do not criminalise lesbians and gays. - *New Statesman*, 1 Nov. 1985

> In recent years policing has been marked by an aggressive territorial imperative which has criminalised the streets for young people through the notorious 'sus' laws, and now seems intent on criminalising people's homes. - *Guardian*, 6 Dec. 1985

► This word was first recorded in the late 1950s, and is a typical *-ize* formation. (This simple and obvious way of producing a verb from a noun is resented and resisted by many, usually solely on the grounds of nervous unfamiliarity.) Its recent vogue, however, may owe something to the influence of the later term *decriminalize.*

Crown School *noun* a proposed British primary school for gifted pupils which is directly financed by the Department of Education and Science

> The Professional Association of Teachers resolved at its annual conference ... to oppose Crown schools because they would promote elitism. Mrs Eileen Barraclough ... said: 'All our schools should be Crown schools'. - *Daily Telegraph*, 30 July 1986

CUG *noun* CLOSED USER GROUP

---

custody suite *noun, euphemistic* a police cell

> A new euphemism was coined at Oxford Crown Court yesterday when, much to the irritation of judge Hilary Gosling, two detectives persisted in referring to 'custody suites'. ... The police claimed that they had been instructed to refer to custody suites since the introduction of the new Police

and Criminal Evidence Bill on January 1. - *Daily Telegraph*, 18 April 1986

► A euphemism which seems incongruously glamorous.
The word *suite* has been stretched somewhat in recent years. Its traditional sense of a collection of something (usually rooms in a context such as this one) has been shifted by the marketing hyperbole of trades such as hotel-keeping to mean a single room.
The terminology has also appeared in the expression *rape-suite* (*The Times*, 3 Sept. 1986). This is clearly more appropriate, as such an arrangement would involve a series of rooms for medical and other purposes. Although there was a proposal that Sussex Police might have one, there have been extensive objections to it. It would cover the whole coast from Chichester to Rye and such a huge mileage would mean that evidence would be lost and that doctors would lose the opportunity of early medical examination.

---

customer-friendly *adjective* see -FRIENDLY

---

custom publishing *noun* the publishing of a specialized magazine in which all the advertising space is sold to a single advertiser

> Associated Newspapers is to expand its magazine interests in Britain early in the new year with the introduction of 'custom publishing'. ... Custom publishing is virtually unknown in Britain except when publishers make an exclusivity offer to one advertiser to help boost revenue in an otherwise slack time. - *UK Press Gazette*, 11 Aug. 1986

---

cyberphobia *noun* fear of or hostility towards computers

> In the previous 48 hours I had seen enough computer hardware and peripherals to bring on a mild bout of what the American Psychological Association has recently identified as 'cyberphobia'. - *Listener*, 15 May 1986

► The Greek word *kybernētēs*, meaning pilot or governor, formed the basis of the English term *cybernetics* in the late 1940s. This in turn led to derivatives such as *cybernation* and *cybernated*, where the *cyber-* element means much the same as 'computer'.
Overcoming this natural fear of highly complex seemingly intelligent equipment is the reason why manufacturers have tried to make the machines user-friendly.

---

cycler *noun* a continuously moving structure in space, equipped with full life-support systems enabling astronauts to live and work there for a number of years while travelling between the planets

> The commission foresees an elaborate system of spacecraft and space stations, with astronauts shuttling between them. It calls this system the 'highway between the worlds'. At the centre of its envisaged system is 'cycler' - a space motel that

travels continuously, like a small comet, in a vast, elliptical trajectory around the sun, and crosses the orbits of both the earth and Mars. – *Economist*, 7 June 1986

DAT *noun* DIGITAL AUDIO TAPE

Technically, DAT is dynamite. In the short term it will confuse the market. In the long term, it could replace the conventional audio-cassette – just as the compact disc will eventually replace the LP. – *Listener*, 31 July 1986

data bus *noun* an electrical pathway between the microprocessor and memory in a computer, consisting of a set of wires, usually tracks on a printed circuit board, along which binary signals flow, one byte at a time, that represent information to or from a piece of external hardware (eg a printer)

The databus, like a motorway, can only handle a certain volume of traffic before all its lanes become clogged. – *New Scientist*, 20 March 1986

► This describes both the pathway and the multiple wires down which data flow. It may be spread and connected by a BACKPLANE.
The data bus is the thing which is likely to delay flow of information between the component parts of the computer, for however speedy the function of the individual parts of the computer, information can never travel along the data bus faster than the speed of light.

data compression *noun* **1** any of various techniques used in computing to save storage space by eliminating gaps, empty fields, redundancies, or unnecessary data, to shorten the length of records or blocks **2** any of various analogous techniques in which data is reduced or transformed for ease of handling

Anyone who wants to record 24 hours of high-quality stereo on a cassette the size of a cigarette packet can now do so. ... Clever data compression techniques squeeze two channels of digital code into this short length of track. To cram 24 hours of sound on a four-hour video cassette, the Sony recorder is switched to audio-only mode. – *New Scientist*, 17 Oct. 1985

DBS *noun* DIRECT BROADCASTING BY SATELLITE

---

debtnocrat *noun, informal* an official of the International Monetary Fund, the World Bank, or a comparable organization, who deals with international debts

> This 'debtnocrat' official was not alone in seeing virtue in the Bradley proposal. - *Guardian*, 1 Aug. 1986

► The *-crat* suffix has been extensively used lately to produce pejorative compounds. The original model of this generation was *bureaucrat*, itself described by the Fowlers in severe language. (*Aristocrat* and so on are much earlier, deriving from the Greek *kratos* (= strength)). *Eurocrat* is a formation favoured by critics of the EEC, who imagine the European Commissions staff to be larger than it is. (In fact, it is the same size as the Scottish Office.) *Debtnocrat* is strangely constructed as it retains a redundant *-n-* in the middle, presumably based on *technocrat.*
The debts of the Third World have generated much emotive reaction. There was at one time a fear that the inability of Mexico and other Latin American nations to discharge debts to British and other European banks might cause a collapse of the City. The lending by the British clearing banks has been scrutinized by those interested in development issues. Many such people avoid banks with a reputation for extravagant and, as they see it, avaricious lending to poor countries which can hardly service the debt, let alone repay it.

---

decerealization *or* **decerealisation** *noun* the conversion of land traditionally used for growing cereals to other uses

> The prospect of 20,000 new golf clubs might strike the Royal and Ancient as a possible threat to the character of the game. It would want to ask questions; but nothing compared to the questions the EEC Commission could contrive about the proper course to follow for the decerealization of farmland. - *Daily Telegraph*, 11 June 1986

► In the light of the CO-RESPONSIBILITY LEVY and other pressures to reduce cereal production, many arable farmers are becoming OUTGOERS.

---

deep litter egg *noun* (the EEC term for) an egg produced by hens kept uncaged in sheds at a density of not more than seven hens per square metre and with at least a third of the floor area covered with litter material - compare SEMI-INTENSIVE EGG, BARN EGG

> In between these two extremes [semi-intensive eggs and barn eggs] came 'deep litter' eggs. Here hens are confined to sheds but the density is a roomier seven hens per metre. - *New Health*, Sept. 1986

---

de-industrialization *or* **de-industrialisation** *noun* the dismantling of much of the industry in an area through the closing down of existing industrial businesses and failure to attract new ones

> Cleveland, the county with the highest unemployment rate in

> Britain, yesterday launched a campaign to pressurise the Government into giving it £50 million-a-year aid. Unemployment, de-industrialisation and dereliction have united all sections of the community in the belief that the county needs urgent help. – *Daily Telegraph*, 19 June 1986

► An extension of the established sense of the word, defined in the *Longman Dictionary of the English Language* as 'the tendency over time for the share of a country's gross domestic product contributed by the manufacturing sector to fall relative to that contributed by the service sector'.

---

de-industrialize *or* **de-industrialise** *verb* to carry out DE-INDUSTRIALIZATION

> Manufacturing accounts for a small and shrinking part of the American economy. The dollar's overvaluation in 1982–85 hastened this change but it did not 'de-industrialise' the United States. – *Economist*, 19 April 1986

---

[1]**demi-veg** *adjective* of or following a diet that is mainly vegetarian but sometimes includes animal products such as poultry and fish

> A new word 'demi-veg' has entered the English language to describe an increasing number of people who are only part vegetarian. The Fresh Fruit and Vegetable Information Bureau shows that over three million people in this country ... have adopted a semi-vegetarian lifestyle by cutting out red meats and foods which are high in salt, sugar and fat from their diets. – *Saffron Walden Weekly News*, 3 July 1986

> One element that ought to disturb the meat trade is that the demi-veg diet is a trendy one. ... So it has become the cool thing not to eat red meat as it is not to smoke. – *Guardian*, 20 June 1986

---

[2]**demi-veg** *noun* a person who follows a DEMI-VEG diet

---

de-modernization *or* **de-modernisation** *noun* a process of making less modern e g the removal of some modern architectural features, such as raised walkways linking tower blocks, in order to render buildings more habitable and less conducive to crime

> ... The announcement of a five year de-modernisation plan for the borough's twelve-year old Mozart estate to be carried out in accordance with Coleman's recommendations at a cost of between £2 and £3 million. – *Guardian*, 13 Jan. 1986

---

depauperization *or* **depauperisation** *noun* the elimination or reduction of poverty

> The depauperisation of China means some Chinese getting less poor quicker than others. – *Economist*, 31 May 1986

---

deselect *verb* to drop from a team or group; *especially, of a constituency political party in Britain* to revoke the official nomination of (a sitting MP or prospective parliamentary candidate); to refuse to readopt as a parliamentary candidate

> In Park ward ... a deselected Labour councillor stood as 'Labour against Militant' and polled 57% against the official candidate's 25%. - *Economist*, 24 May 1986

► The word has come to significance as a result of pressure in many constituency Labour parties for replacement of right-wing candidates. The procedure is not restricted to Labour, however. Sir Anthony Meyer Bt, MP for Clwyd North West (Conservative) was considered for deselection. Indeed, although the word is new, the procedure stretches back some time. The Conservative Association for the Cambridgeshire South West constituency changed their minds and rejected, shortly before the 1983 General Election, their chosen candidate. This - it was said - was because his wife was a member of the League Against Cruel Sports. The constituency is a rural one in which foxhunting is important.
The Chairwoman of Wiltshire Education Committee was faced with the possibility of deselection during 1986 over the still-lingering issue of preservation of grammar schools.
The result of successfully resisting deselection is the procedure described by the more familiar term of *readoption*, as in: 'My readoption as the Tory candidate for Aldershot last month was one in the eye for the "Sunday Express".' (Julian Critchley, *Listener*, 1 May 1986).

---

deselection *noun* deselecting or being deselected

> Mr Cocks believes that the consequence of his de-selection could be the loss of his Bristol South seat, the only Labour seat in the South West. - *Observer*, 6 April 1986

---

designer drug *noun* a synthetic drug that has effects similar to those of an illegal narcotic (especially cocaine and heroin) but is not specifically proscribed by law

> Designer drugs, which can be made in a school laboratory and provide the equivalent of artificial heroin or cocaine, are sweeping the United States. - *Guardian*, 21 March 1986

> The new 'fashion' in drugs soon to hit Britain would be the 'designer drugs' - home-made, synthetic drugs - with similar effects to heroin and cocaine, whose formulation can be tampered with by the individual user to suit his or her taste. - *Daily Telegraph*, 3 Feb. 1986

► The adjective *designer* has been used in many fanciful and astonishing ways. Besides this phrase, *Company* has described *designer water* (Feb. 1986), and the *Guardian* has mentioned *designer movie* (3 July 1986). On 13 May 1986, the *Sun* showed Derek Hatton, the sartorially-sensitive Liverpool Labour politician, as wearing a *designer suit* (presumably closely related to a tailor-made suit). The *Observer* (20 July 1986) extends the vogue to Scottish culinary art: 'There is fast-food haggis and there is a special-celebration '*designer*' *haggis*, which in Edinburgh probably comes from master-butcher John MacSween.' Then there is *designer stubble*, the two or three days' growth of beard carefully nurtured by fashionable men. The *New Statesman* (19 May 1986) is apprehensive about the imminence of *designer socialism*, with gin and tonic at £1.75 a glass. Yet we may have (according to the *Guardian*, 7 March 1986) high hopes of the performance of a *designer bug*. This is a genetically engineered virus which the Ministry of Agriculture has approved in principle. Its purpose in life is to attack the caterpillars of the moth *Panolis flammea*, which vandalizes lodgepole pines.

---

desktop *adjective* **1** of or being a complete computer system usually comprising a keyboard, data and program storage facility, visual display terminal, and often a printer, all in one unit **2** of or being a program, language, etc for use with a desktop computer

> The new, compact Epson 'Taxi' PC ideally suited to accessing these 'electronic libraries' is a powerful, low cost IBM compatible desktop computer that's supremely easy to use - whether or not you have any previous computing experience, and it's available in three configurations from small business to corporate applications. - *The Times*, 11 March 1986

> Programs known as desktop organisers can also include games that can quickly be banished from the screen though they tend to be of the more worthy mental stimulation type. - *The Times*, 11 March 1986

► This derives from the notion that such a computer may be accommodated on a desk-top as opposed to a computer-room. Manufacturers such as IBM and Wang have been making them since 1983 or 1984 and they are now fairly commonplace. They have contracted in size so much that it is now possible to see the desk as well.
It is an instance of VERY LARGE SCALE INTEGRATION. The logic process, the arithmetic process, and the memory storage previously being housed in racks and racks of relays can now sit on one chip.
LAP-TOP takes it one stage further.

---

desktop publisher *noun* someone who carries out DESKTOP PUBLISHING

> 'We're doing more and more of our communication on desktop systems', she said. 'It comes out looking beautiful. Our receptionist is now producing some of our internal material with graphics. Everybody who uses a typewriter can be a desktop publisher'. - *Majorcan Daily Bulletin*, 29 May 1986

---

desktop publishing *noun* an office DESKTOP system essentially comprising a personal computer, software, and laser printer, on which can be performed all necessary stages in the production of printed material

> Desktop publishing, a technology that has only recently

reached the buzzword stage in Silicon Valley, is being touted by high-technology insiders as the industry's latest white knight.... Said John Sculley, Apple's chairman. ... 'What we are doing is coming up with a concept that fills the gap between the typewriter and the typesetter'. ... 'I believe desk-top publishing is far more than a niche market. It's a way to revolutionise the way we communicate on the printed page'. – *Majorcan Daily Bulletin*, 29 May 1986

Desktop publishing basically means using a smallish computer to produce documents with an appearance and a print quality which approaches that of professionally typeset material. Its done in-house, so you aren't paying fees, and you don't have to wait for the print shop. – *Daily Telegraph*, 4 Aug. 1986

► This kind of entrepreneurial activity is the product of simple tools of the trade (a personal computer, the relevant software, and a laser printer) which are easy to use.
Apple of Cupertino, California lead the field in producing this type of equipment. It can be obtained from about £4,000.

---

desmond *noun, British slang* a lower second-class (university or polytechnic) degree

► This is a pun on the name of Archbishop Desmond *Tutu* (2:2). The Archbishop has been prominent in news coverage of the unhappy developments in the Republic of South Africa. For some time the Bishop of Johannesburg, he was preferred to the Archbishopric of Cape Town during the summer of 1986.
The pun reputedly owes its origins to students of Newcastle University.

---

detensify *or* **de-tense** *verb* to relieve of nervous tension; relax

He studied the work of people like Jacobson in Chicago and became expert in detensifying techniques and in the art of meditation. – *Guardian*, 19 Feb. 1986

Relax back. De-tense and tone up with wooden massage rollers. – *Cosmopolitan*, July 1986

---

de-tensioned *adjective* freed from nervous tension; relaxed, especially as a result of relaxation exercises

The Rev Geoffrey Harding, now retired ... pottered amiably around the vestry kitchen preparing tea for the de-tensioned City workers. – *Guardian*, 19 Feb. 1986

---

dieselization *or* **dieselisation** *noun* the act or process of DIESELIZING

---

dieselize *or* **dieselise** *verb* **1** to adapt or convert (eg a petrol engine) to use diesel as a fuel **2** to equip or be equipped with a diesel engine

In Britain, the large car user is cushioned from the harsh

economic realities because ... his fuel bills are met by the company. He has much less incentive to dieselise than his continental counterpart. - *Financial Times*, 10 Feb. 1986

---

digital audio tape *noun* (*abbreviation* **DAT**) tape that records and stores sound in digital form

The DAT (digital audio tape) cassette will record or play-back prerecorded tapes about two-thirds the size of the familiar compact cassette. Maximum playing time will be about two hours, with quality roughly equivalent to compact disc. - *Observer*, 4 May 1986

---

dim-dip *noun* a device on a road vehicle which automatically turns on low-powered dipped headlights when the engine is running and the side lights are switched on, in order to make vehicles more visible to pedestrians and to reduce headlight glare in well-lit streets.

---

direct broadcasting by satellite *noun* (*abbreviation* **DBS**) a system that broadcasts television programmes direct to homes, using artificial satellites in earth orbit

Cable television, which depends largely on programmes beamed by satellite and picked up on commercial-size dish aerials, is the bit of the future that has taken off. The bit that is still waiting to happen is DBS, or Direct Broadcasting by Satellite. This was the brave new venture that required us to install dinky little dishes at the bottom of our gardens so that we could receive three or four extra BBC and ITV channels directly from the sky. - *Daily Telegraph*, 3 March 1986

A substantial step toward realizing that dream will take place this autumn with the launch of the British satellite television service Superchannel. ... It will be the forerunner of a new type of television, Direct Broadcasting by Satellite (DBS). Television channels on high-powered satellites ... will be beamed directly into viewers' homes where they will be received by small dish aerials costing about £500. - *The Times*, 7 July 1986

---

directed-energy weapon *noun* any of a group of weapons used for missile defence, that destroy their targets by directing high-energy beams of radiation or subnuclear particles onto them, can be ground or space-based, and include chemical and X-ray lasers and PARTICLE-BEAM WEAPONS

NATO's top military commander, General Bernard Rogers ... is proposing an improved air defence system that could draw on some of the research into directed-energy weapons ... for the US Strategic Defence Initiative (Star Wars, so called). - *Financial Times*, 1 Aug. 1986

> To leave no technological stone unturned, the SDI organisation is studying about a dozen directed-energy weapon concepts, in various stages of development. Farthest along are infrared chemical lasers. - *New Scientist*, 20 June 1985

► Directed-energy weapons use electromagnetic or accelerated particles of matter so focussed and directed, and at such levels of power, that they cause deliberate damage.
It is intended that the laser weapons and PARTICLE-BEAM WEAPONS which are forms of this weaponry should constitute components of the Strategic Defence Initiative.

---

direct-injection *adjective, of a diesel engine* having the fuel and air mixture injected directly into the combustion chamber

> Competition in the rapidly-growing diesel car sector is also expected to intensify, with the arrival during the course of this year of Austin Rover cars fitted with a new direct-injection diesel engine developed jointly with Perkins. Austin Rover expects to be able to claim a 'world first' for such a unit to be installed in cars which will include the Montego and Maestro. - *Financial Times*, 10 Feb. 1986

► Conventional car diesel engines have a precombustion chamber where the air and fuel are mixed. Direct-injection engines include techniques which increase the air circulation and ensure better combustion, resulting in a performance that is better and uses less fuel than current diesel engines.

---

disintermediation *noun* the practice in corporate finance of borrowing money directly from lenders, thus dispensing with the services of an intermediary (e g a bank)

> Where rules and rulemakers permit, commercial banks will ... search for ways to reverse the 'disintermediation' which has sent corporate clients to the markets rather than their bank managers for cash. - *Economist*, 28 June 1986

► Companies wishing to raise money externally have traditionally borrowed from banks. This situation is changing in many industrial countries, particularly in the USA. The deregulation of interest rates has pushed up the price of bank loans, and often it is cheaper and more flexible to raise money directly from investors by issuing financial instruments (shares, bonds, commercial paper, etc). Among large Japanese companies, for example, the proportion of external finance raised from bank borrowing fell from 60% in 1982–3 to 35% in 1984–5.

---

disinvest *verb* to practise DISINVESTMENT

> The ranks of underemployed apartheid bureaucrats wait

eagerly to nationalise the assets of foreign firms inclined to 'disinvest'. - *Economist*, 21 June 1986

---

disinvestment *or* **divestment** *or* **divestiture** *noun* reduction or ending of investment; *especially* the withdrawal of investment and cutting of other economic links with a company or nation as a form of sanctions

[Frank] Field has written to the 200 voting members of the laity with demands for the Church to carry out its policy of 'disinvestment' in South Africa. - *Daily Telegraph*, 26 Feb. 1986

On July 16th, the regents of the University of California ... enacted the biggest institutional disinvestment measure yet against South Africa, voting to sell off $3 billion in stocks and bonds in companies which had South African dealings. - *Economist*, 26 July 1986

Although American investment in Ulster is relatively small - only $1.2 billion - the potential impact of a campaign that even hints at divestment could be far greater than in South Africa since the 24 American companies in Ulster employ 11% of the workforce. - *Economist*, 3 May 1986

So far nobody has come up with a telling measure of the effectiveness of public or private sanctions. Even the extent of divestiture is hard to measure. - *Economist*, 12 April 1986

► The basic sense of *disinvestment* in economics dates back to Lord Keynes, who alternatively referred to it as 'negative investment'. The word has recently acquired new connotations, particularly in contexts relating to South Africa: rather than simply a failure to invest money in a business (eg by not replacing capital equipment), it now indicates a deliberate severing of economic ties.

---

disinvitation *noun* disinviting or being DISINVITED

For Honeyford, 'disinvitation' is a common experience. When the students of Oxford Polytechnic invited him to a conference, he was not surprised to receive a letter from the dean of the faculty of educational studies suggesting that 'there may be a number of reasons why you might consider it appropriate to decline the invitation'. - *The Times*, 25 June 1986

---

disinvite *verb* to withdraw an invitation to (a guest speaker, conference delegate, etc), especially on the grounds that the invited person's opinions or associations are held to be politically unacceptable

He [Ray Honeyford] was invited recently by Leeds city council to speak publicly on the subject of 'peace education,' and then hastily 'disinvited' when it was discovered that, on

this subject too, his opinions would prove disagreeable to the fascist left. - *The Times*, 25 June 1986
The pressure to 'disinvite' the South Africans and one delegate from Namibia [from the World Archaeological Congress in Southampton], came from the Southampton branch of the Association of University Teachers. - *The Times*, 18 Jan. 1986

► In times of diminishing courtesy, it has become quite common to withdraw an invitation - frequently because circumstances have changed and the visit would no longer be appropriate. Too often, however, it is the result of insufficient consultation by the inviting committee, coupled with aggressive resistance by a minority of agitators.
Several Conservative government ministers endured this rudeness during the first half of 1986 when education budgets were causing unfavourable reactions in universities and schools.

---

disorderly conduct *noun* an offence of public misconduct causing distress, harassment, or alarm

► The Conservative government in Britain has long stressed its emphasis on law and order. This has given the party much electoral appeal. However, such zeal has not always been endorsed by results. A rising crime-rate and increasingly ghastly forms of football hooliganism have been coupled with scenes of unseemly violence in the course of the NUM dispute and the early months of News International's operation from Wapping.
A white paper *Review of Public Order* was published in 1985. This in turn resulted in a Public Order Bill which was going through Parliament during 1986. Various new offences were suggested in the white paper and embodied in the bill. Disorderly conduct is intended to embrace the more nebulous kinds of hooligan or anti-social activity, which previously lay outside the bounds of any defined criminal offence. In particular, it seeks to prevent general annoyance of old people and people of other racial groups. It includes writing and signs which are threatening, abusive, or insulting.

---

distributive sex *noun, US euphemistic* promiscuous sexual behaviour

In America, the term 'distributive sex' is in some places preferred to the word 'promiscuity'. - *English Today*, Jan.-March 1986

---

ditz *noun* a DITZY person

'Meryl Streep is serious, Suzanne Somers isn't. That's the way they're seen. ... I don't think Miss Somers does ditsy tap dances when she gets home. I've been both. I used to be a ditz. Now I'm talented.' [Cher] - *Guardian*, 22 June 1985

---

ditzy *or* **ditsy** *adjective, chiefly US informal* excessively refined or affected; chichi

> Godard's opinions on television are pure middlebrow 'Guardian' old hat - the box is usurping cinema, usurping reality. Though some of the ditzy chatter is deliberately idly amusing, the fact is: most of it is serious in intent. - *City Limits*, 9 Aug. 1985

---

divestment *noun* DISINVESTMENT

---

divestor *noun* a person or organization engaging in DISINVESTMENT

> Along with 12 earlier total divestors and 30 partial divestors, universities have withdrawn some $400m from companies doing business with South Africa. - *Economist*, 12 April 1986

DNA fingerprint *noun* GENETIC FINGERPRINT

DNA fingerprinting *noun* GENETIC FINGERPRINTING

---

dogfood *noun, US slang* BLACK TAR

---

doorstepping *noun* **1** door-to-door political canvassing **2** *derogatory* intrusive tactics (eg besieging people's homes or pestering them with questions) used by journalists to obtain a story

> Admittedly, there was not much sign of a strong anti-Thatcher backlash as Mr Carrington ... went door-stepping around Hurlingham Park. - *Financial Times*, 26 Feb. 1986

> The BBC announced that it was to terminate *Checkpoint*, the programme in which [Roger] Cook made his name by pursuing ... small-town crooks up their driveways and into their mock-Tudor domiciles. Perhaps Auntie ... was growing nervous of the door-stepping antics of Big Roger? - *New Scientist*, 26 Sept. 1985

► The non-derogatory sense of the word has become important as a result of voters' reluctance to attend public meetings. Up to about the Macmillan election of 1959 it was reasonable to expect substantial attendances at public meetings for both local and general elections. These are now exceptional. The importance of television and other domestic entertainments means that constituents expect to be canvassed at home. The term has led to the expression used by political organizations 'on the doorstep' and its logical extension 'leaning on doorbells'.
The derogatory sense is less innocuous. Notwithstanding attempts by the Press Council to impose a reasonable code of morality on journalistic practice, there have been some shameful excesses by less reputable journalists. This particularly applies in cases of scandal, sexual crime, and bereavement.

Whereas in the political sense, most of the conversation does take place on the doorstep (or, if the canvasser is welcome, inside the door), in the journalistic sense such a direct approach is unlikely to be successful. Hence the disc jockey Simon Bates said (BBC Radio 1; 21 Aug. 1986) how agreeable it would be if the press would treat the forthcoming (Bob) Geldof-(Paula) Yates post-nuptial festivities in a civilized way and just 'took the piccies and didn't do the doorstepping; down the chimney and so on'.

---

dp-speak *noun* see -SPEAK

---

dragon lady *noun* a woman who, as the wife of a ruler, has acquired formidable personal power

> In the space of 18 days, two of the 20th century's best-known 'dragon ladies' have seen their power and their sumptuous lifestyles end abruptly and ignominiously. Before dawn on Feb. 7, Haiti's First lady, Mme. Michele Duvalier ... accompanied her husband, 34-year-old Jean-Claude 'Baby Doc' Duvalier, up the steps of an American C-141 military transport for a flight to ... France. It was late evening yesterday at Clark air force base in the Philippines when 57-year-old Imelda Marcos joined her husband. – *Daily Telegraph*, 27 Feb. 1986

► The dragon has been a symbol of power – generally destructive – since the mythology of ancient Greece and the symbolism of the Old Testament, eg Bel and the Dragon. They were usually associated with voracious appetites.

History shows a variety of women in powerful positions achieved through their husbands' eminence. In the Roman Empire Augustus' second wife, Livia Drusilla, used her position to control many aspects of affairs at Court. Eventually she ensured the succession of Tiberius, her son by an earlier marriage, through nepotism. Claudius' second wife, Messalina, found in her position an opportunity for sexual licence of – even by the standards of those times – exceptional athleticism.

The three great revolutions of modern western European history have all been characterized by domineering women: the English revolution (Henrietta Maria, wife of Charles I), the French (Marie Antoinette, wife of Louis XVI), and the Russian (Alix, wife of Nicholas II).

Early in 1986, two of the current specimens came unstuck in dramatic circumstances. Imelda Marcos, wife of Ferdinand Marcos, who had been in power in the Philippines since 1965, fled on 26 February. Ironically, her husband's regime was replaced by that of Mrs Cory Aquino, who was a totally inexperienced – and in some ways naive – politician coming to power on a wave of sentimental support on behalf of her murdered husband.

Michele Duvalier is the wife of Jean-Claude Duvalier ('Baby Doc'), whose period of power in Haiti ran from 1971 (when he succeeded his father) to 7 February. She is a spectacularly beautiful Creole. Creoles are a group feared or despised by most of the island's population, including her husband's family and connections. So her eminence was particularly an object of loathing and distrust, even when her husband's status was tolerated. As the Duvalier regime tottered there was something of a shift in influence from Michele Duvalier to her mother-in-law and sister-in-law; two other dragon ladies.

Both Imelda Marcos' and Michele Duvalier's power featured extravagant parties. Also, in the case of Marcos, colossal wardrobes were discovered and, with Duvalier, highly-priced jewellery.

The popularity of Benazir Bhutto in Pakistan during 1986 has indirect parallels. It is based on the reputation of her dead father. Miss Bhutto has, however, a record of political awareness and academic achievement.

Droppies *plural noun* Disillusioned, Relatively Ordinary Professionals, Preferring Independent Employment Situations: people who leave full-time careers to pursue a more flexible and fulfilling form of self-employment

> Chris [Roberts] can only find one problem to date. 'If I start listing the benefits of my new life I lay myself open to charges of under-achievement, irresponsibility and even parasitism.' ... This leads to a reluctance by Droppies to admit how congenial the new life is. - *New Society*, 5 Sept. 1986

---

druglord *noun* the influential boss of a drug-dealing racket

> The governor of the drug-rich state of Sinaloa ... is thought to be a close accomplice of Mexico's most wanted druglord, Felix Gallardo. - *Sunday Times*, 1 June 1986

► The word has two possible sources. It may be modelled on *landlord*, *slumlord*, etc; or it may be simply a variant of the better-known term *drug baron.*

Dry *noun, British* a Conservative politician who holds hard-line or uncompromising views, especially in supporting the monetarist policies of Margaret Thatcher's government; one who is opposed to the moderate *Wet* faction

> The proportion of Wets and Dries in the Cabinet is still evenly balanced. - *Sun*, 30 Jan. 1986

► The term *wet* is very well-established, having its origins at the time of the 1979 General Election to denigrate a Conservative politician not having the stomach for the more extreme policies of the new Thatcher administration. It derives directly from prep-school slang.

Dry is a straight reverse to describe those who are loyal to Mrs Thatcher and thus reliable. Messrs Tebbit, Lawson, Ridley and Sir Keith Joseph (the originator of Thatcherism) are generally considered to fall safely into this category.

Another entertaining term is slowly emerging from the mass of meteorological analogy: *sogginess*, describing the quality of being (fairly) wet and embracing SDP, Liberal, and (in some opinions) Labour positions.

---

dual capacity *noun* the double role, incorporating the roles previously allotted separately to a stockbroker and a stockjobber, allowed to a member of the London Stock Exchange after BIG BANG – compare SINGLE CAPACITY

> The famous Big Bang ... will involve the ending of the rigid separation of brokers and market makers – bringing in so-called 'dual capacity'. – *Financial Times*, 3 March 1986

Duckathon *noun* see -ATHON

---

ductility *noun* the ability of a structure to absorb and dissipate energy, achieved by incorporating selected weak points which give way first under stress (eg during an earthquake) and thus protect more important parts of the structure

> To get structures to withstand [an earthquake] is a matter of allowing them to move, even if they distort permanently, but not to the point of breaking up. The concept is called ductility. – *Financial Times*, 6 March 1986

---

dumb terminal *noun* a computer terminal that has no processing power and can only transmit or receive data

> When volumes were low, the market was able to cope using a simple batch system. Buyers and sellers presented their sales tickets to order entry clerks on the market floor who put the details into the computer system using a simple 'dumb' terminal – that is, one without its own processor 'brain.' – *Financial Times*, 17 March 1986

---

dwarf-throwing *noun* the sporting activity of throwing a volunteer dwarf as far as possible

> An international dwarf-throwing competition in West Germany next month has been cancelled. ... The Hamburg-based Organisation of People of Restricted Growth protested about what it called a macabre spectacle. – *Daily Telegraph*, 18 Feb. 1986

► This pastime has suddenly become so well-established that it has actually been used under sponsorship to raise money for charity. World championships have been advertised with 90 contests in pubs and clubs. The volunteer wears a helmet, but is still prone to considerable danger to his body. Indeed, the practice has been the subject of extensive protest. Its immediate history suggests origins in 1985 in a saloon bar in Australia. It had been introduced as a means of attracting customers. However, it was witnessed as an informal entertainment as long ago as 1963 in the Black Forest.
'Peter Simple', the *Daily Telegraph* humorous columnist, wrote (29 May 1986): 'I fully expect to see dwarf throwing included as an official event in

the next Olympics and its potential for charitable fund-raising (e.g. 'Dwarf Aid') is immense.'

economic refugee *noun* someone who flees to a foreign country (especially from a Communist or third-world country to the West) mainly to obtain a higher standard of living rather than to escape danger or persecution

> Last week Chancellor Helmut Kohl announced measures designed to discourage immigration. ... The new rules may help deter some of the 30,000 so-called economic refugees who are expected to step into the transit lounges at West German airports this year and request asylum. - *Time*, 8 Sept. 1986

econospeak *noun* see -SPEAK

ecosocialism *noun* a brand of socialism which emphasizes ecological issues

> Ecosocialism has undermined the Greens, who won only 2.5% of the vote last year and so have no seats in the state parliament. - *Economist*, 10 May 1986

educationspeak *noun* see -SPEAK

EFA *noun* EUROFIGHTER

egomyth *noun* an elitist belief about a person's worth eg the belief that an Oxbridge education is always the most desirable academic background

> H. Williams ... explores some of the elitist barriers that still exist in UK business society: the so-called 'egomyths'. - *Financial Times*, 24 Feb. 1986

electroantennogram *noun* a tracing of the electrical activity of an insect's antenna

> Tiny probes inserted into the antennae of insect pests could show how they home in on their favourite crops. Researchers at the US Department of Agriculture are experimenting with the probes on the Mediterranean fruit fly - the scourge of California fruit growers - the cotton boll weevil and a variety of other pests. Eric Jang of the Tropical Fruit and Vegetable

> Research Laboratory in Hawaii presents fruit flies with a selection of smells. When the insect detects a smell it triggers an electrical response which is picked up by the probe and recorded as an 'electroantennogram'. - *New Scientist*, 26 June 1986

---

electronic erosion *noun* the breaking down of barriers, eg between countries, by the frequent use of quick and easy electronic communication systems

> Small towns and cities become more important relative to nations, whose frontiers are broken down by 'electronic erosion', money and information swirl around the globe, in defiance of all political controls. - *Daily Telegraph*, 14 June 1986

---

electro-thread *noun* a security device consisting of a short strand of wire which can be attached to or built into products in a shop and will set off an electronic alarm at the shop door unless deactivated by a shop assistant on payment for the item

> Unlike conventional hard tags, the electro thread can be disguised as a price ticket or label or even sewn unobtrusively into clothing and textiles. - *Daily Telegraph*, 1 Jan. 1986

Elginism *noun* the practice of stealing antique fixtures and fittings from old houses

> A. J. Amos of the London Architectural Salvage and Supply Co., puts the cost of replacing a stolen antique fireplace at £20,000. 'It's Bill Sykes all over again,' he says, 'It's been graced with the name of Elginism.' - *Daily Telegraph*, 13 June 1986

► From Thomas Bruce, 7th Earl of Elgin (1766-1841), and the Greek artefacts which he removed from Athens and the surrounding area.
At the time he was Ambassador to the Ottoman Porte and he removed the items with the full authority of the Porte at various dates between 1803 and 1812. They largely ended up in the British Museum, where they have remained ever since.
The most important pieces were portions of the frieze and other sculptures of the Parthenon. They also included some segments of the Athenian temple of Nike Apteros and various bits and pieces from Attica.
The subject is currently relevant as the Panhellenic Socialist Greek government has been making attempts to recover them, largely through the person of Melina Mercouri, the actress, their Minister of Culture. The British government has, however, rejected the claim on the grounds that return of the marbles would set a precedent resulting in the passage of a colossal number of antiquities all around the globe back to their places of - sometimes historically remote - origin.

Elves of Wall Street *plural noun, informal* the market analysts on the New York Stock Exchange, usually considered to be the grey eminences controlling the state of the market

> Volatile share prices stabilised last night after Wall Street's record drop this week which was attributed to bearishness on the part of ... the so-called 'Elves of Wall Street'. - *Daily Telegraph*, 10 July 1986

► Modelled on Sir Harold Wilson's coinage *gnomes of Zurich* in 1956 (speech in House of Commons): 'All these financiers, all the little gnomes of Zurich and the other financial centres, about whom we keep on hearing.'

---

email *noun* electronic mail

> Telecom Gold is a good email system because it allows you to configure it to suit your own terminal and your own method of working. - *Practical Computing*, March 1986

Eminent Persons Group *noun* (*abbreviation* **EPG**) the group of seven statesmen from Commonwealth countries who visited South Africa in 1986 in an unsuccessful attempt to negotiate a peaceful settlement of the country's political crisis

> Members of the Eminent Persons Group ... refused to abandon their efforts in spite of Pretoria's destructively-timed raids on the principal black opposition movement. - *Scotsman*, 21 May 1986

> Part of the trouble with the debate was that everyone felt compelled to pay tribute to the work of the Eminent Persons Group. I am not sure whether Eminent Persons should be encouraged to go about in a Group. For group travel tends to reinforce their sense of eminence, their consciousness of destiny sitting on their shoulders. - *Spectator*, 21 June 1986

► The Commonwealth leaders' summit at Nassau in December 1985 tasked the team to visit South Africa and to submit a report on what they found there. After a courteous exchange of letters with President P.W. Botha, the team paid their visit.

Few questioned their integrity or their motivation. However, their title was the subject of some ribald jocularity because of its apparent pomposity. The sexually impartial *persons* was made necessary by the Group's composition of six men and one woman (Nita Barrow).

The group operated under the co-chairmanship of Malcolm Fraser (Prime Minister of Australia 1975–83) and General Olusegun Obasanjo (Head of the Federal Government of Nigeria 1976–79).

Their report, *Mission to South Africa*, published in June 1986, dwells a great deal on the undoubtedly moving nature of the group's experiences. They recommended - probably somewhat ambitiously - that the South African government should dismantle Apartheid, release Nelson Mandela (and others), lift the ban on the African National Congress and other parties, and establish a more representative government.

---

enhancer *noun* a region of DNA in the nucleus of a cell, that stimulates other nearby segments of DNA to synthesize RNA during replication of the cell's genetic material

> This is a characteristic of 'enhancers' - the regions of DNA that stimulate transcription of nearby segments of DNA into RNA; antibody genes are partially controlled by these enhancers. - *New Scientist*, 13 June 1985

E number *noun* a number, preceded by the letter E, which is found in lists of food ingredients and denotes a certain food additive

> From July, all caramels used as colours ... will have to be listed on labels either by name or E-number. - *Which*, June 1986

► *E* indicates European, the number being part of a scheme of harmonizing EEC food control regulations.

Environmentally Sensitive Area *noun* (*abbreviation* **ESA**) an area of the United Kingdom which has been specified by the Ministry of Agriculture for restraint in agricultural techniques in order to preserve the environment

> Sussex Downs have been chosen as one of six environmentally sensitive areas in England and Wales, it was stated yesterday. ... One aim of the designation is to reduce the acreage of crops and to reintroduce sheep grazing, traditional role of the Downs. - *Daily Telegraph*, 28 Aug. 1986

► The Ministry of Agriculture has identified certain areas, such as the Yorkshire Dales and the Norfolk Broads, in which the preservation of a spectacular environment is considered more important than intensive agricultural production. Farmers have been urged to eschew the more dramatic kinds of fertilizer and intensive farming techniques in return for financial compensation. This accords obviously with the embarrassment of European Community surpluses of agricultural produce and the current need to promote employment opportunities through tourism. However, the 1986 allocation of £6 million for compensation seems somewhat modest.

---

environment-friendly *adjective* see -FRIENDLY

EPG *noun* EMINENT PERSONS GROUP

> The six-month deadline by which the EPG should report to the six Commonwealth states monitoring their progress

> technically expires at the end of June. - *Scotsman*, 21 May 1986

---

episcopi vagantes *plural noun* bishops of minor Christian congregations who are unrecognized by, or have no authority within, any major Christian Church

► Latin, literally 'wandering bishops'.

Various breaches in the line of consecration have given rise to these unconventional prelates. The first was the schism in AD 312 between Saint Augustine and the Donatists. In this century the consecration of the Old Catholics in Holland and the schismatic bishops in the east of Ceylon (now Sri Lanka) are examples.

Some adopt fantastic titles and they are generally not associated with territorially definable dioceses. They are consecrated in an irregular or clandestine manner, passing on their authority in equally irregular ordinations. Such congregations as they have are minimal.

A.N. Wilson gives an entertaining explanation of their position in a charmingly ponderous dialogue between Norman Shotover and David Mason in *Unguarded Hours* (early in Chapter 3). Mason describes the bishops as 'harmless enough'. However, Mr (Bishop) Skegg causes havoc which keeps the plot flowing on through the rest of the book and indirectly into its sequel *Kindly Light.*

ESA *noun* ENVIRONMENTALLY SENSITIVE AREA

---

estatescape *noun* the appearance and design features of a housing estate

> It was 25 years ago in New York that researchers first alerted us to the disadvantages of modern 'estatescape' as compared with traditional 'streetscape'. - *Best of Health*, May 1986

► Formed by analogy with *landscape.*

The notion was developed in the 1960s in the United States. The term is new in the United Kingdom.

However, many demographic studies in Britain have been highlighting the dangers of the housing estate way of life for some time. The new towns (eg Basildon, Bracknell) particularly highlighted the psychological and social drawbacks. Cumbernauld was said to give rise to 'new town blues'. Research in the 1960s showed them to be 'socially sterile', and this criticism has been levelled against the artificial community created at Milton Keynes.

The Parker-Morris Committee in 1961 pointed out in its report *Homes for Today and Tomorrow* the dangers of estatescapes (without using that term), and suggested various ways of limiting these problems. Many have since been adopted: the use of more colour, a village style of layout, punctuation of the building with trees, and the use of fences for control of children and greater privacy.

---

ester pulping *noun* a technique used in the paper industry for obtaining fibre pulp from wood, in which wood chips are cooked in a liquor containing ethyl acetate, acetic acid, and water to break down the lignin and hence release the fibres

> The paper industry, an energy intensive consumer of trees, is set to benefit from a new sulphur-free pulping technique that promises to increase productivity, lower energy costs and virtually eliminate pollution problems. The advance, dubbed ester-pulping, came as a result of work by Tim Young, a student at the University of Wisconsin in Madison.
> - *Financial Times*, 22 April 1986

---

ethical *adjective* of or being an investment policy which avoids investment in companies whose activities the investor considers morally objectionable (e g tobacco companies, or firms having links with South Africa)

> If you hanker after the puritan vigour of hard work but prefer your money to work for you, the latest crop of 'ethical' investments might appeal. ... The price of a clean conscience is no higher than for other investments. - *The Times*, 19 July 1986

► A typical ethical fund is the Stewardship Unit Trust (run by CC Lee and Company of Cambridge). It claims to be the only organization which satisfies the whole range of moral requirements which it has set itself; i e avoidance of South African investments or those trading in armaments, tobacco, or alcohol. It offers 'profitable investment with firm ethical guidelines'.
This type of investment is a pleasant luxury for those able to indulge their principles in such a way.

---

ethnic weapon *noun* a chemical or biological weapon designed to attack a specific ethnic population known to have a hereditary susceptibility to its effects

> There are new and even more toxic nerve gases than the present generation of British invented V-agents ... and perhaps even poisons targetted to attack specific populations - the so-called ethnic weapons. - *New Socialist*, Feb. 1986

► This is probably a fanciful and speculative nonce-word. There are at present no known ethnic weapons in the arsenals of the UK, NATO, USA, or USSR.
They appear to be seen as the heir of the V-agents which were, in fact, invented by American not by British scientists.
Presumably some diseases could theoretically be incorporated in weapons if the target population was known to be susceptible to their effects. They could cause havoc as European explorers did to the natives of various parts of north and south America and certain Pacific islands through measles, chicken pox, and venereal diseases. Possibly something could be made of the varying resistances of different ethnic groups to radiation.
Such a system would clearly cause such moral outrage and such administrative problems after hostilities that its use - if not its manufacture

administrative problems after hostilities that its use - if not its manufacture - would undoubtedly be counterproductive.

Eurofeebleness *noun* EUROWIMPERY

> Fear of terrorist attacks is not the only reason why Americans are deciding to stay at home. ... Indignation about what many Americans regard as Eurofeebleness towards terrorism is another. - *Economist*, 26 April 1986

Eurofighter *or* **European Fighter Aircraft** *noun* (*abbreviation* **EFA**) a fighter aircraft planned for joint development by the UK, West Germany, Italy, and Spain, and intended to operate chiefly in ground attack and fighter cover

> The Eurofighter (also known as the European Fighter Aircraft or EFA) is a £10bn plan ... to build up to 800 aircraft between now and the end of the century to replace ageing Phantom, Jaguar and Lockheed L-104 fighters. - *Financial Times*, 1 Aug. 1986

► Compared with the Warsaw Pact, Nato has lacked an orchestrated policy of common equipment. Lately there have been some improvements in this respect, such as the production of an anti-tank guided weapon system by Britain, France, and West Germany; an Anglo-Italian helicopter; and the Tornado aircraft produced by Britain, Italy, and West Germany. The project definition of the Eurofighter began in September 1985 and has been progressing through 1986. Such co-operation not only improves the solidarity of the North Atlantic alliance (notably, in this case, including Spain, whose loyalty has been tested by a referendum); it also makes economic sense.

European architecture *noun* the systems necessary for the integrated defence of Europe within the context of a strategic defence system for the defence of the continental United States and its allies against ballistic missiles

> The larger of the two new contracts deals with what is known in the trade as a 'European architecture' for Star Wars - that is, a conceptual and technical structure that may or may not succeed in relating ambitious anti-missile technologies such as high energy lasers and particle beams to the real problems of defending Europe against nuclear attack. This study will be sub-contracted to industry and is expected to last 22 months. - *Guardian*, 25 June 1986

Eurosclerosis *noun* a condition of sluggishness or rigidity in the economies of western Europe

> The term 'Eurosclerosis' is often used to describe how

inflexible attitudes and excessive regulation have dampened economic growth in the EEC. - *Guardian*, 20 June 1985

The Continent has been slow to adapt or innovate as economic events moved rapidly, a condition that was dubbed Eurosclerosis. - *Time*, 28 July 1986

Eurowimp *noun* a cowardly or vacillating Western European; *specifically* one who does not support US military action against terrorism (eg the attack on Libya in April 1986)

The rude words fly about the Libyan bombing - 'cowboy!', 'Eurowimp!' - *Economist*, 26 April 1986

He [Lord Carrington] warned that popular support for the Western alliance was in danger of being eroded by 'megaphone cartoonery - Euro-wimps in one set of newspapers and American cowboys in the other.' - *Daily Telegraph*, 29 May 1986

► Slang and highly derogatory.
The word *wimp*, meaning a pathetic or wet person, is still regarded as highly colloquial and does not find a place in many standard dictionaries. At the time of the American attack on Libya in April 1986, the majority of European opinion inclined to *laissez-faire.* The British government's decision to offer airbase facilities for the American venture attracted support from Republicans in the USA but split the public in the UK. Conversely, such vacillating as this Eurowimpery was castigated by Colonel Gadaffi of Libya when he addressed what he saw as his potential allies (in his struggle against the USA) at the Non-Aligned Movement conference in Harare (4 Sept. 1986): 'I go out from here saying goodbye to this funny movement. ... There is no place for neutralist non-alignment.'

Eurowimpery *noun* the acts and ideas characteristic of EUROWIMPS

West Europeans are still strong supporters of the Atlantic alliance - and they still believe that America would come to their help if there were a war in Europe. This may be some comfort to Americans furious about 'Eurowimpery' in the Libya affair. - *Economist*, 26 April 1986

---

excimer laser *noun* an ultraviolet laser which is designed as a ground-based DIRECTED-ENERGY WEAPON

The technology involved in the Star Wars programme is, to say the least, arcane. The research programme has been divided into five areas, which can roughly be described as sensors (optical, infra-red, radar etc), directed-energy weapons (including spacebased chemical lasers and neutron particle beams, ground-based excimer and free electron lasers, and nuclear-driven X-ray lasers), kinetic energy weapons (rockets and spacebased guns), information technology (ie, computers) and supported systems (like spacebased power reactors). - *New Socialist*, Feb. 1986

---

exfoliator *or* **exfoliant** *noun* a substance or device (eg a SCRUB or an abrasive glove) which removes dead skin cells and thus improves skin tone and complexion

In the old days, it had to be a wet flannel, but now there's a host of tools to keep skin in perfect condition from top to toe. Use them to work body exfoliators and toners, face masks and scrubs, or lather them with soap to shift dead cells and make skin squeaky clean. - *Options*, March 1986

The Pier Ange exfoliant is an exotic mix of sweet clover and rock seaweed with clay extracts. - *Daily Telegraph*, 14 Aug. 1986

---

expert system *noun* a computer system containing specialized information and designed to mimic human thought processes so that a user can conduct an apparently intelligent dialogue with the system

The most important applications of computerbased expert systems may not be in high-technology industries. Marvin Denicoff from Massachusetts Institute of Technology told a conference in Boston that industry in the US is turning to expert systems to preserve the expertise collected over many years by skilled factory workers. - *New Scientist*, 26 Sept. 1985

Expert systems have been described as the next major advance in computer technology. ... Already they are helping farmers fight crop disease, scientists make soap powders and engineers fix faults in everything from telephone equipment to helicopters. - *Listener*, 26 June 1986

► Such systems are apparently intelligent means of storing knowledge and rules. They are used for particular purposes of problem solving. Mycin is a medical expert system. BL have such a system for making decisions of programming their body-painting schedules. There are indeed parallels with a simple medical diagnosis. Certain questions are posed, thus directing the line of inquiry and restricting potential answers

---

eyemap *noun* a computer-coded picture of the eye made by scanning the retina with a special machine, which can be used as a means of identification

No two eyes are alike, and the map of the retina is said to be as individual as a fingerprint. Once the representatives have their eyemaps in the computer, they may look into a device similar to a View Master to see if the computer recognises them. – *New York Times*, 20 May 1986

Factor 8 *noun* a blood-clotting agent used in the treatment of haemophiliacs

> As well as the pain and suffering caused, they want compensation for the social consequences of being tainted by the so-called 'gay plague'. And their main target will be local health authorities who issued contaminated batches of the blood clotting agent Factor 8 to haemophiliacs. – *Mail on Sunday*, 17 Aug. 1986

► Haemophiliacs and others receiving blood donations have been consistently at risk during the AIDS epidemic. It was alleged during August 1986 that about 800 haemophiliacs had an unusually high (1 in 100 was suggested) chance of contracting AIDS, as a result of using the agent. Various companies in the United Kingdom and the United States produce it. Although they have been threatened with legal action, it is considered that local health authorities are more vulnerable in this respect.

farmerceutical *noun, informal* a growth-promoting hormone (e g ZERANOL) used to improve meat production

> Mr Harrington omits to mention the urgent research being directed into growth-promoters 'safer' than today's 'farmerceuticals.' – *Listener*, 14 Aug. 1986

farmer-friendly *adjective* see -FRIENDLY

Father *noun* a member of a group of conservative black vigilantes in South Africa who are in conflict with the COMRADES

> Bishop Tutu had flown to Cape Town to bring together the two warring factions in the Crossroads squatter camp area. He succeeded, and the conservative vigilante 'Fathers' agreed on a truce with the radical 'Comrades', bringing an uneasy calm to the devastated camps. – *Daily Telegraph*, 14 June 1986

feature-itis *noun, humorous* the tendency of newspaper editors to fill their pages with an excessive number of feature articles

> One of the great strengths of the *Daily Telegraph* was that it steered clear of this kind of flatulent journalism. ... There have

> been signs of late that even this excellent newspaper is not immune to feature-itis. – *Listener*, 7 Aug. 1986

---

firmware *noun* a computer program or data stored on a chip in a read only memory, as opposed to software which is stored on magnetic tape or disk

> The new Spectrum also has some radical improvements in its firmware, thanks to the new 32K 'Derby' ROM (read only memory). – *Guardian*, 20 Feb. 1986

---

fixed link *noun* a permanent link (e g a bridge or tunnel) constructed between two pieces of land separated by a stretch of water

> The idea ... was one of six winning projects when a competition was held in 1969 to design a fixed link across the strait [of Messina]. – *Financial Times*, 26 Feb. 1986

► This has been made particularly topical by the revival of plans for a Channel tunnel linking Kent with the Pas de Calais. It is fixed in that the proposed tunnel is in place and available for regular use permanently, as opposed to the occasional facilities offered by ferries and hovercraft.

---

flaky *also* **flakey** *adjective* unstable, unreliable

> More flaky rate rises can only confirm that we live in a high interest society. – *Guardian*, 9 Jan. 1986

> Calling Libya an outcast nation led by a barbarian, he [President Reagan] described Colonel Gadafy as irrational and 'flaky' (unstable). – *Guardian*, 9 Jan. 1986

> British Telecom's Multi-User dungeon adventure ... has finally moved from the alpha-test to the beta-test stage. It has the weapons installed plus new rooms, spells and objects. It is playable, but still too flakey for BT to charge people for playing it. – *Guardian*, 16 Jan. 1986

► Both *flaky* and *flakey* are well-documented in American reference books. Its use in Britain was given an impetus by President Reagan's description of Colonel Gadaffi in a speech at the beginning of January 1986. The context and tone of its use indicated that he thought that the Libyan leader was mad.

The diversity of definition given by American works indicates that the spread of meaning is less specific. *2nd Barnhart Dictionary* gives a 1973 citation and speaking of 'flaky behaviour' suggests an interpretation of 'very unconventional, eccentric'. Wentworth and Flexner's *Dictionary of American Slang* (2nd edition, 1975) shows it, in its supplement, with three separate senses: (1) 'Colourful, eccentric' (2) 'Screwy, crazy' (3) 'Easygoing, carefree', and has a citation from 1964. *Random House Dictionary* (1982) shows it as slang; first as 'eccentric, peculiar, non-conformist'; second as 'questionable, unreliable'.

Webster's supplement 6,000 *Words* (1970) gives it as 'markedly odd or unconventional, crazy'. Its *Ninth New Collegiate Dictionary* (1983) is more

mealy-mouthed, describing it as 'distinctly and often amusingly eccentric', which seems somewhat at variance with Reagan's sentiments. It shows *offbeat* and *wacky* as synonyms.
In Alison Lurie's *War Between the Tates* the precocious 13-year old Matilda tells her mother that she looks 'flaky'. Erica Tate questions the meaning of the word, but is not favoured with an answer.
The term is generally taken to derive from the condition of brick, slate, or other material that has become brittle and fissile from age and weathering. But it may well have originally suggested a drug-induced state, since *flake* is a slang term for cocaine.

---

flightswitch *noun* a switch of traffic from one air terminal to another

► In April 1986, the fourth terminal at Heathrow Airport was opened by the Prince and Princess of Wales. As it is the world's busiest airport, the extra facilities were well overdue.
The terminal was arranged to serve British Airways intercontinental flights, KLM (Royal Dutch Airlines), and Air Malta. Consequently, extensive rerouting of ground traffic was necessary and the term *flightswitch* appeared pasted over existing Heathrow signposts during the spring. Initially, widespread chaos was reported as the new terminal sorted itself out. However, as the summer proceeded a more organized regime established itself.

---

flip-in *noun* a POISON PILL that gives shareholders of a company threatened by takeover the right to buy additional shares in the company at half price – compare FLIP-OVER, BACK-IN

---

flip-over *noun* a POISON PILL that gives shareholders of a company threatened by takeover the right to buy shares of the purchasing company at half price – compare FLIP-IN, BACK-IN

---

flirtyfishing *noun* a method used by the Children of God and other religious sects to recruit new members, involving young girls talking to, reading the Bible with, and in some cases sleeping with potential recruits

► This is a blend of the verb *flirt* and the concept of *fishing* as a form of Christian evangelism (as in Christ's words 'Follow me and I will make you fishers of men', Matthew 5:19). An older related term is *love-bombing*, i e the technique of overwhelming a potential recruit with gestures of affection and (often sexual) love.
The rigorous and sometimes sinister methods used by some Christian groups to recruit and retain young and impressionable people have aroused much public interest. Harrowing stories told by parents who have been unable to disentangle their children from the control of such groups have been widely reported in the media. Such an incident has also been given considerable mileage on the ITV (Central) soap-opera *Crossroads*.

---

flops *noun* floating-point operations per second: a measure of computer power used for very powerful computers

Floating point operations per second (flops) are a

conventional measure of supercomputing power. Each flop represents a mathematical operation, addition, subtraction and so on, carried out with a very high degree and demonstrably correct measure of precision. ... The fastest supercomputers to date, the Cray 2 and the CDC Cyber 205 have a top performance of about 1bn flops. - *Financial Times*, 10 April 1986

---

fly-by-light *noun* a computerized flight-control system in which commands are transmitted by optical fibres

---

fly-by-wire *noun* a computerized flight-control system in which commands are transmitted electrically

> Airbus Industrie is represented at the 1986 Farnborough Air Show by its A100 demonstration aircraft, displaying the latest 'fly-by-wire' technology. - *Daily Telegraph*, 1 Sept. 1986

---

foodie *noun, informal* someone having an avid interest in food, especially in rare or exotic dishes

> Unpretentious, carefully seasoned and served dishes, made of cheap ingredients, are what avant garde foodies are taking to more and more. - *Cosmopolitan*, June 1986

> It's an open secret that the Queen Mother is the foodie of the royal family. - *Observer*, 24 Aug. 1986

---

foodism *noun* preoccupation with and above-average interest in food, especially natural, additive-free food

> The joke used to be that 'foodism' was the cult of Guardian-reading trendies, otherwise known as the Islington Organic Left. - *Guardian*, 4 July 1986

► The health enthusiasts of the BRANWAGON are sometimes restricted in their choice by their political inclinations. These may make them eschew, say, South African sherry or oranges.
Those who are keen on their food may be known as FOODIES. British Rail free magazine *Inter City* carried an article (July/August 1986) on SNCF (French railways) gourmet dining facilities under the title 'Moveable Feasts for Fast Foodies: Michael Raffael boards France's sophisticated gourmet super-train'.

---

food terrorist *noun, derogatory* someone who tries to bring about changes in eating habits and food manufacture by publicizing the health hazards associated with certain foods and food additives

> Who is responsible for this profit-threatening reform in eating habits? Most visible is a small band of determined activists - dubbed the 'food terrorists' by the more sour defenders of the food industry. - *Guardian*, 4 July 1986

---

foppy *noun* a fogey-hippy: someone who, at a relatively late age, has left the rat race to live a simple and peaceful life

> The Formentera foppy is likely to be a Conservative impatient with Conservatism. He is never without yesterday's Financial Times or today's El Pais. From both he tries continually to reassure himself that his new carefree existence has been justified by the conditions he fled. - *Sunday Times*, 17 Aug. 1986

---

force goal *noun* a policy presented to NATO by a member state for adoption as a common objective

> Congress voted the money but said it could not be spent unless NATO adopted a 'force goal' which included the binary bombs and shells. ... Along with about 1,000 other force goals, this one will be laid before the NATO ambassadors in mid-May and before the alliance's defence ministers a week later. - *Economist*, 3 May 1986

> NATO defence ministers ... will be asked to 'note' the acceptance last Friday by their ambassadors of the new United States 'force goal' for the introduction of modernised chemical weapons. - *Daily Telegraph*, 20 May 1986

---

fourth-generation language *noun* (*abbreviation* **4GL**) any of several high-level computer programming languages for commercial data processing that are capable of complicated handling of data from databases and that allow programs meeting the user's precise requirements to be written, often by the end-user him- or herself

> Mention the phrase 'productivity tools' and the reaction may be a politely stifled yawn. But drop 'fourth-generation' languages into the conversation and the response is likely to be more enthusiastic. - *Practical Computing*, March 1986

---

fractal *noun* a line, surface, figure, or other form whose dimension is fractional and which cannot be represented by conventional 3-dimensional geometry

> Not until the concept of Fractals was introduced had geometry been able to come to terms with the complexity of nature's shapes. - *Scientific American Spring Books*, Jan. 1986

---

fraudster *also* **fraudsman** *noun* somebody who commits a fraud; a swindler, impostor, or conman

> The RSPCA said yesterday that it had had more complaints this year than ever before about bogus inspectors. ... Most of the impersonators tricked people into giving them money to get rid of unwanted pets, which they then sold through pet shops or newspaper advertisements. Others were hoaxers

> attempting to alarm neighbours they disliked, or animal activists taking pets they believed were being mistreated. The society said it had yet to take legal action against the fraudsters. – *Guardian*, 20 March 1986
> The inquiry ... follows a report by EEC auditors that fraudsters have swindled the Common Market out of £57 million. – *Star*, 13 Feb. 1986
> Hunt for rat and maggot fraudsters ... Detectives are hunting gangs of conmen who use rats and maggots to trick pensioners out of their life savings by persuading them that their homes are infested and charging thousands of pounds to 'clear up.' – *Daily Mail*, 13 Jan. 1986

---

[1]**free-base** *verb, slang* **1** to purify (cocaine) by mixing it with ether or ammonia and allowing the chemical to evaporate **2** to smoke cocaine produced by free-basing

> At first ... the chemical process for purifying cocaine – called free-basing – was complicated and potentially dangerous – *Guardian*, 5 June 1986

---

[2]**free-base** *noun, slang* purified cocaine produced by FREE-BASING

> The 'freebase' is then smoked in a pipe. This produces irritation of the tongue and can damage the mouth, throat and lungs. – *Today*, 10 April 1986

---

free-electron laser *noun* a very high energy laser that uses a focussed beam of free electrons and is designed as a ground-based DIRECTED-ENERGY WEAPON

> The work on the free-electron laser is now the basis for a major weapon under development for the star-wars arsenal. The objective is to create a laser that could knock out a Soviet missile within one minute of takeoff. – *New Scientist*, 26 June 1986

-friendly *suffix* helpful to; inclined to favour, assist, or protect; in sympathy with

► The suffix *-friendly* probably owes its origins to the computer world. Users were initially – and to some degree still are – afraid of the unfamiliar and daunting technology.

Thus the US expression *user-friendly* emerged. It was no longer enough for the user to make the machine do its job. He had to feel happy and comfortable while this was happening. More facilities were added. Such things as the ability to produce pie-charts intrigued and amused the user and gave him greater incentive to use the machine. Entirely non-technical users employed computer power to communicate with other people rather than just to solve problems.

The friendliness related both to simplicity of use and relevance of the facilities. However, as is evident from the examples below, the analogy

now extends well beyond computers.
In the computer field, the term now seems to appear in isolation rather than just as a hyphenated suffix. Partially jocular, it is a convenient way of referring to an affectionate familiarity with the machines. James Innes writes (*Spectator*, 26 July 1986): 'Ellis senior was in computers and junior was 'friendly' with them at a young age.'

audience-friendly On the credit side is John Napier's audience-looping set, whose shimmering tracks and spinning bridge make ... a more audience-friendly affair than *Time*. – *Listener*, 15 May 1986
customer-friendly Hence our determination to understand and accommodate your actual needs. ... To paraphrase the familiar jargon, we are extremely customer-friendly. – *Financial Times*, 17 Jan. 1986
environment-friendly [Baden-Württemberg's] premier, Mr Lothar Späth, likes to stress the environment-friendly character of the high technology firms he is busy encouraging. – *Economist*, 21 Dec. 1985
The European Commission has just published a new structural plan, in which we suggest ... EEC subsidies for farmers in environmentally sensitive areas who undertake to follow environment-friendly practices. – *Economist*, 28 June 1986
farmer-friendly These were ominous words for those inside the Community who have over the past three years been patiently trying to reform the EEC's profligate and farmer-friendly common agricultural policy. – *Economist*, 29 March 1986
girl friendly There is some dispute ... about how far those campaigning for girls in science and technology can or should aim to make the physical sciences more 'girl friendly'. There is ample evidence that text book examples and illustrations tend to ignore girls and women entirely, and that such materials can, and should, be changed. – *Guardian*, 11 March 1986
Labour-friendly The cycle stunt was Labour-friendly too – the Greater London Enterprise Board puffing a cycle parts firm it supports. – *Guardian*, 5 March 1986
nature-friendly The Labour programme seems genuinely intended to be 'nature friendly', trying to strike a reasonable balance between growth and pollution and anxious to avoid exporting ecological misery to other countries. – *Guardian*, 21 April 1986
newspaper-friendly The Display Ad Make-Up System is simple, fast and cost-effective because it is the only system that was built from the ground up to serve the needs of the Newspaper and Print Industry. Unlike any other graphics or word processing system, Display Ad Make-Up System is truly 'newspaper-friendly'. – *The Display Ad Make-Up System* (*Digital Publishing Systems Ltd*), 1986

fuck-off *noun, Frenglish* a British tourist

> She sai [sic] at a cafe table while a group of French youths discussed the nationality of her husband, who had gone over the road to take some photos. Dutch? German? 'Non, il est un *fuck-off*' declared one youth authoritatively. Our informant says it's a slang-phrase she heard several times, engendered no doubt by the oft-declared love of the average Brit for sex and travel. – *Guardian*, 13 Aug. 1986

gamete intra-fallopian transfer *noun* (*abbreviation* **Gift**) a technique for the treatment of infertile women, in which eggs and sperm (the gametes) from the prospective parents are injected, via a catheter, directly into the woman's fallopian tubes where fertilization can occur naturally without the gametes having first been subjected to the hazardous journey through the woman's reproductive tract

> A new variant at this stage, developed largely by Ricardo Asch of the University of Texas in San Antonio, is to suck up egg and sperm together in a tube and replace them, via laparoscopy into the top of one of the fallopian tubes. Then, in theory, the egg is fertilised in its normal environment. The procedure, known as GIFT (for gamete intra-fallopian transfer), has its supporters, but some question its value, given that an embryo can more easily be transferred via the cervix. – *New Scientist*, 3 July 1986

GCSE *noun* General Certificate of Secondary Education: a system of examinations for secondary schoolchildren in Britain, intended to replace the existing GCE 'O' Level and CSE examinations

> Members [of the Schoolmasters and Women Teachers' Association] predicted that the September start of the General Certificate of Secondary Education would be 'chaos', 'confusion', a 'half-baked, botched experiment' and 'a dog's breakfast.' – *Daily Telegraph*, 2 April 1986

> There are still people who question how far the GCSE will be superior to present or past 16+ examinations. There will still be differentiation between abilities, in the form of different exam papers, more demanding for the more able pupils. – *Marxism Today*, Sept. 1986

► The system is the brain-child of Sir Keith Joseph (Secretary of State for Education & Science 1981–86). Teaching towards the new syllabus began in September 1986. The first exams are scheduled for 1988.
Its aim is to provide a fairer commentary on true abilities than that provided by the outgoing system. It seeks to tell employers, by reference to specific targets, what skills their potential employees have. It places greater emphasis on practical and oral work than the old system did, and results are based on continuous assessment as well as on written exams.
£20 million has been invested in books, in addition to £10 million on the relevant teacher-training.
It was originally greeted with great enthusiasm by the teaching unions, but the larger unions (NUT and NAS/UWT) have become more cautious about some of the details of its implementation. In particular it has met criticism from a variety of sources, in both the independent and the state sectors, about the slender preparation time allowed for transition.

---

gender-bender *noun* a person whose appearance and behaviour are sexually ambiguous or do not conform to the norms of his/her sex

> Outrageous gender-bender Pete has dented more than the charts. He has lashed lots of his fellow stars with a tongue well known for bitchiness. – *Star*, 13 Jan. 1986

---

gender-bending *noun* obscuring the distinction between the two sexes, eg by transvestism or bisexuality

> Representations of masculinity are changing for young working class men. ... Pale pinks and soft blues are this year's colours for casual shirts and fashion jeans. ... It may not be Boy George's idea of gender-bending, but the visual reassembly of masculinity through popular fashion is becoming a real feature of the 1980s. – *New Socialist*, Feb. 1986

► This concept suggests that the inter-sexual divisions need not be as rigid as conventional attitudes have indicated. The approach is currently epitomized by the pop-singers Boy George and Marilyn.
Yet the phenomenon has appeared in most, if not all, societies of the world. For example it is evidenced in a lot of Red Indian tribes, such as the Dakotas, whose berdaches were men wearing women's clothes and doing what was traditionally regarded as women's work. Their sexual performance is uncertain as is that of the cudirias of Brazil. In Bengal, however, bisexuality was formerly believed to indicate enhanced power.
Various causes have given rise to this eccentricity. It may just be for preference, although it is now usually for entertainment. It may be to demonstrate some social point. For example, the virgins of Albania used to dress as men after they had rejected marriage. It may be to provide some more specific service to a community, such as the Sakpota dancers in Dahomey who banish evil spirits. It may be for sexual titillation: some women are aroused by men in drag.

---

geneism *noun* discrimination against a person on the grounds that his/her genetic constitution indicates a susceptibility to a particular disease

> After racism and sexism, geneism? Medical science is about to set another teaser for lawmakers. ... It is posed by advanced genetic-screening techniques that promise to revolutionize medicine by showing how susceptible a person is to this or that disease. Which is marvellous, so long as people are not denied jobs or insurance just because of their genes.
> – *Economist*,19 July 1986

The word seems to be a semi-jocular invention by the author of the cited article, and is perhaps unlikely to find a foothold in the language. Nevertheless, the concept is significant: increasingly, employers and insurers are rejecting applicants because of (sometimes incorrect) suppositions about their susceptibility to specific diseases.

---

gene therapy *noun* a method of treating certain diseases, using techniques of genetic engineering to insert new genes into nonreproductive (somatic) cells in specific parts of the patient's body. Such new genes are not inherited by the patient's offspring. – compare GERM-LINE THERAPY

> And now six research groups in the United States are preparing to carry out human gene therapy. Their first targets are two rare hereditary diseases. – *Listener*, 9 May 1985

---

genetic fingerprint *noun* a unique pattern of repeated DNA sequences (MINI-SATELLITES) in the genetic makeup of an individual, that can be used to identify that individual or his/her offspring

> In theory, there is an alternative. Everybody has a unique set of genes, so why not take 'genetic fingerprints' and identify a person from his DNA? The trouble is that the genetic differences between people are very small. That is not surprising, because the job of most genes is to tell the body how to be a person rather than a seaslug. – *Economist*, 4 Jan. 1986

---

genetic fingerprinting *noun* the act or process of taking GENETIC FINGERPRINTS

> Four-year-old bloodstains and semen stains on cotton cloth yielded sufficiently intact DNA to discover the 'fingerprints' of their original owner. Genetic fingerprinting is a lengthy skilled-labour-intensive business. But it will help juries long baffled by forensic scientists' cautiousness. – *Economist*, 4 Jan. 1986

---

germ-line therapy *noun* a method of treating certain diseases, using techniques of genetic engineering to insert new genes into the reproductive cells of the patient. Such new genes will then be passed on to all future generations. – compare GENE THERAPY

But what about 'germ-line' therapy, in which new genes are added to the reproductive cells (sperm or egg) and are therefore passed on to all future generations? This would raise ethical issues greater than any other procedure in the history of medicine. – *Listener*, 9 May 1985

---

gesture politics *noun* the practice of taking a political action for the sake of appearances, e g to show public support for or censure of someone or something while knowing that that action will have little real effect

Mrs T[hatcher] announced last week that the government will spend £15m on scholarships for black South Africans and to help the front line states with their communications problems. ... The Director General [of the British Council], cautious Sir John Burgh, admitted his outfit hadn't been consulted before ... about this example of those 'gesture politics' Mrs T claims to detest. – *New Statesman*, 11 July 1986

---

ghetto blaster *noun* a large portable stereo radio, usually incorporating a cassette tape recorder

BR yesterday had another embarrassment with the disclosure that the Queen's ears had been assaulted by a loud radio, known as a 'ghetto blaster'. ... A BR spokesman said that playing music too loudly or being 'naked in a carriage' were breaches of railway by-laws and that those responsible could be prosecuted for causing a nuisance. – *Daily Telegraph*, 26 Feb. 1986

A jury at Birmingham Crown Court heard from witnesses who described a limping youth clutching a 'ghetto blaster' radio. – *Star*, 22 Jan. 1986

► All leading manufacturers produce equipment to meet this description. Its use is not exclusively restricted to black ghettos. The *Sunday Times Magazine* carried a picture caption (11 May 1986): 'Ghetto-blasting in Ballymun, north of Dublin, is measured less in decibels than by anarchic fervour'.

Part protest, part entertainment, this fashion seeks to draw attention by loud aggressive music to circumstances which are no more drab than slums have been in the past, but which are horrific compared with more prosperous circumstances which can be seen regularly on the TV.

The lack of entertainment (other than TV) for young (frequently unemployed) people in most of the inner cities is a well-recognized problem to which local authorities have responded with varying degrees of success. It has been acknowledged by many commentators since the high-rise flats of the early 1960s, in reports such as that by the Ministry of Housing & Local Government 'Families Living at High Density' (1970) and in protest songs such as Cat Stevens' 'Where Do the Children Play?' (1973).

Gift *noun* GAMETE INTRA-FALLOPIAN TRANSFER

---

gigadisc *noun* an optical disc that is capable of storing large amounts of data (usually about 1000 megabytes)

> For big users there are 'gigadiscs' ... which can store 1,000 megabytes of data. - *Guardian*, 5 June 1986

---

gigaflops *noun* a thousand million FLOPS

---

girl friendly *adjective* see -FRIENDLY

---

gizmology *noun, informal* technological gadgetry

> Great excitement at the arrival of *Today*, Britain's first high-technology newspaper. ... The paper's editors invited John Stansell ... to write a gee-whiz piece for *Today's* second issue about the gizmology that brings the newspaper out. - *New Scientist*, 13 March 1986

► The slang word *gizmo* or *gismo*, meaning a gadget, has been common in the USA since the 1940s. It is relatively unfamiliar in Britain, however. (A particularly unappealing character in the early days of the Channel 4 soap-opera *Brookside* was so named.)
The combination is new on both sides of the Atlantic.

---

glasnost *noun* the willingness of the Soviet government to be more open about its affairs

> All of this does not excuse the Soviet Union's behaviour but it may help to explain it. What seemed to be at risk was Mr Gorbachev's 'glasnost' policy, the essence of which is more openness. - *Scotsman*, 9 May 1986

► The Russian word meaning openness or frankness has gradually come into current usage during the Premiership of Mikhail Gorbachev. His apparently friendly and almost avuncular manner attracted a favourable press at the time of his visit to Britain in 1985 and his summit meeting in Geneva with President Reagan.
Glasnost was best demonstrated in 1986 by the startlingly honest public admissions on the Chernobyl disaster. To a lesser extent, uncompromising recriminations and the relevant announcements on a Black Sea ship collision in August 1986 followed the same line.

---

glitterati *plural noun, informal* **1** celebrated and fashionable authors and scholars as a social group **2** celebrated and fashionable people; media celebrities and jet-setters

> Soon the good little girl at glitterati gatherings [Princess Stephanie of Monaco] - like that with the Sinatras, her parents and brother - gave way to a sulky, sultry siren. - *Woman*, 8 March 1986

Daniel Haberman ... has never met the men from the New York Review of Books. No one has asked him to join the glitterati at the Institute for the Humanities. 'It's nice to be left alone,' he says, 'but I do want to be listened to.' - *Guardian*, 30 May 1984

PR agencies seldom employ the Johns, Bills, Maries or Daphnes of this world. I seek Torquil Fanshawe-West, or Alexia Vronsky-Adams, or some such Damien or Ffiona or apparent representative of the glitterati. - *UK Press Gazette*, 4 August 1986

► A blend of *glitter* and *literati*; but the second element seems to have been almost forgotten in the newer sense 2. It seems, indeed, that a suffix *-erati* is entering the language; see also SLOPPERATI.

---

[1]**glitz** *noun* conspicuous showiness; glitter, gaudiness

Behind the flurry of walkabouts and TV news conferences ... behind the comparative youth and glitz, behind sarcasm and the sackings, the question remains ... how far down the road of change Mr Gorbachev wants to take the Soviet Union. - *Listener*, 30 Jan. 1986

A minor revolution is taking place in fashion jewellery for spring and summer. The glitter and glitz of the fake has been ousted by the natural and ethnic. - *Daily Telegraph*, 29 Jan. 1986

► It is a formation based on *gl*amour and R*itz* (with its associations of wealth and splendour), or perhaps on the German word *glitzern* (= to glitter).
The current obsession with American TV soap operas of highly glamorized and increasingly improbable story-lines may have something to do with the popularity of this word.
It is also possibly an indirect result of the atmosphere of prosperity which the Reagan administration seeks to promote. The celebrations for the 100th anniversary of the Statue of Liberty, coinciding with the 1986 Fourth of July, was described in the USA as 'the most revolting display of glitz this century'.
Elmore Leonard's novel *Glitz*, published in the USA and Canada in 1985, also appeared (Viking) in the UK in 1985 and became more widely read in paperback (Penguin) in 1986.

---

[2]**glitz** *verb* to dress or adorn with gaudy finery; tart up

Dynasty and The Colbys also quite literally double the real world, glitzing up the kind of emotional and domestic problems that are the stuff of everyday life. - *Listener*, 6 Feb. 1986

---

glitzy *adjective* showily attractive in a superficial or deceptive way; glittering, gaudy

---

go-go *adjective* **1** dynamic and up-to-date **2** fast-growing; *especially* of or being a financial concern involved in high-yield speculative investments

> Donny Dingle – the company's bearded Glaswegian Creative Director, who's so go-go that even his secretary has a Porsche 944. – *Guardian*, 6 Feb. 1986

> His [Girolami, chairman of Glaxo] view of biotechnology ... is typical. 'It's really only an approach rather than a research method in itself. It reminds me of the days when operations research was the go-go area in management.' – *Financial Times*, 17 Jan. 1986

► New senses of a word previously associated with vigorous and vaguely erotic dancing (usually by a small troupe of girls) in the late 1960s.

Go Go *noun* a form of HIP HOP music that originated in Washington DC and that differs from Hip Hop chiefly in the use of acoustic rather than just electronic instruments

> From a band who took metal bashing to the masses to another about to do it in an even bigger way, the Junkyard Band's 'The Word' ... is a hook-ridden slice of Go Go. – *City Limits*, 14 Aug. 1986

---

golden handcuffs *noun* a large payment made to an employee as an inducement to continue working for the same company

> He [Sir Lawrence Airey] accepted that there was a limit to what he could do to prevent the loss of staff. Unlike a commercial boss, he doesn't have at his disposal 'golden handcuffs' to counter the temptations of the private sector. – *Listener*, 13 Feb. 1986

> Golden handshakes and golden handcuffs are now part of every headhunter's vocabulary. – *Business*, July 1986

► High salaries earned in the City of London have been the subject of several press reports in 1986. A survey found that 7% of City executives earned over £100,000 a year. One financial group, probably quite typical, pays its chairman £213,000 a year, six directors over £180,000 each, and five other employees more than £100,000. Profit-related bonuses can give top dealers substantially more than this; one is reported to be earning a million pounds in 1986.
Banking and broking firms competing for a leading place in the City after BIG BANG have spent heavily to attract and keep expert staff. The seemingly exorbitant salaries have been criticized in some quarters, although others seek to justify them by pointing to the extraordinary demands of the work and to the short working life which results.

---

golden hello *noun* a large payment made to an employee joining a company; a signing-on fee

> So the Tories' friends in the City got away scot-free: stamp duty halved, and contrary to many predictions, nothing extra on the banks, the brokers, or those disgusting young men with their golden hellos. – *Daily Telegraph*, 24 March 1986

> Salomon Brothers, the Wall Street investment house specializing in bond markets, has recruited a leading City economist for its London gilt-edged operation. ... No signing on fee, or 'golden hello,' is involved. – *The Times*, 6 March 1986

---

golden parachute *noun* a contractual guarantee of compensation to an employee in the event of dismissal or demotion following a takeover or merger

> More than a third of the top 100 United States industrial companies now offer 'golden parachutes' to key executives, according to management consultants Towers, Perrin, Forster & Crosby. – *Daily Telegraph*, 21 July 1986

► It has been current in the USA since 1982 but has only just appeared in Britain.
This is part of the prolific range of related vocabulary: GOLDEN HANDCUFFS, GOLDEN HELLO, etc. All these owe their origins to *golden bowlers* (i e bowler hats), which reflected the change from military to civilian dress in the well-remunerated military redundancies of the late 1950s.

---

golden share *noun* strategic control held by a national government in a privatized company, as a safeguard against a takeover by foreign or undesirable interests

> The government may take a 'golden share' in the companies set up to run airports after the privatisation of the British Airports Authority, Mr Michael Ancram, the Scottish Office minister with responsibility for airports, told the Commons yesterday. – *Financial Times*, 10 April 1986

-gram *suffix* a jocular greeting on a special occasion, delivered by a costumed person to the amazement and embarrassment of the recipient

> Tarzangram man Paul Winters has hung up his chilly loincloth until the spring and now delivers messages ... as Huggy, the cuddly huggogram bear. – *Star*, 17 Jan. 1986
> 'Happy birthday! It's a phobiagram!' – *Daily Mirror*, 30 Jan. 1986

> Bagpipe player, Alan Hunter of Edinburgh ... provides an authentic Scottish atmosphere at weddings, parties, fairs etc

> and operates a 'pipe-o-gram' greetings service. – *Business Success*, July/Aug. 1986

► This enterprise fills the void left by the end of the inland telegram service.
The heir to the tradition of the singing telegram, the first variant was the simple *kissogram*. The search for originality has now produced the cruder *boobagram*, and numerous others. A *gorillagram* tends to be less of a fearsome beast than of a hot and bothered man inside a hairy costume and plastic mask. The *Daily Telegraph* even reports a *Sara Keaysagram* (after Miss Keays, former mistress of Cecil Parkinson, sometime Chairman of the Conservative Party and Cabinet Minister), whereby 'a country-looking lady, no longer young and at least eight months pregnant, gives a smart knock on the door and says 'I have bad news for you...'. BBC Radio 1 offers *tranagrams*. One can even risk *Roly Poly Grams*, whereby a female visitor of 25 stone and dimensions 60–40–60 will express goodwill and, if desired, strip.
A character (Pat Hancock) in the Channel 4 (Mersey Television) soap-opera 'Brookside' recently demonstrated the problems of providing this kind of service as a source of additional income. He found it exhausting, time-consuming, frequently ill-received, and not very remunerative.
See also POTATOGRAM.

Gramm-Rudman *noun* the Gramm-Rudman law, which provides for an automatic across-the-board reduction in US government spending when the Federal budget deficit exceeds a set annual limit

> The Gramm-Rudman approach to statecraft is so crazy that one is amazed that a free people should have enacted it. Prof. [Lester] Thurow likens its philosophy to a man threatening to cut out his stomach if he cannot lose weight. – *Daily Telegraph*, 7 July 1986

> There, in the marble-columned reading room [of the Library of Congress] ... congressmen may dream in peace and breathe the mustiness of ancient values. Except that at 5.30 p.m. every day, save Wednesdays, the wisdom-seekers who used to stay till 9.30 have to go home, because Gramm-Rudman has cut $18m out of the library budget. – *Economist*, 19 April 1986

► This extraordinary measure, the brainchild of senators Phil Gramm and Warren Rudman, was passed by Congress in 1985, apparently as an act of desperation. Shock-waves followed, as people came to realize that the Law – whatever its honourable intentions – could leave the country without prisons, defence, or anything else. Massive spending cuts were implemented, despite a ruling by the Supreme Court in July 1986 that the Law's major provision was unconstitutional.

---

graphite-moderated *adjective, of a nuclear reactor* having a moderator (substance for slowing down neutrons) made of graphite

> There are other parallels, too, between our Magnox reactors and Chernobyl. Both are graphite-moderated, and therefore

subject to the kind of fire raging at Chernobyl, which proved so difficult to put out at Windscale. - *Guardian*, 5 May 1986

---

gravitipole *noun* a hypothetical single concentrated gravitational charge; *also* a hypothetical particle having such a charge

More than 50 years ago, Paul Dirac showed that he could explain the existence of electric charge in discrete 'quantised' units if there also exist particles carrying single magnetic poles - 'monopoles'. Following Dirac, Zee speculates on the possibility of analogous 'gravitipoles', which require that mass, like electric charge, is quantised. - *New Scientist*, 16 Jan. 1986

---

gray *noun* (*symbol* **Gy**) the SI unit of ionizing radiation equal to an absorbed dose of 1 joule per kilogram

See quotation at BECQUEREL

► It is used as the basic measure of radiation absorbed by the body. It is 100 times larger than the old measure (the *rad*).
It owes its name to Louis Harold Gray (1905-65), a prominent Cambridge physicist whose principal work was on absorption of gamma radiation into the body.
He has left another eponymous memorial. His first published paper described what was known as the cavity ionization principle. Wretchedly for him, Bragg had already described the principle. A happy compromise was reached by naming it for posterity the Bragg-Gray principle.

---

graze *verb* to eat (especially Spanish hors d'oeuvres, known as *tapas*) standing up

People under 30 don't eat in America any more. They do something called 'grazing'. To graze is to eat the entire meal standing up ... while you sip a glass of wine or mineral water and survey the scene. - *Punch* (*Food and Booze Extra*), July 1986

---

grazer *noun* someone who GRAZES

Specialities include fresh sardines, octopus, clams, mini-omelettes and chicken wings. But while in Spain these are supposed to be a snack to whet patrons' appetites for pigs' trotters and paella, in the States and here they are being presented to appeal to the 'grazers'. - *Sunday Times*, 27 July 1986

---

green *verb* **1** to make urban areas greener and more rural in appearance by the addition of trees, plants, grassy areas, etc, and a reduction in the number of buildings **2** to cause to become concerned about environmental and ecological issues

In support of the Groundwork programme, the government

has allocated extra funds for local authorities to clear the appalling legacy of industrial growth and decline. ... With their special expertise in restoring polluted land, in low-cost greening and community involvement, the Trusts are injecting a new dimension to conventional restoration. - *Guardian*, 5 March 1986

The RAS ... moved away from their Ratepayer Association origins and priorities, towards a gradual greening of their outlook. - *Guardian*, 5 March 1986

---

green glue *noun* plant cover that binds and prevents soils from being eroded by water or especially wind; *also* any of various plant species capable of such action

Experts at the Kew herbarium, transferring archives on to a computer, have found one species they call 'green glue'. The ugly, spiky plants will grow in arid wastes and bind shifting desert sands. - *Daily Telegraph*, 11 March 1986

---

[1]greenmail *noun* **1** the business tactic whereby a company buys a substantial block of shares in another company and threatens to make a takeover, so forcing the threatened company to repurchase the shares at a premium **2** (in Australia) the business tactic whereby a company buys a substantial block of shares in another company with the intention of selling them to a third company at a profit

The controversial American takeover tactic known as 'greenmail' has surfaced for the first time in a British bid battle. - *Guardian*, 14 Aug. 1984

The critics of the raiders' activities look at the vast sums of money that are being made - particularly with the use of such tactics as 'greenmail' ... - and shake their heads. In Washington, the legislators have stirred this year, with a string of bills aimed at slowing the raiders down or stopping them in their tracks. - *Listener*, 5 Sept. 1985

The Australian invaders are ... likely to prove adept at exploiting the regulations abroad. Many have already indulged in Australian-style 'greenmailing' (ie, buying stakes in companies and selling to a third party at a profit). - *Economist*, 4 Jan. 1986

---

[2]greenmail *noun* to practise GREENMAIL on

This is not the first time that Mr Steinberg has successfully 'greenmailed' companies into buying back his shares at a profit. - *Economist*, 16 June 1984

---

greenmailer *noun* a person practising GREENMAIL

Mr Holmes à Court decides what he is going to do and proceeds methodically from one stage to the next. ... This has helped earn him a reputation, perhaps unfairly, as a greenmailer. - *Economist*, 4 Jan. 1986

---

gullie *noun* a metal tray used as the goal in the game of OCTOPUSH

---

gumball *noun, US slang* BLACK TAR

Guppie *noun* an ecologically-minded Yuppie

Designer Katherine Hamnett ... is bringing fashion and politics together in a magazine aimed at Yuppies ... and Guppies. - *Guardian*, 18 May 1985

► Derived from *G*reen + *Yuppie.*
The extended acronym *Yuppie* stands either for *Y*oung *u*rban *p*rofessional or *Y*oung *u*pwardly-mobile *p*rofessional *p*erson. Rather like the origin of *quango* (non-governmental or national governmental?), both sources of origin are extensively documented. The *OED Supplement* favours *urban.* This social description is North American in origin and Yuppies first appeared as a conscious group in support of Senator Gary Hart's unsuccessful campaign for the US Presidency in 1984. In 1986 they were said to hold a balance of power in a British by-election in the Fulham constituency.
The stereotype is alleged to interest itself in a vague way in a variety of well-intentioned causes, such as the protection of whales and of the environment generally (green being the broad description of those engaged in ecological politics or work). They are considered to be supportive of the SDP in the main, although the result of the Fulham by-election (a convincing Labour victory) did not bear out this generalization.

---

[1]hack *verb* to gain unauthorized access to computer systems through a telephone connection

Users actually choose passwords that are easy to remember, so they are also relatively easy to hack. - *Guardian*, 27 June 1985

---

[2]hack *noun* an act of HACKING

The two great British hacks - Prince Philip's Prestel mailbox, and the BBC TV's Microlive mailbox on Telecom Gold - seem both to have resulted from password misuse.
- *Guardian*, 27 June 1985

---

hacker *noun* **1** someone who studies and programs computers purely as a hobby **2** someone who gains unauthorized access to computer systems through a telephone connection

> Computer hackers have been running a brisk racket 'cleaning up' the driving licences of wealthy businessmen. For a charge of £100 a point, endorsements have been erased from the files of the British government's Driver and Vehicle Licensing Centre at Swansea. - *Business*, April 1986

► Presumably this derives from someone who hacks his way into a system. It started to be heard around 1984 and 1985 but was then still considered to be part of the arcane argot of computers. It is now commonplace.

---

handicappism *noun* discrimination against handicapped people

> Ageism's lagging behind sexism, racism, and handicappism because even the oppressed seem to accept the discrimination. - *Guardian*, 11 June 1986

HARM *noun* HIGH-SPEED ANTIRADIATION MISSILE

---

headage *noun* a uniform per capita payment for animals; capitation

> Under the present sheepmeat regime I shall be receiving a headage payment of £7.32 on each of my breeding ewes. - *Financial Times*, 11 March 1986

► This formation on the *-age* analogy of *acreage* was noted in the late 1950s but only in highly specialized agricultural contexts. It is now commonplace because of EEC payments which are based on the number of head of animals, for example beef headage payments.

---

hearing-impaired *adjective, euphemistic* hard-of-hearing; suffering from a hearing loss that falls short of total deafness

> In England and Wales ... there also exists a profession of trained counsellors with particular relevance to the hearing impaired - the hearing therapist. - *Guardian*, 11 Feb. 1986

---

heli-stat *noun* an airship with added helicopter rotors

> The 343ft long experimental 'heli-stat' consisted of the familiar cigar-shaped balloon on an elaborate aluminium frame with four helicopters mounted on it to provide lift and drive. - *Daily Telegraph*, 4 July 1986

---

heterosexism *noun* discrimination against a person on the grounds of his/her homosexuality

> We should be struggling against racism and heterosexism. - *Spare Rib*, June 1985

> The issue of sexism brought us on to the far more contentious issue of heterosexism which does not mean, whatever The Sun

might say, compulsory homosexuality for all. - *Sunday Express Magazine*, 30 March 1986

► The Gay Rights movement has kept up pressure for about a quarter of a century to ensure that homosexuals are treated on the same basis as those of received sexual tastes.
The Greater London Council was, before its abolition, particularly generous in securing this kind of equality. Its leader, Ken Livingstone, was consistently forthright in his support for Gay Rights (along with many other minority causes). However, of late this has been taken to extremes which have rendered the cause ridiculous in some people's views and the effort has therefore been, in some respects, counter-productive.

---

heterosexist *adjective* of or showing HETEROSEXISM

... beliefs rooted in the heterosexist and unequal society in which we live. - *Guardian*, 25 Feb. 1986

HG list *noun* Hypocritical Gestures List; the range of options open to someone who is using GESTURE POLITICS

[Mrs Thatcher] has made Sir Geoffrey Howe's task as conciliator in Southern Africa almost impossible by her implacable response to those who want sanctions. Why, one minister whispered, can she not just pick some from the Foreign Office's HG list? - *Listener*, 17 July 1986

---

high definition *noun* a technique used in the manufacture of flat-screen televisions, that produces pictures of very high quality

Imagine a flat picture-like object, two and a half by three and a half feet, hanging on the sitting-room wall, picture-thin too - only not a picture. This is the likely pattern for the TV set of the next decade. It will replace today's bulky box on a stand and, thanks to a new technique called High Definition, the picture quality will be so good that we will actually be able to see the ball as Botham's son hits it for six. - *UK Press Gazette*, 2 June 1986

---

high-dread *adjective* causing much fear

The scientists and engineers who work in the field [of nuclear power] still have immense confidence in the safety of the plants they design and run. Even after Chernobyl they talk of it as a 'low-risk, high-dread industry'. - *Listener*, 3 July 1986

---

high-end *adjective* of or being goods, merchandise, etc that are at the top end of the market and are very expensive

British companies didn't meet the Japanese offensive early enough; instead of reliable, low-cost equipment, they produced only very expensive, 'high end' goods. - *Observer*, 4 May 1986

---

high-speed antiradiation missile *noun* (*abbreviation* **HARM**) a missile comprising a two-stage rocket carrying high-explosive warheads and designed to home in on radar emissions

> HARM, the gold-plated ($283,000) high-speed antiradiation missile, which has been criticized by some Pentagon officials ... succeeded in twice disabling a Libyan SA-5 radar station. - *Time*, 7 April 1986

Hip Hop *noun* **1** a youth subculture, originating among black and Hispanic teenagers in New York City, which embraces distinctive styles of music (often using a montage of records and sound effects), dancing (flamboyant breakdancing and body-popping), graffiti art, and dress, and often expresses iconoclastic socio-political views through rhythmically chanted verse (rap) **2** the music of Hip Hop, characterized by a very heavy disco beat and rapping over a staccato electronic background

> Hip Hop has not gone away. A phenomenon of many dimensions, with its own art, dress sense, and dance styles as well as DJs, rappers and revolutionary recording studio operatives, it has either been regarded as insubstantial or unmarketable beyond aficionados. ... Hip Hop's deep cultural and political meanings are less easily denied. - *Guardian*, 14 March 1986

> More and more contemporary music - from glossy UK pop to streetwise American Hip Hop - is taking TV values, images and references as a source of inspiration. - *Listener*, 21 Aug. 1986

HIV *noun* human immunodeficiency virus: the virus which causes AIDS

> The thinking behind the BMA proposal is that a fear of loss of employment puts people off being tested for HIV (human immunodeficiency virus, formerly HTLV-3), the virus which causes Aids and a range of other, milder, conditions. - *New Statesman*, 11 July 1986

---

hobby terrorist *noun* someone who engages in terrorist activities while living a conventional life and remaining in regular employment

> On the rear walls of the building [the Hamburg police centre fire-bombed on 17 Aug.] were daubed slogans ... and the five-pointed star symbol of an extreme-left group, Revolutionary Cells. This group allies itself to the more ruthless Red Army factions and its members are known as 'hobby terrorists' because they work normally and meet only infrequently in

small groups to plan and commit political crimes. - *Daily Telegraph*, 18 Aug. 1986

---

hollowization *or* **hollowisation** *noun* the loss of capital, technology, and talented people from a country

Some top executives and business groups have already begun to speak darkly about the so-called 'hollowization' of Japan. - *Newsweek*, 23 June 1986

---

homesit *verb* to act as a HOMESITTER

He [William Brown] and his wife ... are fond of animals, particularly horses and dogs. 'So homesitting for us often includes mucking out stables, feeding, grooming and exercising horses - and catching them if they stray onto someone else's farm.' - *London Standard*, 18 Dec. 1985

---

homesitter *noun* someone who is employed to live in a house and act as a caretaker while the owner is away

Christmas is one of the twin annual peaks (the summer holiday period is the other) of the homesitter's year, though fortunately things aren't always so dramatic. - *London Standard*, 18 Dec. 1985

► *Babysitters*, required by law for children under 11 years old, have been so described since the 1920s.
The need for homesitters is the result of increasing crime rates and the vulnerability of empty houses to squatters exercising their legal right to occupy and remain in empty property. The need for security of empty houses is related to NEIGHBOURHOOD WATCH schemes.
Town-centre churches often maintain a rota of *churchsitters*, as a defence against vandals and thieves. This is particularly necessary in the case of churches which are much used for casual prayer and in which the Blessed Sacrament is reserved.

Home Watch *noun* NEIGHBOURHOOD WATCH

Whenever Mrs Dina Jones ... gets up at night to feed her baby, Hayley, she makes a point of looking outside to see if anything suspicious is happening. If there is, she phones the police and informs her neighbours. That is what the Home Watch scheme is all about. - *Today*, 24 June 1986

---

homing overlay device *noun* a KINETIC-ENERGY WEAPON that carries a homing device to guide it towards its target, and no warhead

The Pentagon tested another device last year designed to knock down objects in space. Known as the 'homing overlay device', it is little more than a metal projectile, but it poses one more threat to the Anti-Ballistic-Missile Treaty that bars weapons against missiles. – *New Scientist*, 30 May 1985

---

homoeotic gene *noun* a gene that is responsible for regulating the structural development of an organism, such that a mutation within that gene causes radical alterations in appearance

> It soon became clear that not all the genes were equally important. There were a handful of 'master genes' whose effects seemed to far outweigh all the others – in particular the genes known as homoeotic genes. A change or mutation in one of these genes would radically change the appearance of the fly. A fly which normally had two wings could be changed by a simple genetic alteration into a fly with four wings. – *Listener*, 16 Jan. 1986

---

horseculture *or* **horseyculture** *noun* the practice of dividing farmland into small plots which are sold as grazing land for horses

> Local councils and conservation bodies are becoming increasingly worried about the growth of 'horseculture'. – *Daily Telegraph*, 20 Aug. 1984

> Green Belt farmers, frustrated by not being able to cash in on the value of their land for houses, have long encouraged horseyculture by selling an acre or two at premium prices to absentee horse-owners. – *Daily Telegraph*, 12 April 1986

► A semi-jocular formation on the model of *agriculture, horticulture,* etc. The suburbs of London, Birmingham, and other major cities, particularly in the south of England, include many citizens who are intent on social climbing or, indeed, SOCIAL MOUNTAINEERING. As part of this they consider that a rural association can be achieved through the children riding. Furthermore the children may like riding.

Their houses seldom have sufficient grass acreage for keeping ponies. Landowners in such suburban areas see a means for satisfying this taste by selling their fields in small plots. These are then occupied by the owners of ponies or by riding establishments of varying degrees of efficiency.

Very frequently fields are used inefficiently in this way, with less consideration for the horse than is appropriate. Ragwort and hemlock abound and the heavy proportion of docks means that they are worm-infested. The grass is seldom rested or fertilized and often there is little or no shade. Poor drainage often exacerbates laminitis and other foot-conditions prevalent in ponies.

The financial prizes of this kind of enterprise are encouraging to the landowners. A four-fold increase in the price of an acre of land resold with a modest bit of fencing is not unusual.

---

hot key *noun* a facility that allows access to a computer program (eg a spreadsheet) while using a different program (eg a word processing program), and enables the user to switch instantly between different activities

---

Hotol *noun* Horizontal Take-off and Landing: a SPACE PLANE powered by an air-breathing engine (one that takes oxygen from the atmosphere, instead of carrying liquid oxygen, to burn its hydrogen), that is designed to use normal runways for takeoff and landing and to carry payloads into low-Earth orbit

> British Aerospace reckons that Hotol could launch satellites into low earth orbit for a fifth the price of using the shuttle. ... Unlike the shuttle, which jettisons its main fuel tank, Hotol will be entirely reusable. - *Economist*, 15 Feb. 1986

► Hotol is currently being developed by British Aerospace and Rolls-Royce. Details of its revolutionary engine have not been made public. The *Daily Telegraph's* science correspondent calls it 'Britain's great industrial hope of the Nineties'. Unfortunately it faces competition from a similar US project dubbed 'Orient Express'.

---

hot particle *noun* a discrete particle of radioactive material

> Instead of being uniformly distributed, the accumulations of radioactive material are distributed as 'hot particles' throughout the inshore marine sediments and generally in the environment over a very wide area around the nuclear reprocessing plant. - *Guardian*, 1 March 1986

---

hot rock *noun* rock that is naturally hot and can be used as a source of geothermal power (eg for providing district heating)

> There are distant hopes of a new industry for Cornwall - the provision of power from hot rocks ... deep beneath the earth's crust. - *Listener*, 5 June 1986

► This source of power has been developed by the Camborne School of Mines and experiments have been carried out at the Rosemanoes Quarry near Penryn. Proponents of this worthwhile alternative form feel that the Department of Energy would do well to offer them more encouragement and tangible assistance.
The heat produced is the result of granite heated naturally by its innate radioactivity. It should be available from all granite areas of Cornwall and Devon, or presumably any other granite-based region.
The system requires three boreholes. Cold water is pumped down one. A natural radiator is formed and hot water comes up the other two at temperatures between 70°C and 90°C.

Huppie *noun* a young upwardly mobile person who has a largely conventional lifestyle but spends some of his/her leisure time living as a hippie

> They do not regard themselves as hippies; to stretch a point

they might, at most, be called holiday hippies. Some ... might be better described as huppies: young, upwardly mobile, and living free from routine until the middle of next week.
- *Guardian*, 16 June 1986

---

hwyl *noun* emotional ardour, usually associated with fervent eloquence - used especially in referring to Welsh people

'Forensic' is not the word that springs to the lips about Neil Kinnock's style. He has too much of the hwyl in him, too many echoes of Lloyd George and Aneurin Bevan, for his oratory to be easily encompassed by the courtroom.
- *Listener*, 30 Jan. 1986

Welsh hwyl is also much in evidence in Far From Paradise (BBC 2) a new seven-part ecological series from Cardiff unveiled last night. - *Daily Telegraph*, 17 Jan. 1986

► This is a long-established word in the Welsh language.
It has been attributed with a remarkable breadth of meaning. The basic sense is 'mood' or 'sail'. (The latter enjoys combinations such as *hwyl flaen* = foresail and *yr hwyl fawr* = mainsail.) The 'mood' meaning can also be combined in phrases such as *mewn hwyl dda* = in a good mood.
In conversation the farewell *hwyl*! may be translated 'best of luck' or 'have fun!' (or arguably, in the American English idiom, 'have a nice day!').
The word is frequently found in Lloyd George's papers (eg his letters to Dame Megan, which are generally written in English but are extensively punctuated with Welsh phrases). These occurrences illustrate its extraordinary variety. Of a fellow Liberal MP's performance in the House (1896) he says *mewn hwyl faur* = in great form. Of himself he writes (1899) *a chefais hwyl anarferol* = in unusually good form. He found a political meeting (1902) *hwyl campus* = excellent fun.
The word features in a jocular description of Ieuan Jenkins in Kingsley Amis' *That Uncertain Feeling* (set in Swansea): 'He's always been a great one for the hwyl - you know the old Welsh oratorical fire and the rest of it'. This is an isolated use in the spirit of its Welsh context and the word has not appeared generally in English writing until recently.

---

hypercharge *noun* an interaction between elementary particles that is held to be the fifth force acting with gravity, electromagnetism and weak and strong interactions, and is a weak force tending to oppose the gravitational attraction between objects

Instead of the four forces - gravity, electromagnetism, and strong and weak nuclear forces - which they are now struggling to combine in one unified package, [physicists] will have five. The 'new' force, provisionally dubbed 'hypercharge', has a range of about 200 metres, and tends to push things apart.
- *New Scientist*, 16 Jan. 1986

---

hypercube *noun* **1** a 4-dimensional analogue of a cube **2** a pattern for wiring a computer based on the theory of the hypercube

> What does a four dimensional 'cube' (or 'hypercube') look like? How can you visualise four dimensional space? To the mathematician there is no great problem involved. Indeed, mathematicians routinely make use of 'spaces' of many more dimensions than three, sometimes even infinitely many. This is because a visualisation of a high dimensional space is not necessary for the mathematics involved. - *Guardian*, 23 Aug. 1984

> Three years ago Dr Charles Seitz and Dr Geoffrey Fox at the California Institute of Technology built a computer, uncommonly powerful for its price, wired together in the pattern known as a hypercube. It was modelled on one of the beautifully symmetrical ways you could wire up a computer if hyperspace were real. ... The geometry of hypercubes taxes human spatial intuition, but the subject can be approached by analogy. If you take two squares, position them one above the other, and create four new edges to join the four pairs of corresponding corners, you get a cube. Take two cubes and join the corresponding corners, and you get a four-dimensional hypercube. - *Guardian*, 15 May 1986

---

hyperkinesis *noun* an abnormal condition of children, marked by hyperactivity associated with delayed development and impaired learning

> The book's author, Dr Eric Taylor, who is senior lecturer in child and adolescent behaviour at London's Maudsley Hospital, explained, 'A lot of children exhibit behaviour that could be described as over-active, which really just means they move about a lot, but a lasting pattern of chaotic and inattentive over-activity could be described as hyperactive. But the serious cases, more correctly called hyperkinesis, are where such behaviour goes hand-in-hand with delayed development and learning'. - *Daily Telegraph*, 29 Jan. 1986

---

hypersonic *adjective* of, being, or moving at a speed five or more times that of sound in air

> A Lockheed Aerospace executive has ... predicted that routine hypersonic flights - about five times the speed of sound - would be a reality by the year 2000. - *Daily Telegraph*, 22 Jan. 1986

Hystar *trademark* - used for an aircraft that is a cross between an airship and a helicopter, has a toroidally-shaped helium-filled envelope powered and controlled by propellers and/or rotors, can be either piloted or remotely controlled, and, because of its vertical takeoff facility and great manoeuvrability, is used for lifting heavy loads of logs out of forested areas

> A cross between an airship and a helicopter, called Hysta, could soon help the Canadian forestry industry. It can reach

trees that other aircraft cannot reach - at least not economically. - *New Scientist*, 3 April 1986

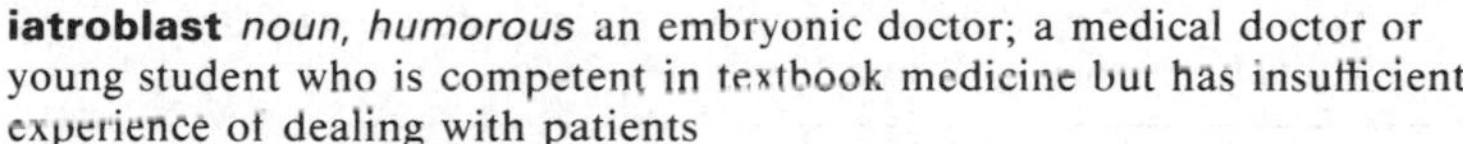

iatroblast *noun, humorous* an embryonic doctor; a medical doctor or young student who is competent in textbook medicine but has insufficient experience of dealing with patients

> In front of our very eyes the Professor [Tony Glenister, Professor of Anatomy and Dean of the Charing Cross and Westminster Medical School] produced from his hat the word 'iatroblast', a new scientific term for a new scientific phenomenon. ... The medical student might well become a well-motivated, scientifically-competent houseman but has far to go before becoming a proper doctor. - *Bookseller*, 7 June 1986

► From Greek *iatros* = doctor + *blastos* = bud, shoot.

iceball *noun* a game played on an ice rink by two teams of five players on skates who attempt to score goals by throwing a studded ball into an elevated box

► This hybrid sport, a creation of the Mecca leisure company, combines characteristics of basketball and American football and is played by two squads each of 15 players on skates.
It has been introduced by Mecca to six British stadiums of their own and they hope that it will appeal to the management and patrons of council-operated and other rinks. But in Oxford rink managers and city officials have banned it for being overviolent.

icon *noun* a symbolic representation on a visual display unit of a facility available to the user of a computer system

► These demonstrative symbols are designed to be universally understood and, above all, to be user- FRIENDLY. For example, instead of the word 'file' it will show a filing cabinet.

ideas processor *noun* OUTLINE PROCESSOR

> Brainstorm was described as an 'ideas processor', the first of its kind in the UK, and a new type of application that would join the likes of word-processors and spreadsheets to become

an essential part of any micro-computer system. - *Guardian*, 6 March 1986

---

index fund *or* **indexed fund** *noun* an investment trust holding a wide range of shares calculated to reflect accurately an index of share prices, so that the value of the investments rises or falls in accordance with the movement of the stock market as a whole

> Index funds may be big internationally, but an international index fund still has few friends at home. - *Daily Telegraph*, 30 July 1986

> In the United States indexed funds represent about 8 p.c. of the total, and half the new money is going into such funds. - *Daily Telegraph*, 17 July 1986

---

inerrantist *noun* someone who believes in the infallibility and literal truth of the Bible; a fundamentalist

> The essence of fundamentalism is the belief in the 'inerrancy' of the Bible as it was originally written. ... The Southern 'inerrantists', as they have become known, are authoritarian and intolerant in their beliefs. 'If you don't stink like them, you don't stink at all', one earthy Virginia preacher told me. - *Guardian*, 23 June 1986

► This new derivative of the established term *inerrancy* (= infallibility) may be the result of the strict meaning of *fundamentalism* having become somewhat diluted.

---

inflation tax *noun* a proposed tax to be levied on companies that give their employees wage increases in excess of a statutory level, unless because of increased profits or a profit-sharing scheme

> The Social Democrat-Liberal Alliance wants to apply stick as well as carrot. Its latest blueprint for an election manifesto calls for an 'inflation tax'. ... The passing of inflation and the erosion of union power in Britain have undermined a main argument against inflation taxes - that they burden companies with large penalties they are powerless to resist. - *Economist*, 9 Aug. 1986

---

infopreneur *noun* someone engaged in INFOPRENEURIAL activity

> American makers have used their knowhow to better commercial ends. ... Other countries - Britain and West Germany particularly - have been inexplicably making life as difficult as possible for their own infopreneurs. - *Economist*, 23 Aug. 1986

---

infopreneurial *adjective* of or being business development and activity in the field of information technology

> To compete with AT & T, IBM, NEC, Fujitsu and Hitachi in

the infopreneurial revolution, GEC and other European high-tech businesses will have to pick their partners with an eye for technological strengths to plug their most serious weaknesses. ... Both Plessey and GEC ... might then be one, or a significant part of one, of the survivors when the infopreneurial industry experiences the sort of consolidation the motor industry has gone through. - *Economist*, 2 Aug. 1986

---

informatics *noun* the science of electronic information processing

The system of rights, privileges and obligations which ... enabled English society to provide stability without tyranny through the ages, has now come unstuck in the age of informatics. - *Listener*, 16 Jan 1986

---

information services *noun* an industry combining the high-technology industries of computing, office automation, and telecommunications

All that noisy jostling going on right now between the IBMs, Xeroxs and AT&Ts of the corporate world is merely the clatter of these three industrial sectors ... being forged together by their underlying technologies into a single, ultra-tech activity called information services. - *Economist*, 23 Aug. 1986

Inheritance Tax *noun* a tax in Britain levied on transfers of capital (eg by gift or inheritance), replacing the previous Capital Transfer Tax

The Chancellor yesterday abolished Capital Transfer Tax for all lifetime gifts between individuals. ... The tax, which will continue to apply in the case of gifts on death and for various transfers into trusts, is also to be renamed Inheritance Tax, representing a shift back to the days of the old Estate Duty Tax, which was replaced by CTT in 1974. ... It will make it easier for home owners to gift their homes to their children without any tax penalty and in many cases make long-term provision for children's education simpler to organize. - *The Times*, 19 March 1986

Though the castrated CTT has now been cheekily renamed an Inheritance Tax, the reality is that it is a charter for any heir with a somnambulant accountant to avoid any impost whatsoever. - *Guardian*, 20 March 1986

► Attempts to simplify taxation are a generally popular relish to the more solid meat of a budget. Reduction or elimination of taxes is a particular pledge of the current British government.
The 18 March 1986 budget removed lifetime gifts from tax (formerly Capital Transfer Tax). Gifts on death are now subject to Inheritance Tax. Special provision is made for lifetime gifts in cases in which the donor dies within seven years of the gift: a tapering scale applies. There are also particular restrictions to prevent the donor enjoying or retaining any benefit.

The arrangements were received by the press with predictable clichés according to political alignment.

---

innoventure *noun* an innovative venture

> In post-tax-reform America ... profit-sharing arrangments ... will spread through the ordinary ranks of workers in what will really be co-operative innoventures. - *Economist*, 2 Aug. 1986

---

intra-ocular lens *noun* a lens implanted into the eye after the removal of the natural lens, that helps in focussing

> Every year in Britain, about 50,000 people have a cataract removal operation. For more than half of them, a lens is inserted at the time of the operation. It is called an intra-ocular lens. - *Woman's Own*, 8 March 1986

---

intrapreneur *noun* somebody who initiates or manages a new business or division within an established company

> We should break up the hierarchical mega-corporation into co-operating networks of 'intrapreneurs.' Then everybody will become individualists again, and work twice as hard and twice as inventively. - *Guardian*, 13 March 1986

► The coinage of this word has usually been attributed to Gifford Pinchot III, an American management consultant whose book *Intrapreneuring* was published in 1985. However, others were using the word at about the same time. It is a central term in the book *Future Work* by James Robertson, a speaker and consultant on work and its future pattern, who feels that conventional attitudes to what is meant by work need to change. He examines the possibility of more feasible working hours and the need for greater recognition of family responsibilities of male employees.
Most significant is Robertson's discussion of intrapreneurship, whereby there is acceptance of entrepreneurial activity (especially by former employees) within a large organization, possibly part-time. This concept has been successful in some companies in the USA and Sweden. He also mentions the quasi-synonym *skunkworks*, which is an American description of this type of contribution.
He predicts some resistance from trades unions (presumably on the grounds of restrictive practice and levels of remuneration) and from management (presumably on the grounds of loss of control).
He uses the expression *ownwork* to describe the type of activity to which companies might encourage their employees to move when they wish to thin out management.

---

intrapreneurial *adjective* of or being an INTRAPRENEUR

---

intrapreneurship *noun* the condition, status, or skill of being an INTRAPRENEUR

---

intron *noun* a section of a nucleic acid (eg DNA) that does not code information for protein synthesis

> And if all modern organisms are descended from shared ancestors, are introns ancient structures that have been lost by bacteria, or are they a novelty discovered only by the 'higher' forms of life? – *New Scientist*, 26 June 1986

---

ipse *noun* integrated project support environment: software designed to streamline and semi-automate some aspects of the development and writing of integrated systems of computer programs (eg for the command and control system of an aircraft)

> Programmers seeking the leading edge in software development can now choose from two off the shelf integrated project support environments. GEC Software last week announced the availability of Genos, its framework for an ipse. The concept of an ipse is to surround the software developer with a set of integrated tools that plug into a portable framework. ... Derek Alway, md at GEC Software, said that the design of Genos was based on the specification laid down by the US DoD for an Ada Programming Support Environment. The GEC ipse will be pitching at defence and aerospace environments in which the Ada language is a crucial element. – *Datalink*, 26 May 1986

---

iridologist *noun* someone who practises IRIDOLOGY

---

iridology *noun* a technique of diagnosis based on the belief that illness in any part of the body is reflected by markings on a part of the iris thought to correspond with that part of the body

> She was tired, lacked energy, was putting on weight, suffered from digestive problems and had a severe bout of pancreatitis. The real worry was that she couldn't find out what was going wrong. So she turned for help to a special form of diagnosis called iridology where conditions of the eye – especially the iris – can give information used in the diagnosis of physical and mental disorders. – *Here's Health*, Feb. 1986

---

irradiate *verb* to treat food by IRRADIATION

---

irradiation *noun* exposure of food to low levels of gamma radiation in order to sterilize and preserve it

> 'Irradiation' of foodstuffs by an intensely radioactive byproduct, such as Cobalt-60, could, it is claimed, prevent some deaths and much misery from food poisoning every year. – *Financial Times*, 25 March 1986

► The irradiation of food is an extremely emotive subject, made more so by the Chernobyl disaster. It is already practised in 39 countries and the

US Food and Drug Administration recently permitted the irradiation of pork, fresh fruit, and vegetables.
In the UK, the Advisory Committee on the Safety of Irradiated and Novel Foods has come down in favour of irradiation, with the dose they recommend ten times the kiloGRAY allowed in the US. The committee has been widely criticized for the close links of some of its members and advisors with companies dealing in irradiation technology.
Irradiation is already used in the UK for sterilizing medical supplies. It could lead to a decreased reliance on pesticides and reduce the incidence of food poisoning. However, it could also be used to 'clean up' contaminated food (see ZOMBIE FOOD) and two companies are at present facing fines and possible prison sentences for importing irradiated prawns which had originally failed quality control tests.
Irradiation has been found to lower the level of some vitamins and damage polyunsaturated fats. Widespread public alarm about nuclear issues in general and worry about the unknown long term effects of irradiation have led to the creation of the euphemistic term PICO-WAVE.

---

isoprinosine *or US* **isoprinocine** *noun* an antiviral drug that is used to treat the early stages of AIDS

> There have been preliminary reports showing that patients infected with the AIDS virus (at a relatively early stage of infection) are less likely to progress to frank AIDS if treated with isoprinosine, though the drug has no role in the treatment of AIDS itself. – *New Scientist*, 2 Jan. 1986

---

jalapeño *noun* a short and thick green chilli, often used in Mexican cooking

---

jarming *noun* exercising the upper body, especially the arms (eg by swimming)

> American doctor Joseph Wasserug believes that health benefits not from a lot of legwork but from regular exercise of the upper body, in particular the arms. He cites the longevity of many orchestral conductors, solo violinists and pianists ... as examples of the benefits of 'jarming,' jogging with our arms. – *Options*, April 1986

► This humorous expression for jogging with the arms is reminiscent of the handjive. That absurd sedentary dance was briefly fashionable in the late 1950s and involved extensive gesticulation and movement with the hands.

Exercising with the arms is a somewhat specialized extension of the passion for physical exercise which has been evident since the mid-1970s. It is frequently to be seen, albeit not under the title jarming, in the activities of the aerobics expert Lizzie Webb on *TV AM.* Her exercises are designed to appeal to a wide variety of participant, including sometimes those who are too old or infirm for more complete exercising.

---

jar wars *noun, humorous* the controversy in the US over drugs tests which President Reagan is urging everyone to take and which involve providing a urine sample

> In what has been dubbed 'jar wars' 78 White House staff have obeyed the call, starting predictably with the compulsively obliging Vice-President Bush (he would have peed into his leader's bottle if there was any danger that Mr Reagan might be emulating Jack Kennedy's occasional resort to a joint with a girlfriend.) - *Guardian*, 27 Aug. 1986

► In September 1986 President Reagan and his wife, Nancy, appeared on television to appeal for public support in a 'national crusade' against drugs. Afterwards he ordered drug tests for all government employees engaged in sensitive jobs. Anti-drug education is planned to extend even to kindergartens.

J curve *noun* a model of the supposed effects of devaluation on a balance of payments deficit, with an initial downturn (caused by a devaluation of exports and a rise in the price of imports) followed by an upturn as exports are boosted and consumers change to buying cheaper home-produced goods

> Australia's Federal Treasurer Paul Keating ... coined the phrase 'J curve' to describe what he said were devaluation effects. ... The failure of the J curve to materialize has produced some of the raunchiest political cartoons seen in the traditionally irreverent Australian press for some time. - *Daily Telegraph*, 28 May 1986

> Recent statistics show a clear increase in the volume of Japan's imports of manufactured goods, and the volume of Japan's exports is either levelling off or declining. But, because of the J-curve effect, the price of exports denominated in American dollars has increased. - *Economist*, 5 April 1986

► The term has become popular in economics, and has been applied to the Japanese and American economies as well as to that of Australia. It is based on the shape of the letter J with its initial downward curve followed by a sudden sweep upwards.
Graph-curves attract numerous titles representing their apparent shape. The best-known include *convex*, *concave*, and *bell-shaped.*

---

job splitting *noun* dividing a job between two employees in such a way that little cooperation is needed between them, as opposed to job sharing where much cooperation is needed

---

jumbo *noun, US slang* CRACK

> In the past six or eight months crack or jumbo as it is sometimes called has become the hottest drug on the market. - *Guardian*, 16 June 1986

---

junk bond *noun* a high-yield speculative security, especially one issued to finance an intended takeover

> Mr Rupert Murdoch, the Australian-born media entrepreneur, has raised more than $1bn in one of the largest offerings of high yield securities, commonly referred to as 'junk bonds', in the New York financial markets. - *Financial Times*, 3 March 1986

> The Federal Reserve chairman, Mr Paul Volcker, yesterday won a critical skirmish with the Reagan White House when the board of the US central bank voted to curtail the use of junk bonds in American takeovers. - *Guardian*, 9 Jan. 1986

► Bonds of this type were invented in the late 1970s by the Wall Street investment bank Drexel Burnham Lambert. The derogatory name bestowed upon them is often unfair, and their supporters prefer to call them simply 'high-yield bonds'. Strictly speaking, they are merely securities which have been given an inferior rating ('below investment grade') by the major rating agencies.
Some of them are risky, but statistics suggest that their annual return is 6% greater than that of bonds rated fist-class.

---

kamikaze legislation *noun* legislation which may have immediate benefits but which will be disastrous in the long term

> 'The democratic leadership may think this is clever politics in an election year, but the American people see this for what it is - kamikaze legislation that could take their jobs down in flames,' he [President Reagan] said. - *Daily Telegraph*, 30 May 1986

► Kamikaze is a Japanese word meaning divine wind (*kami* = god + *kaze* = wind). Japanese kamikaze pilots were a tragically heroic feature of the 1941-45 war in the Far East. Amongst other things they deliberately crashed their aircraft onto the decks of enemy warships (sometimes with

the aeroplanes overloaded with ammunition). As a result, extensive figurative use of the word has been made since the end of the Second World War.
President Reagan was referring to a protectionist trade Bill passed by the Democratic majority in the House of Representatives.

---

kamikaze protein *noun* an enzyme produced by cells, that repairs damaged DNA, especially that caused by carcinogenic agents

> A recently discovered 'kamikaze protein', which appears able to repair cancer damage to DNA molecules in the body's cells before dying itself, may offer hope for the prevention and treatment of cancer, a specialist said yesterday. - *Daily Telegraph*, 31 July 1986

---

keypad *noun* a device resembling a small (section of a) keyboard for interfacing with electronic (eg teletext) systems

> Prestel, by contrast, is pre-computerate. It assumes you are using a keypad to select a number. - *Guardian*, 13 Feb. 1986

► While it is not new, this is an example of a technical concept which is now commonplace in layman's parlance.
It generally takes the form of a miniature keyboard. It probably has some specialization of function or arrangement. For example, it will often not be in the traditional QWERTY format. It may have only numbers or will show a range of unusual characters. A numeric display at the side is usual.

---

kinetic-energy weapon *noun* any of a group of non-nuclear weapons, including SMART ROCKS and RAIL GUNS, that destroy their targets by the force of impact

---

knave *noun, slang* an innocent person duped by terrorists into travelling by air with a suitcase containing a bomb primed to explode in mid-flight

> In the suitcase bomb business, these innocent couriers are called 'knaves'. A successful knave never does a second run. - *Listener*, 8 May 1986

► This term became notorious when in spring 1986 a girl was deluded by an Arab terrorist, who was masquerading as her boy-friend, into thinking that she was smuggling diamonds. In fact she was taking a bomb on board an El-Al aircraft. This kind of activity has led to the need for CONDOR and other devices.

---

knowledge engineer *noun* a computer expert who gathers and arranges information so that it can be used in an EXPERT SYSTEM

> One of the biggest bottlenecks in the building of expert systems is caused by the difficulties of capturing the knowledge of human experts. The task often requires lengthy in-depth interviews between a knowledge engineer and a

> human expert, as a prelude to the transformation of the knowledge thus elicited into a form that can be readily processed or manipulated by an expert system's inference engine. – *Guardian*, 23 Jan. 1986

► In the preparation of a computer system to serve in some technical role, there are likely to be two sources of expertise.
There will be the *domain expert*, who knows about the subject in question, such as medicine. Balancing that competence there will be a knowledge engineer whose business is codifying the information. It is most unlikely that both functions will be carried out by the same individual.

---

kyokushinkai *noun* an aggressive form of karate in which no protective clothing is worn and the object is to knock out the opponent by any means short of blows to the head or testicles

> Many, like Vic Charles, who regards himself as an athlete, regard karate as a sport like swimming or athletics. Others such as members of the kyokushinkai style (whose founder, Oyama, was famed for felling bulls with a single blow), take a harsher line. – *The Times*, 10 April 1986

► This Japanese word means 'The peak of truth'. The style was developed by Masutatsu Oyama, born in 1923.

Labour-friendly *adjective* see -FRIENDLY

Lanark Blue *trademark* used for a ewe's-milk cheese which is made in the Lanark Hills of Scotland and is similar to Roquefort

> The new Scottish cheese Lanark Blue is ... a genuinely new cheese in my experience of British cheeses. – *Glasgow Herald*, 25 April 1986

---

landside *noun* the area of an airport before the passport control – compare AIRSIDE

> By having no shops on the landside we encourage people to pass through passport control and keep the check-in area spacious and flowing. – *Daily Telegraph*, 11 March 1986

---

lap-held *adjective or noun* (of or being) a portable computer small enough to be operated on a person's lap; a 'deskless' computer

The Typecorder was a lap-held computer word processor. - *Personal Computer World*, Feb. 1986

---

lap portable *noun* LAP-HELD

The Tandy 100 and NEC PC-8201A lap portables are primitive by today's standards, but the right software helps to bring them up to scratch. - *Practical Computing*, March 1986

---

lap-top *adjective or noun* LAP-HELD

The SMC-T11 ... is described by Sony as a 'second generation lap-top'. - *Personal Computer World*, Feb. 1986

► A somewhat absurd word based on DESKTOP.
The first was manufactured in 1984. However, now that they are in fairly common use, it has become clear that quite a robust lap is needed.
It is meant to indicate that the equipment is reasonably portable. Compare LUGGABLE and TRANSPORTABLE.

---

larder fridge *noun* a fridge which does not have a freezer compartment

---

LaRouchie *or* **LaRouchite** *noun* a follower of the American politician Lyndon LaRouche

With major mid-term elections coming up in November for the Senate, the House, state governorships and a host of lesser jobs, some politicians believe the LaRouchies could exercise real influence and even power. - *Listener*, 8 May 1986

In California the LaRouchites claim a membership of 10,000 with 200 candidates running in the state elections; they also say that they have more than 120,000 signatures out of the 393,000 needed to put an initiative on the November ballot that would require a universal test for AIDS. - *Economist*, 26 April 1986

► This bizarre faction believes a number of obscure and unlikely things. As a generalized description of their attitudes, they may be said to be extremely right-wing. They tend towards an overstated fear of Soviet agents and their influence and what they see as pan-global alliances involving Israel.
Particular suspicion is cast on a number of prominent public figures in the USA. They also believe that the British royal family heads an international drug-smuggling ring. In September 1986 the Prince of Wales, visiting Chicago, was subjected to hostile demonstrations by LaRouchies.
Lyndon LaRouche, 63 years old, is of Quaker lineage, and was a Communist and Trotskyite before adopting his present individual beliefs. His followers' principal tactic is a system of entryism into every conceivable organ of the American establishment.

---

laser mass spectrometer *noun* a highly sensitive instrument that can detect the presence of a substance (eg a chemical element) at extremely low concentrations. The mass spectrometer incorporates a pulsed laser which produces positive ions from even a single atom or molecule of the substance, which can then be detected.

> The laser mass spectrometer will be 10,000 times more sensitive than existing techniques for detecting liquids or gases and 1,000 times more efficient in the case of solids. The team envisages applications in electronics, medicine, security and environmental protection. – *Sunday Times*, 1 June 1986

---

laser scanning *noun* a system for monitoring and checking goods and supplies (eg items in a supermarket) in which a laser is used to scan bar codes to provide information for stocktaking, pricing, etc

> Laser-scanning electronic tills probably costing a total of more than £220m are likely to be installed at three-quarters of all main check-outs operated by leading supermarket chains before 1990. – *Financial Times*, 10 Feb. 1986

---

laser shopping *noun* a system of shopping where goods are subjected to LASER SCANNING at the checkout to determine their price

> Stringent checking procedures are vital if shoppers' confidence in 'laser shopping' is to be maintained. ... There's no easy way for shoppers to be sure that the prices they see displayed are the same as those at the checkout. – *Which*, Sept. 1986

---

launch constraint *noun* an order or restriction preventing the launch of an air- or spacecraft

> But he noted that the design flaw which caused the accident, the leaky O-rings in the joint between the segments of the booster rocket, was well known in advance. As a result officials had imposed a 'launch constraint' meaning in Nasa parlance a restriction debarring a launching until a particular technical fault was corrected. – *Daily Telegraph*, 11 June 1986

---

leaksmith *noun* somebody who leaks information

> Proposals for new roads across London costing nearly £200 million are under discussion between the Transport Department and London Docklands Development Corporation. ... 'The implications are immense,' says Transport 2000, the pressure group which describes itself as 'leaksmiths to the Transport Department'. – *Daily Telegraph*, 23 June 1986

► A simple *-smith* formation on the pattern of *blacksmith*, *goldsmith*, and so on.
Leaks have become so commonplace in government, industry, commerce, and even apparently from Court, that they are becoming a recognized form of public relations (usually disguised as informed predictions). Indeed, it is unusual not to learn from the Press of the general drift, if not the detail, of

public announcements (such as the Budget and ministerial changes) before they are made.

---

lean-burn *adjective* of or being an internal-combustion engine that uses a reduced proportion of fuel in the fuel-air mixture, thus lessening fuel consumption and pollution from exhaust fumes

> Unleaded petrol will be the rule of the road by the 1990s. By then all new cars are expected to have 'lean-burn' engines which run on the lower octane fuel. - *Today*, 24 June 1986

► This technique is favoured by the British motor industry, as opposed to that in Germany, which uses 10%-15% more petrol.
It has been developed by Austin Rover and Ford on the basis of an American system involving a 3-way catalytic converter and fuel-injection system.

---

leisure suit *noun* a loose-fitting suit similar to a track suit, consisting of a matching top and trousers in a soft fabric, which can be worn for exercising or as a casual garment

> You'll be looking good and feeling great in this superb Umbro leisure suit. Wear it for your daily fitness routine or simply for relaxing round the home. - *Woman*, 8 March 1986

► This is also known as a *jump-suit*, which presumably sounds rather too energetic or too physical for some tastes. It can be made of cotton, denim, or just about any other material as dictated by price. It can be worn with or without a belt according to convenience, figure, or desired appearance. They are certainly not a representation of ANTI-CHIC. Such garments can be both highly practical and very attractive. With a scarf and other accessories they can be worn on quite smart social occasions.

---

lentivirus *noun* any of a group of RETROVIRUSES that include the AIDS virus and those which cause disease in cattle, goats, and sheep

> The virus that causes AIDS was first identified only two years ago. It belongs to an unusual family called lentiviruses that cause a variety of unpleasant diseases in sheep, goats and cattle. The discovery of this relationship ... provides a clue to the long-term course of the disease in humans. Sheep infected by a lentivirus called visna suffer from a chronic illness that they never shake off. Symptoms include paralysis resulting from damage to the brain and nervous system - direct effects of the virus which are now being found in people with AIDS. - *Listener*, 27 March 1986

Leopard *noun* a member of the police anti-narcotics squad in Bolivia

> Bolivian anti-narcotics policemen, known as Leopards, and an adviser from the United States Drug Enforcement Administration found two big Brazilian generators supplying shacks where coca paste had been filtered, purified in ether and acetone, and dried into crystals. - *Economist*, 26 July 1986

> American soldiers will remain in Bolivia for at least two months, transporting the Leopards on search-and-destroy missions into the countryside. - *Time*, 28 July 1986

► This word came to prominence during a joint American-Bolivian campaign in July 1986 against drug traffickers in Bolivia. Unfortunately, the campaign was too large to maintain secrecy; it found plenty of evidence of cocaine manufacture, but no cocaine and no traffickers. It is alleged that the production and movement of cocaine are now an inextricable part of the infrastructure of the Bolivian economy.

---

leverage *verb* to raise money (for a buy-out or other speculative business deal) largely by borrowing, on a relatively small capital base, in the expectation that interest repayments on the loan can be paid out of the profits of the deal

> Highly-geared firms, particularly those which built up debts during leveraged buy-outs, cannot easily use cheaper money to refinance debts run up when interest rates were higher in 1984–85. - *Economist*, 29 March 1986

> Some bankers are worried that if the present trend in 'leveraged' buyouts continues, a significant proportion of British industry could become overburdened with debt. ... In the US, where the number, size, and experience of leveraged deals is much greater than in Britain, this is already causing serious concern. - *The Times*, 12 May 1986

► As a noun, *leverage* has long been used in finance as the American equivalent of the British term *gearing*. As a verb, it entered American English in the 1950s but has only recently become prominent in Britain.

LHRH agonist *noun* LUTEINIZING HORMONE-RELEASING HORMONE AGONIST

---

liberation theologist *or* **liberation theologian** *noun* an adherent of LIBERATION THEOLOGY

---

liberation theology *noun* a theory, associated especially with the Catholic clergy in Latin America, that theology involves a political commitment to change society by liberating mankind from social and political injustice

> Liberation theology, born in Latin America more than two decades ago, links spiritual freedom to liberation from social and economic oppression. The Vatican applauds some parts of liberation theology, such as its concern for the poor, but condemns Marxist elements often associated with it. - *Guardian*, 14 March 1986

► The first instance of the expression was in Gustav Gulierrez's *Teologiá de la liberación Perspectivas*, published in Lima in 1971. It demanded a commitment through faith to abolish injustice in order to build a new society.

It is not particularly anti-left wing or anti-right wing. The church in Nicaragua has got into a great deal of trouble with the left-of-centre regime in that country. Clergy whose ministry is under an authoritative right-wing government are obliged to come to terms with the ambivalent Christian view of Marxism.
The liberation to which it refers is not only liberation from politically extremist governments. It also relates to an indirect dependence on trade with Europe and the USA. Its interpretation is sometimes connected with black theology and feminist theology.
Although its origins were in the Third World, especially Latin America, it has lately aroused much interest in Britain as the affairs of those countries (particularly Nicaragua) have been given increased attention.

LIC *noun, chiefly US* LOW-INTENSITY CONFLICT

---

lig *verb, British informal* to obtain refreshment or entertainment at another's expense; freeload

► Two established senses are (1) to steal, and (2) to lounge about. This appears to be an extension of both those.
It stems from an old dialect word meaning to lie, which in turn comes from Old English *licgan.*

---

ligger *noun, British informal* a person who LIGS; a freeloader

> Of course the Paris hotels were full of fashion writers, buyers and liggers ... from all over the world, in town to view the next season's collections. - *Listener*, 27 March 1986

Lindow Man *noun* the Iron Age Briton, apparently a victim of a ritual killing, whose well preserved body was found in 1984 in a peat bog at Lindow Moss in Cheshire

> Lindow Man (alias Pete Marsh), the much-televised body from a Cheshire bog, has pride of place in the exhibition [at the British Museum]. ... He will certainly be a crowd-puller. But I did not find him at all appealing; seeing the wretch 'in the flesh' for the first time reminded me instantly of a squashed Gladstone bag that had seen better days. - *New Scientist*, 17 July 1986

► Lindow Man caused a great sensation on discovery because of his excellent physical condition. This interest was heightened by the violent manner of his death. For a year or so afterwards and when on initial display in the Natural History Museum he was known by the name Pete Marsh, as a pun on his erstwhile resting-place. However for long-term use a more dignified title was felt to be appropriate.

---

lite *adjective, informal* light: eg **1** *of food and drink* not fattening or full-bodied; easily digested; of low alcoholic content **2** not serious or severe **3** generally YUPPYISH

> The new in-word ... is 'lite', as in lite white wine, lite

mayonnaise and lite classics: life without commitment or consequences. - *Guardian*, 26 Aug. 1986

What the neon-ised Bar Escoba is conscious of ... is the 'lite' factor. Said André Plisnier: 'Spanish food can be very heavy and fatty. We knew that ... we had to have a healthy menu, and one which let people eat a little but often.' - *Sunday Times*, 27 July 1986

► A trivial and trendy spelling on the *tonite* analogy. *Tonite* goes back several decades and was probably intended to draw the reader's attention to an advertised event by its unusual informality.

---

lithotripter *noun* a device for treating kidney stones, without the need for surgery, which uses shock waves to reduce the stones to particles of very small size

The most important joint venture so far has been the installation of a £1m lithotripter, bought by Bupa, in St Thomas's Hospital, London. - *Financial Times*, 22 Jan. 1986

► Not the same as a *lithotriptor*, which is a surgical instrument (known since the 19th century) for crushing stones.

Livingstonization *or* **Livingstonisation** *noun, British* the control of companies by local Labour councils

The Labour party's new policy will be that of nationalisation plus - in other words, nationalisation plus what Aims [of Industry] has termed 'Livingstonisation'. - *Daily Telegraph*, 23 June 1986

► Based on the name of Ken Livingstone, last leader of the Greater London Council (dismantled March 1986). A witty and eloquent man, Livingstone embodied for many people the more startling and extreme policies of Labour councils. Possibly his actual influence was less than his reputation and his immortality through this eponymous term suggest.

---

logic bomb *or* **logic time-bomb** *noun* an instruction secretly programmed into a computer, as an act of sabotage or fraud, that will cause the system to break down in specific circumstances

'Logic bombs' have forced at least six companies out of business in the last two years. ... One contract programmer is alleged to have planted periodic failures in a system so that he'd be called out again and again to fix them. - *Computer Weekly*, 8 May 1986

It was becoming increasingly common for disgruntled staff to program instructions into the computer that would be triggered only after their departure. Most companies had no insurance for the consequences of such logic time-bombs. - *The Times*, 11 Aug. 1986

Lolobal *trademark* - used for a ball surrounded by a hard plastic platform on which the user stands while gripping the ball between his/her feet and attempting to bounce, either as a means of exercise or as a competitive sport

> And from Holland there's the Lolobal, an intriguing looking device which has already brought hours of amusement to the staff of *New Health*. – *New Health*, June 1986
> Flying high on the Lolobal, the latest craze after the skateboard is Glen Cassidy, watched by another enthusiast, Alison King. The youngsters were demonstrating the versatility of the Lolobal outside the Lewis Meeson Newsagent shop. – *Herts and Essex Observer*, 14 Aug. 1986

---

loop *noun* a self-contained series of computer program instructions that is repeated until some specific or terminal condition occurs

> The fateful decision was taken on Thursday to add ... two more personal computers to the network. Both were well tried machines which had been in use on other projects. ... When they were added to the network, however, it went into a 'loop', a critical condition in which the software talks endlessly to itself and where no information can get in or out. ... It took the exchange team four hours to break into the loop and establish that one of the additional personal computers had an as yet undiagnosed fault. – *Financial Times*, 17 March 1986

► Loops are used to avoid duplication in a program when different sets of data require the same instructions. However, should a bug occur in the system, programs can become trapped in a loop from which it is difficult and time-consuming to escape.

---

low-intensity conflict *noun, chiefly US* (*abbreviation* **LIC**) the use of adequate, but not excessive, force to repulse or neutralize terrorism

> In the corridors of the Pentagon, low-intensity conflict (or LIC as it's now commonly known) has become the hottest new military theory. The old counterinsurgency doctrine stressed the threat to American interests posed by Third World revolution. But LIC shifts the focus of concern to another target: paranoid fear of an international terrorist plot against the free world. – *New Internationalist*, July 1986

► The current euphemism to describe what was known as *counter-revolutionary warfare* in the 1950s and 1960s
The post-Vietnam anti-militarism in the USA has called for careful choice of terminology to describe military expenditure and military effort outside the USA. This term appears to be suitably anodyne.
George Schultz, Secretary of State, favours this kind of minimum force approach. Hawks, such as Caspar Weinberger of the Pentagon, favour something less deliberate to control the activities of the USSR, Libya, Cuba, Iran, and other regimes seen as hostile to US interests.

---

luggable *adjective or noun* (of or being) a mains-powered microcomputer comprising all the components of a DESKTOP computer integrated into a single unit which can be carried a short distance

> Luggables provide the utmost in features and functionality but are heavy. ... While the drawback of luggables is weight and size, 'laptops' score on weight and size but can have drawbacks in screen quality. - *Money Management*, July 1986

---

lumpectomy *noun* surgical removal of a tumour, especially in breast cancer, together with only a small amount of surrounding tissue

> Some surgeons favour a so-called radical mastectomy, which involves removing not only the entire breast but also much of the surrounding tissue. ... At the opposite extreme to this disfiguring procedure is the 'lumpectomy'. - *Daily Telegraph*, 17 Sept. 1986

► The medical profession has gone to great lengths to research and promote forms of treatment for cancer which stop short of amputation. (Chemotherapy is one of the best known and now one of the most successful examples.) It is a particular triumph to have produced a technique which obviates breast mastectomy, the psychological effects of which are particularly harrowing for many women. The results are nearly as good as radical surgery, and continue to be improved.

Lundy *noun, NIrish* a traitor who collaborates with invaders; a quisling

► This eponymous term derives from Lt Col Robert Lundy who was the Governor of Londonderry at the time of the siege in 1689.
At first he was popular with the Protestant citizens and declared his loyalty to William and Mary. However, from the beginning of the siege his attitude was equivocal. It seems unlikely that he had Jacobite sympathies. He probably just felt inclined to keep out of trouble.
Whatever other interpretation is put on his behaviour, it is certain that he dampened the enthusiasm of the Protestants in the city. He corresponded with the enemy and inadvertently or deliberately encouraged them. He excluded the hawks from his council and eventually fled Londonderry, leaving the siege to others. The House of Commons investigation into his performance found - with masterly understatement - that his conduct had been 'very faulty'.

---

luteinizing hormone-releasing hormone agonist *or* **luteinising hormone-releasing hormone agonist** *noun* (*abbreviation* **LHRH agonist**) a hormone that regulates the action of the ovaries through the pituitary, and can be used as a contraceptive

> In fact LHRH agonist represents the use of far lower levels of hormones than the conventional Pill or even the so-called mini-pill because it works directly on the pituitary rather than flooding the system to produce a feed-back effect. - *Scotsman*, 22 May 1986

► A synthetic version of this hormone, taken as a nasal spray, acts on the

ovaries to prevent ovulation. It has fewer dangerous side-effects than the contraceptive pill and because very low levels of the hormone are involved it is of interest as a contraceptive for breast-feeding women as only very tiny amounts pass into breast milk.
It was developed by Dr Hamish Fraser in Edinburgh.

---

magalog *noun, US* a magazine issued by a shop and combining miscellaneous general-interest features (eg travel articles and short stories) with a list of products for sale

> K-Mart, a giant supermarket chain, is launching a magazine-cum-catalogue (the word that is being used here is magalogs) to be called *American Lifestyles.* ... A big toy chain, Toys R Us, is also launching a magalog aimed at school-kids. – *UK Press Gazette*, 23 June 1986

► Although the concept is familiar in the UK, the word itself does not seem to have crossed the Atlantic yet.

---

magnometer *noun* a device for measuring the yang (male energy) that is held to be emitted by ley lines

> A certain extra briskness comes into Symes' voice at times like this but he conscientiously tested the Salisbury Plain ley lines with a magnometer for yang. – *Guardian*, 12 Feb. 1986

► If one believes that ley lines exist, and that they emit yang, then one may also believe that this device works. Many people remain sceptical on the first count, let alone the others.

---

mailmerge *noun* a program used in word processing for producing letters, in which a name and address file is merged with the text file containing the letter

> For some users mailmerge is vital. This is the program which enables the setting up of a list of names and addresses. The program can automatically send a personal but otherwise identical letter to each – in other words the letter is topped and tailed from the list. – *Daily Telegraph*, 30 June 1986

Mamba *noun* Middle-Aged Middle-Brow Accomplisher: an unflamboyant, conformist, conservative, professionally successful, and prosperous middle-aged person

> To say Mambas rule OK would not suit their rhetorical style;

rather they prevail. ... Seldom have Mambas enjoyed such relative strength. – *Glasgow Herald*, 3 May 1986

► Probably nonce. However, there is a vogue for bizarre acronyms to describe social groups. This is perhaps a *yuppy* or a GUPPY grown up.

Mandela Town *noun* an imitation shantytown built by anti-apartheid demonstrators to draw attention to the condition of blacks in South Africa

> Mock shanties have become the seasonal symbol of protest as anti-apartheid campaigners have set up camp on dozens of university campuses across the country [USA]. When deans have lost their cool and demolished these 'Mandela Towns', demonstrators have acquired an even more potent metaphor of oppression. – *Economist*, 12 April 1986

► From Nelson Mandela, the black activist imprisoned in South Africa.

---

manufacturing automation protocol *noun* (*abbreviation* **MAP**) a scheme to standardize the manufacture of automated shopfloor systems (eg robots and machine-tool controllers) to ensure that all products conform and are fully interchangeable and substitutable

> The exercise, at AutoFact '85, is intended to show how far General Motors has come in persuading computer and factory equipment manufacturers to produce products to the Manufacturing Automation Protocol (MAP) – a standard for factory communications. – *New Scientist*, 7 Nov. 1985

► The system is a form of computer *lingua franca.*
It owes its origins to General Motors, who recognized the potential chaos which would arise from use of a variety of computer systems of different manufacturers. They appreciated that these should be able to talk to each other and they needed a common means of communication. Subsequently Boeing have been working on TECHNICAL OFFICE PROTOCOL (TOP), which will deal with office chaos in this way, as opposed to factory chaos.

MAP *noun* MANUFACTURING AUTOMATION PROTOCOL

> The National Computing Centre in Manchester and University of Leeds Industrial Services are jointly trying to define the requirements for setting up a MAP test and conformance centre in the UK. – *Financial Times*, 22 Jan. 1986

---

marathoner *noun* someone who runs in a marathon

> You may have read that marathoners go out bingeing on pasta the night before a big race. There is evidence that loading up with carbohydrates helps increase the body's store of glycogen, the major muscle fuel which runs very low from

> around the ten-mile mark, sometimes called the 'wall'. – *She*, April 1986

► The term *marathon* has its origins in the battle of Marathon in 490BC in which the Athenians defeated the Persians. It is alleged that after the battle Pheidippides ran from Marathon to Athens with the news (but this story is virtually demolished in Brian O'Kill's recent book *Exit Lines*). The original distance was 26 miles, and when the race was revived at the 1896 Athens Olympics that distance was used; later, another 385 yards were added. However, many less formal and less arduous imitations have followed, including *half-marathons* and *mini-marathons*. Some of these bear only a token resemblance to the original distance.
The word *marathoner* dates from 1923 in the USA, but is new in Britain. This reflects the current interest in this pursuit, largely the result of the popularity of athletic activities for charitable fund-raising which has given rise to the various newer versions of the event.

Marfan syndrome *noun* a congenital disturbance of the tissues (mesoderm) which provide the fundamental supporting structures of the body, that is marked by arterial and cardiac defects and dislocation of the lenses of the eyes and occurs in patients who are typically tall and slender with very long spider-like fingers and toes

> There was no immediate evidence to indicate whether Bias suffered from Marfan syndrome, a congenital disease that weakens the body's connective tissues and primarily affects tall people. – *International Herald Tribune*, 1 June 1986

► Curiously this condition affects only tall people.
It is alleged that it accounted for the sudden death of the 6ft 5ins tall American volleyball player Flo Hyman who collapsed during a match in Japan in January 1986. It is also blamed for the death of an American basketball player in the mid-1970s.
It was recognized as long ago as 1896 by Bernard Marfan, a French paediatrician (1858–1942), but has only recently come to the attention of the layman. Its symptoms are abnormally long fingers and toes (known as arachnodactyly), and its most serious manifestations are through cardiac and aortic defects.

---

marginalization *or* **marginalisation** *noun* the division of an area of interest (eg music) into specialized areas which appeal to only a small number of people

> The true dilemma of pop is its current marginalisation. While [Paul] Weller's gang goes for ex-Jam fans, Red Wedgers and nascent politico teenies ... Bronski Beat are forced into the teeny/clone corner. – *Blitz*, June 1986

Marinespeak *noun* see -SPEAK

---

marzipan layer *or* **marzipan set** *noun* the stratum of high-ranking specialist staff (eg brokers and market analysts), below the level of director, employed by financial institutions in the City of London

> The most sought-after people are known as the 'marzipan set' - high flyers who are below the icing but above the cake. - *Listener*, 20 March 1986
>
> When all the rules were thrown away, big buyers rushed for broking partnerships. ... Those just below partnership level, often the ones generating much of the business, got none of the capital windfall. They were the marzipan layer. - *Daily Telegraph*, 26 Aug. 1986

---

mega- *prefix* great; extremely large in size or quantity

► The prefix *mega-* (Greek *megas* = great) generated several scientific words in the nineteenth century, such as *megascope* (1831) and *megalops* (1855). However, in this decade it has been a prolific parent, increasingly consorting with non-Greek and non-technical words. In the 1983 Darlington by-election one of the unsuccessful candidates was described by a member of his own party as a *mega-wally*. In 1985 Virgin Megastore reopened. On 12 September 1986 the New Statesman was able to report 'Tower Records ... opened its flagship megastore in the old Swan and Edgar building in the heart of Piccadilly Circus.'
The words listed below are merely a selection of the *mega-* formations which have been noted in 1986. This trend towards hyperbole is also shown in the longer-running saga of SUPER-.

> **megabid** The change comes against the background of the past year's surge of megabids and the trend towards larger scale and more globally integrated securities markets. - *Investors Chronicle*, 13 June 1986
> The mega-bid boom may slow down, but is unlikely to stop. Still in train is Lloyds Bank's £1.3 billion bid for Standard Chartered Bank and the City is busy guessing the next victims. - *The Times*, 2 July 1986
> **mega-blockbuster** *Commando* is the latest mega-blockbuster to storm America - and it's on the way to Britain. - *Sun*, 8 Feb. 1986
> **megabrand** Chairman Roberto Goizeuta later announced, when he reintroduced Classic Coke, 'the concept of multiple product entries under the one large megabrand is the new game'. - *Financial Times*, 10 April 1986
> Woltz [chairman of London International], trained in the marketing school of Seagrams and Unilever, recognises a mega brand when he sees one. - *Observer*, 4 May 1986
> **megabuck** 'Listen man, America has more emotion and a better outlook. If I had mega-bucks I'd be thinking of getting some of it out of Britain.' [Ken Miller, real estate dealer] - *Today*, 25 March 1986
>
> The truth is that this fight is life and death for both men, in terms of megabuck contracts. King is hoping to pull a $20 million plus deal with cable TV. - *Star*, 17 Jan. 1986

mega-city An urban population explosion creating Third World 'mega-cities' with teeming squatter shanty towns rife with malnutrition, disease and poverty, has brought problems beyond all human experience, says a United Nations report issued in London yesterday. - *Daily Telegraph*, 9 May 1986
megaloan Today's credit-card megaloan is tomorrow's bad debt. - *Economist*, 17 May 1986
mega-merger As big bang looms closer the large financial service companies are straining harder at the leash. At the same time the wave of mega-mergers is producing new practices which the regulators must also keep up with.
- *The Times*, 6 March 1986
It was a mega-merger on the lines of that between the Halifax Permanent and Halifax Equitable in 1982 - which created the Halifax Building Society, still the world's biggest.
- *The Times*, 14 April 1986
mega-millionaire By amazing coincidence the first person at the St. James's club to learn that the Secretary of State for Defence had resigned was Lindsay Masters ... who had made Michael Heseltine into a mega-millionaire through their magazine company. - *Daily Mail*, 17 Jan. 1986
megaplan Science's reputation - after *Challenger* and Chernobyl - could do with an altruistic megaplan. - *Economist*, 24 May 1986
megasulk Mr Tony Marlow ... accused the BBC of an 'obsessive and, therefore, possibly misleading view' of South Africa. ... 'Is their approach motivated merely by an institutional megasulk, part of it a vindictive crusade against any policy advocated by the Prime Minister [?]'. - *Guardian*, 1 July 1986
mega-terror The promises of mutually-assured destruction are but exercises in mutual mega-terror. - *Economist*, 9 Aug. 1986
mega-trendy Once again, however, men - and not only the mega-trendy - are once again decked out in floral prints from top to toe. - *Guardian*, 11 July 1986
mega-worry Today's 'mega-worries' for Americans revolve around the environment and nuclear war, the Pennsylvania team has found. - *Daily Telegraph*, 21 July 1986

---

megaflops *noun* a million FLOPS

---

meltdown *noun* **1** the melting of the core of a nuclear reactor **2** an economic collapse (eg of a currency, industry, or market)

When the Russians smothered the fire in the Chernobyl reactor ... they in effect ... opened the door upon a nightmare ... called meltdown. - *Guardian*, 9 May 1986

The prospect of a speculative 'meltdown' of the dollar against the yen confronts the authorities. - *The Times*, 7 July 1986

Industrial meltdown: a bankruptcy petition may protect LTV's giant Cleveland Works. - *Time*, 28 July 1986

► In its literal sense (1), the term has been used since the mid-1980s but was particularly conspicuous in 1986. The extended sense (2) is novel.

---

melt-through *noun* MELTDOWN 1

Soviet authorities apparently fear that the white-hot core of the Chernobyl reactor could melt through its concrete floor in what is known as the China Syndrome, threatening radioactive contamination of ground water supplies. ... Speculation that a total melt-through was imminent yesterday sent grain prices soaring on the Chicago Board of Trade. - *Guardian*, 9 May 1986

---

menu-driven *adjective, of a computer, piece of software, etc* having or using a number of menus to guide a user through the system

In common with Prestel, CompuServe users navigate round the system by the use of menus, hence the system is termed 'menu-driven,' although, like Prestel, users can access a page, or screen of data directly, using the CIS command 'GOTO.' - *Guardian*, 23 Jan. 1986

► The analogy of a menu is based on the user's choice, just as a diner has choice on a restaurant menu. Originally it was devised to avoid the prodigious feats of memory which early users were being forced to achieve.

---

mergermania *noun* a wave of enthusiasm for business mergers

Mergermania is spreading to the publishing industry's publicists. The latest joining of forces is between Judy Dobias's Camron Public Relations and Penny Phipps. - *Publishing News*, 15 Aug. 1986

---

metapower *noun* control or influence existing outside, and usually in opposition to, the established structure of groups holding power

Far from obscuring our understanding, I feel that a concept such as metapower serves to add clarity and precision to the analysis. ... The term is included to distinguish between the 'power' of those who win one or several rounds of a game using certain given rules and those who can alter the outcome by altering such rules. - *New Internationalist*, July 1986

► The combination of *meta* (Greek = among, with, after, change) + *power* has been used extensively by Jorge Nef of the University of Guelph, Ontario, and other political scientists. It is employed to describe the indirect influence of such functions as terrorism or multi-nationals on the conventional national governmental power structure. This type of concept has lately become more important for the same reasons as STATE TERRORISM.

---

methanol-to-gasoline process *noun* (*abbreviation* **MTG process**) a chemical process for converting methanol to gasoline using the catalyst zeolite (a compound of silicon and oxygen containing a small percentage of aluminium)

> South Africa has no crude oil but it does possess large amounts of coal which it could convert to methanol. The process, developed by AECI, begins with a vapour of this methanol mixed with water. ... Varying the parameters, such as the ratio of water to methanol, temperature or pressure, changes the ratio of its products. The cycle is thus very flexible. New Zealand's methanol-to-gasoline process, known as MTG, is less flexible. – *New Scientist*, 3 July 1986

Mexican mud *noun, US slang* BLACK TAR

Mexican Wave *or* **Mexico Wave** *noun* a spectacular wavelike motion among a crowd of people (eg spectators at a sports match), produced by sections of the crowd standing up from their seats in sequence

> It has become the sporting highlight of the summer ... and very soon it could be the thing that brings the fun back to football. It's the Mexico Wave, that wonderful movement when sports fans take over the action from the figures on the field. – *Daily Express*, 5 Aug. 1986

> There was the uncertainty among us media people [at the royal wedding] about whether to stand when the congregation did. Half of us would rise, a third sit confusedly down again, then a fifth struggle to their feet. The Queen must have thought we were trying out a Mexico Wave. – *Sunday Times Magazine*, 27 July 1986

► This act of audience participation, which calls for full terraces of seating for maximum impact, was brought to British attention by TV coverage of the football World Cup finals in Mexico in June 1986. Eagerly adopting it, the crowd at the second test match apparently wrecked the concentration of an Indian batsman, who was out immediately after the wave. (This seems to be part of the current trend for cricket crowds to make themselves felt by visible or noisy expressions of comment.) Audiences at pop concerts have taken up the wave. It was also much in evidence at the Commonwealth Games at Edinburgh in July 1986. On the wet and windy final day it was achieved colourfully with umbrellas. Theatrically and carefully choreographed movement actually on the turf of the stadium is not new, going back to the opening and closing ceremonies of the Moscow Olympic Games of 1980 and probably much earlier.

---

microburst *noun* extreme turbulence consisting of a downward rush of cold air travelling at speeds of over 180 kilometres per hour (100 miles per hour) followed by a sudden shift in its velocity as it nears ground level

> One form of shear was the 'micro-burst' – a jet of air propelled rapidly downwards from a high convective cloud

system. An aircraft taking off or landing could meet head wind, down draught, and tail wind, all within a minute. - *Guardian*, 6 Sept. 1986

► Aeronautics experts have been paying increased attention to the sudden changes in the wind's direction which are known as wind shears. These are blamed for at least 29 accidents involving jet aircraft since 1955.
A microburst is the most extreme form of wind shear, and is reputedly the weather hazard that pilots dread most. The danger received considerable publicity after the crash of a jumbo jet at Dallas - Fort Worth airport in August 1985.

---

micro-floppy *noun* a floppy disk between 75 and 100 millimetres (about 3 and 4 inches) in diameter used for storing programs

► These were originally a response to the demand for physically small discs to go into small boxes. However, they have now achieved particular importance in the context of DESKTOP and LAP-TOP equipment.

---

microgravity *noun* almost zero gravity (eg as experienced by an astronaut in an orbiting spacecraft)

> The reason why microgravity makes it possible to obtain materials of high purity rests on the better mixing of liquids that occurs in containers in space. The advantages of microgravity research present a strong argument for the European Space Agency to develop a free-flying laboratory that would be used in conjunction with the international space station as a base to work from, with new and completed experiments carried between the ground and the station by a manned vehicle. - *The Times*, 2 July 1986

---

midi-bus *noun* a single-decker passenger vehicle, larger than a minibus but smaller than a conventional bus or coach, designed for use on urban routes and typically holding 25-30 passengers

> London Transport is to order hundreds of traffic-beating 'midi-buses'. ... There will be two initial midi-routes in central London - one a new service from Parliament Square to Kensington. - *Daily Telegraph*, 26 June 1986

► A number of services using this interesting compromise vehicle operate, notably in Cheltenham, Exeter, Norwich, Oxford, and Worcester. Bus travel has become extremely unpopular, largely, but not exclusively, as the result of increased car ownership and the greater independence which that brings.
Less than one journey in twelve is now made by bus. In 1953, 42% of passenger traffic went by bus. By 1983 it was down to 8%.

---

midi-route *noun* a route plied by a MIDI-BUS

---

mini-satellite *noun* a stretch of DNA that is repeated in certain regions of a gene, the number of repetitions, when measured for several of these regions for any one individual, forming a unique pattern for that individual

> Dr Alec Jeffreys and his colleagues at the University of Leicester have now found a way to seek out the few parts of the genetic code that vary greatly among individuals. They found that many such 'hypervariable' regions are similar, consisting of stretches of DNA repeated several times. The repeated stretch, known as a mini-satellite, has almost the same sequence wherever it occurs, but the number of repeats is extremely variable. - *Economist*, 4 Jan. 1986

MIPS *noun* million instructions per second: an indication of the power of a computer's central processor

> The computer industry and its analysts agree that demand for mips ... is growing in such installations by an average of 50 per cent a year and in some instances by 100 per cent. - *Financial Times*, 6 May 1986

---

mix nick *noun, informal* a prison where both men and women are held

> Abolish women's prisons and replace them with 'mix nicks'. ... That's the revolutionary message of a recent report [by the Howard League] on women in the penal system. - *Cosmopolitan*, May 1986

► Jocular rhyming term joining *mix*(ed) and *nick* (the slang word for *prison*).
The Howard League for Penal Reform has produced innumerable reports on both policy and minutiae of prison accommodation and routines. One of their reports in 1986 was by a committee chaired by the Lady Seear. It recommended mixed prisons as having many significant social advantages.

---

mobile communications *noun* communication systems, eg CELLPHONES and radiopaging systems, that can be used in different places or while moving, as in a vehicle

> It is only 18 months since cellular radio made mobile communications fashionable in Britain, yet its successor for the 1990s is already on the drawing board. The key advantage of the new system is that it will cover the whole of Europe, including Scandinavia. - *Financial Times*, 6 May 1986

---

monergy *noun* energy equated with money - used as the slogan of a British government campaign to persuade consumers to economize power resources

> Saatchi and Saatchi scratched their twin heads and came up with a buzzword: Monergy. It meant that we would all save money, save energy and save nuclear power by demonstrating that there was no need to spend on building new sources like

> wave-power generators and wind turbines. - *Private Eye*, 19 Sept. 1986

► Blend of *mon*ey + en*ergy*, to identify energy with the pound in the consumer's pocket.
1986 was designated Energy Efficiency Year. The energy economy campaign pursuant to this was aimed at both private consumers and industry.
An Energy Saver Show aimed at the domestic market visited over 200 locations. Regional energy officers have provided help to companies. The whole effort is coordinated by the Energy Efficiency Office. Friendly counsel is given in cheerful leaflets. One item which has surprised many users is advice not to switch off too frequently.
The whole enterprise follows the general trend towards energy economy which has characterized the whole decade, now that a certain end to fossil fuel resources has been detected.

---

motherboard *noun* a printed circuit board that is plugged into the back of a computer and into which can be slotted other boards (daughter boards) so that the computer can operate various peripherals (eg a disk drive or tape recorder for increased program storage)

> By adopting a 'Back-plane' databus with a number of slots for plug-in cards instead of the usual motherboard, AM Stearn has made it possible to upgrade the machine to any future standard in micro technology keeping the existing monitor, hard disk, tape streamer and the like to run under the new system. - *Personal Computer World*, Feb. 1986

---

mountain bicycle *noun* a wide-tyred heavy-duty bicycle, designed to cope with rugged terrain

► The machines were first produced several years ago in the course of exuberant play by American youth. Conventional bicycles were used over sand dunes and rough terrain, so that wide tyres were added. It was then found that the original frames were not strong enough for such rugged activities. So the species of mountain bicycle evolved gradually.
Their use is now a formal sport and they are also used for touring, and even for commuting. Terminology has become more elaborate. *Stumpjumpers*, which can refer both to the particular type of bicycle and their user, surmount large logs. There are also *breezers*, *trailblazers*, and *ridgerunners*.
The pursuit has even spawned literature. The definitive work is probably Rob Van Der Plas' *The Mountain Bike Book* (New York, 1984).

---

mouse *noun* a small box, connected to a computer, which causes a corresponding movement of a cursor on a VDU when it is moved across a table or desk, and bears buttons enabling the user to execute commands

> The most beneficial spin-off from the current interest in personal computers that use a mouse ... is that it allows specialized units for severely disabled people who cannot use

> computer keyboards to be developed much more easily.
> - *The Times*, 12 Aug. 1986

► This nickname is not new to computer specialists but has now come into general layman's usage, particularly as a result of the introduction of PULL-DOWN menus
The zoological name comes from their (approximate) similarity to the rodent, although a likeness to chocolate mice is more apparent.

---

mousse *noun* a cosmetic preparation in light frothy form; *especially* a foamy substance applied to the hair to hold it in the desired style

> Mousse is the magic ingredient of 1986. ... The humble foam formulation can now adorn the body from top to toe.
> - *Observer*, 15 June 1986

> With Alberto's VO5 Alive colour styling mousse you can send spring colours straight to your head - a colour styling mousse which tones your hair as brightly as you wish until the next shampoo. - *Company*, April 1986

> Hot on the heels of mousses for hair and moisturising mousses for the body comes Elizabeth Arden's Simply Perfect Mousse Makeup - *Options*, May 1986

► After lurking in the cosmetic sidelines for some time, mousses are suddenly fashionable. They are generally applied after washing and their principal purpose is to give the hair body.
Although the substance is white, it can be used to impart colour to the hair and a rainbow of choices is available; such as chestnut, plum, mahogany, blonde, silver, and pearl grey.
The products may be used by men and women. They are the work of a wide range of manufacturers, such as Klynol, Tressemme, and Wella.
Mousse is very different in substance and use from *gel*, which stiffens the hair and gives it the appearance of having treacle poured over it.
The term mousse is drawn from its similarity to the food of that name. The same expression is used in an environmental context to describe the mixture of oil and sand which results from an offshore oil spillage.

---

movement conservative *noun, US* someone who is right wing through deep philosophical commitment

> The brand label preferred by many of the men and women of the new right is 'movement conservatives'. This is an awkward mouthful that others decline to adopt. - *Economist*, 4 Jan. 1986

> Though both of them are 'movement conservatives' ... they disagree on many issues. - *Observer*, 11 May 1986

MOW-ist *noun* a member of the Movement for the Ordination of Women

> Later ... she [Dr Margaret Hewitt, national organiser of Women Against Women's Ordination] mused: 'Is there no way of stopping this? It's gone on for so long. Perhaps synod

> should ask itself whether this elaborate copy of parliament is relevant.' She meant, with more kindliness than malice, putting the MOW-ists out of their misery once and for all. - *Guardian*, 7 July 1986

► The seemingly perpetual debate about the ordination of women in the Church of England has generated a great deal of acrimony and has caused many people to leave the Anglican communion, in particular High Church priests alarmed by what they see as the impending approach of female clergy. Several prominent ones have joined the Roman Catholic Church. At the moment, although women priests are readily accepted in the Anglican communion in other parts of the world (particularly the Old Commonwealth), the General Synod blocks further innovations in the Provinces of Canterbury or York. At the summer 1986 meeting of Synod the issue was avoided by being postponed.
The strongest objections come from the Anglo-Catholic wing of the Church. They base these on theological arguments about the maleness of Christ, coupled with various principles regarding the Blessed Virgin Mary and the more pragmatic obstacle that introduction of women priests would preclude union with Rome. They have given rise to the formation of the Movement Against the Ordination of Women, readily known by its approximate but obvious acronym of MIAOW.

MTG process *noun* METHANOL-TO-GASOLINE PROCESS

---

muesli belt malnutrition *noun* a condition of undernourishment in children, caused by following a supposedly healthy diet (eg one very low in fat and sugar) which is in fact only suitable for adults

> Children of food faddists are in danger of suffering from 'muesli belt malnutrition' which can lead to stunted growth and weight loss, Prof Vincent Marks, professor of biochemistry at Surrey University, said yesterday. - *Daily Telegraph*, 2 June 1986

► Previously there had been virtually universal unquestioning confidence in the medical benefits of the various severe diets favoured by social groups such as yuppies.
Prof. Marks' startling allegation caused widespread shock around Parsons Green and Putney and, for a time at least, upset the BRANWAGON.

---

muesli left *noun, humorous or derogatory* those (usually middle class) socialists who are seen as rather trendy and particularly interested in issues such as ecology and healthy eating

> You report ... Kim Howells' attack on the 'awful smugness' of the 'Muesli left', coupled with his plea to lay off John Cunningham. - *New Statesman*, 25 April 1986

---

multiplexed harness *noun* a motor vehicle's wiring harness (prefabricated wiring system with insulation and terminals ready to be attached) which, instead of having separate switches and power cables for each electrical load, has just one time-shared power cable and a few electronic signal cables shared by all loads, thereby reducing the length of wiring, saving space, and allowing innovations in interior design and development of further electronic equipment - called also MULTIPLEXED LOOM

> All over the world motor manufacturers are about to change radically the manner in which they wire vehicles. Out will go conventional wiring looms with their separate switches and power cables for every electrical load. They will be replaced with multiplexed harnesses with just one power and a few signal cables shared by all the loads. ... The biggest advantages, however, will be cost savings to the manufacturer and an easier life for the service mechanic. In fact the gains are said to be so big, that multiplexed looms are tipped to become a world-wide industry with a turnover of billions of pounds by the end of the century. - *New Scientist*, 13 June 1985

---

multiplexed loom *noun* MULTIPLEXED HARNESS

---

multiprocessor *or* **multiprocessing system** *noun* a computer system having a number of separate microprocessors cooperating with each other to process information rapidly

---

multi-task *verb, of a computer* (*system*) to execute a number of tasks simultaneously

► The tasks are only seemingly simultaneous, since no two tasks are ever actually performed precisely simultaneously in a computer.

---

multi-tasking *noun* the execution of a number of tasks simultaneously by a computer

> Multi-tasking is simply the ability to do more than one task, so practically all computers are multi-tasking in that they can be easily programmed to do several things. - *Personal Computer World*, Feb. 1986

---

multi-user *adjective, of a computer* (*system*) able to serve a number of users simultaneously

> Aimed at both single and multi-user environments, the enhanced product allows multiple users to access the same data files without data corruption. - *Personal Computer World*, Feb. 1986

> Unlike the PC/AT, the Great Communicator makes no attempt to be a multi-user machine. - *Personal Computer World*, Feb. 1986

In future, Apricot will concentrate on IBM-compatible multi-user systems (computers capable of being used by several people at once). – *New Scientist*, 26 June 1986

nacho *noun* a corn tortilla chip topped with cheese and chilli

namby not in anyone's back yard – compare NIMBY

NAPS *noun* Nerve Agent Pre-Treatment Tablet Set: a packet of pills designed to allow soldiers to survive exposure to nerve gas which would normally prove lethal

> Packets of the new pills, known as NAPS ... are now being stockpiled by the British Army in Germany. – *Daily Telegraph*, 11 June 1986

nastify *verb* to become more unpleasant

> Attendances [at football] declined and nastified almost everywhere, except in 1982's winning country (Italy) and 1982's host (Spain). – *Economist*, 28 June 1986

► This is probably a back-formation from *denastify*, a vogue word of 1984-5 which was presumably a blend of *nasty* and *denazify*. Referring to football hooliganism, the *Economist*, 8 June 1985, spoke of 'the wider denastification of British society'.

Natal option *noun* a proposed merger of the South African province of Natal with the homeland of KwaZulu, to form a semi-autonomous region with a multiracial legislature

> President Botha seems for now to be at the limit of the reforms he is prepared to make. Some opposition whites ... are therefore looking at an idea known as the 'Natal option' as a possible way out of the impasse. – *Economist*, 12 April 1986

nature-friendly *adjective* see -FRIENDLY

[1]necklace *noun* a tyre placed round the neck of a victim and set alight, used in black townships in South Africa as a means of lynching suspected government collaborators

> The charred bodies of four more black 'necklace' victims ... were found elsewhere. – *Daily Telegraph*, 27 March 1986

> Mrs Mandela was reported to have said: 'With our matches and our necklaces we will liberate this country'. - *Glasgow Herald*, 24 May 1986

► This unsavoury form of penalty attracted public attention during the early months of the year, when violence in the black South African townships increased both in its extent and its ferocity.
The rubber tyres are usually filled with petrol for ease of ignition. Victims are known as *Kentuckies* after Kentucky Fried Chicken.
People's Courts have been established since early 1986 to effect the punishment.
Administration of the discipline is comparable to IRA kneecapping (in its ultimate form kneecapping-in-the-head).

---

[2]**necklace** *verb* to kill by means of a NECKLACE

> Their first statement on the discovery of 32 charred bodies suggested that the victims had been 'necklaced'. - *Guardian*, 16 April 1986

---

neighbourhood watch *noun* a scheme by which residents in a district form a voluntary association, in cooperation with the police, intended to prevent crime by keeping an eye on each other's property, reporting suspicious activities to the police, etc - called also HOME WATCH

> Some brokers have recently gained support from Lloyd's underwriters for policies giving a 10 per cent. discount to householders who join neighbourhood watch schemes. - *Daily Telegraph*, 13 Jan. 1986

> Terraced houses are ideal because the residents can easily keep an eye on their surroundings. Neighbourhood watch schemes which consist of a block of flats and a bit of street would have been impossible to evaluate. - *Illustrated London News*, Sept. 1986

► By July 1986 there were 14,500 such schemes in England and Wales. In July 1985 there had been about a third of that number.
An example of its success is an estate in Chatham, where the scheme was supported by 90% of the 1,250 houses. The level of crime was halved during the first nine months of operation.
Some people have, however, expressed anxiety that it might prove too much of a boon to vigilantes or nosy parkers. In a recent incident in Hertfordshire, an innocent window-cleaner was arrested after a householder precipitately phoned the police on seeing an unknown man scaling a ladder.

---

[1]**nematic** *adjective* of or being the phase of a liquid crystal characterized by having the molecules orientated in parallel lines rather than in layers

> Scientists have known since the 1930s that a suspension of tobacco mosaic virus (TMV) in water can behave like the

> simplest of liquid crystals, the 'nematics'. In nematic liquid crystals the rod-like molecules align in one direction, rather like matches in a box, but show no further periodic behaviour. In water, TMV particles behave in the same way, provided the concentration lies within a fairly narrow range of values. – *New Scientist*, 24 April 1986

---

²nematic *noun* a NEMATIC substance

---

neo-apartheid *noun* the modified system of apartheid introduced in the Republic of South Africa under the presidency of P.W. Botha, including reforms such as the ending of segregation in public places and the abolition of the prohibition of mixed marriages

> Both the HNP and the Conservatives claim the legacy of Hendrik Verwoerd, the father of 'classical' apartheid. Both think that President Botha's 'neo-apartheid' is an inevitable step to black majority rule. – *Economist*, 31 May 1986

---

neurophilosophy *noun* the study of mental processes in terms both of the neuroscience of the brain and of the philosophy of the mind

► This is the title of a book by Dr Patricia Smith Churchland, published in 1986, which attempts to draw neuroscience and philosophy together in 'a unified science of the mind-brain'.

---

new-collar *adjective, US* of or being a class of upwardly mobile people of working-class origin employed in skilled and mainly non-manual jobs

> Reagan ... has secured the loyalties of the burgeoning working-class suburbanites who fall between traditional blue and white collar workers. Called 'New Collar' by pollsters, they ought to be Democrats. – *Daily Telegraph*, 6 Sept. 1986

New Georgian *noun* someone who lives in a renovated Georgian house, in a manner as close to the Georgian lifestyle as possible

> The New Georgians are offshoots of those earlier up-market urban tribes, Sloanes and Young Fogeys. But never before has the saving of a slice of architecture gone so far as to re-invoke a whole anachronistic way of existing. There are people living by candlelight and cooking by wood-fuelled stoves in elegant houses which have been dragged back into the 18th century. – *Guardian*, 10 April 1986

---

newspaper-friendly *adjective* see -FRIENDLY

---

new-tech *adjective or noun* (of, using, or produced by) new technology

> Another new-tech daily is on the move today, though there's no good news in the fact for Britain. *USA Today* is to start

European printing on May 6 – in Switzerland. – *Guardian*, 13 Jan. 1986

Newzak *noun* filmed news coverage whose original impact and significance are dulled by repetition, so that the images become merely evocative or decorative

> The first television showing of the end of Challenger was news of great importance. The second time we saw it, we were given the opportunity ... to reflect on the bravery of the astronauts. ... But from then on, with each subsequent showing of the fireball that became a shroud, news gradually degenerated into Newzak. ... Newzak is to news what Muzak is to music. – *Listener*, 6 Feb. 1986

► The analogy here is with *Muzak*, the meaningless background music which is played in supermarkets and middle-priced hotels. The mind seldom reacts to it either favourably or unfavourably, and the listener becomes accustomed to it in a much shorter time.
The incident which gave rise to the expression was the loss of the American spaceship *Challenger* with its crew of seven astronauts. The disaster was seen by a large crowd and a vast TV audience worldwide. The event was given greater poignancy by the inclusion in the crew of a schoolmistress who was to have taught her class from space. However, after the accident, television audiences became bored by the excessive repetition and at every showing the impact was diminished. As Colin Morris, Head of BBC Religious Broadcasting, said, the disaster was turned into no more than 'a puff of pretty white smoke'.
Other continuing sagas have likewise lost their media impact, even if the situations themselves have not diminished in gravity. The sorrows of Ulster and of South Africa are examples of subject-matter which has suffered in this way.

---

night terror *noun* a nightmare-like dream from which the dreamer awakes but the fear and anxiety of which continue causing a marked reaction which later cannot be recalled. In adults this reaction may include occasions of physical violence.

> A husband who strangled his wife in his sleep while in the grip of a harrowing nightmare walked free from the Old Bailey in London yesterday after being cleared of murder. Colin Kemp ... wept after he heard that the jury had accepted his rare defence of 'night terror' against charges of unlawfully killing his wife Ellen. – *Scotsman*, 3 May 1986

---

nimby not in my back yard: a slogan used to express the sentiments of those who support the concept of a certain issue (e g nuclear power) in principle but do not want anything to do with it near their home

> I would like to take issue on only one point with your leader ... on the disposal of nuclear waste. That is to suggest that

> that Nimby ... is rapidly being superseded by Namby. ... Over the last decade or more the nuclear enthusiasts have, I believe, consistently underestimated public concern about this technology. – *Guardian*, 27 Aug. 1986

► Public protest has increased in recent years over such issues as energy generation and other hazardous forms of industry. As this pattern of reaction has developed, there has also evolved a somewhat less logical and consistent line of thinking. Its protagonists accept the need for, say, the defence of the kingdom by nuclear weapons but do not want the inconvenience or perceived danger of the relevant equipment near their homes.
The Nimby syndrome, as it is sometimes described, has been applied to military installations, nuclear power stations, landfill rubbish disposal, and even wild life parks.
In its more plausible form, it has been addressed to the plan to open four sites for subterranean disposal of nuclear wastes.

---

ninjutsu *noun* a martial art based on the killing techniques of the Ninjas, members of an ancient society of Japanese assassins

> Ninjutsu ... has replaced the Kung Fu cult started by the Bruce Lee films in the 1970s as the latest craze among young martial arts enthusiasts. – *Daily Telegraph*, 28 June 1986

---

no-fault compensation *noun* a state-funded compensation scheme for people injured or disabled by medical treatment, that awards damages according to a fixed scale, does not involve litigation, and does not require proof of negligence or malpractice by a doctor

> The British Medical Association is seeking a meeting with the Law Society to discuss the implications of introducing a 'no fault' compensation scheme for victims of medical accidents. – *Guardian*, 30 July 1986

> The Medical Defence Union's secretary, Dr John Brooke-Barnett, said that in New Zealand no-fault compensation cases are automatically reviewed by the General Medical Council, the doctors' disciplinary body. – *Daily Telegraph*, 19 Aug. 1986

---

northern soul *noun* mainstream soul music from the 1960s, popularized again in the early 1980s by disc jockeys in the north of England

> Assorted Joboxers control the northern soul, jazz and funk sounds. – *City Limits*, 14 Aug. 1986

► The original impetus for the reawakening of interest in soul music came from the Wigan Casino, a disco in Wigan which played 60s' hits from Motown stars such as Smokey Robinson, the Supremes, and Marvin Gaye. The Casino has since closed, but interest in the music has spread and is now a feature of many clubs and discos throughout the country.

North-South *adjective* concerning the relationship between the affluent industrialized nations of the Northern Hemisphere and the underdeveloped nations of the Southern Hemisphere

> Books on development issues appear to account for a significant portion of the current output of geography texts. The growing interest in and awareness of the 'North-South' problem has rightly become a key topic on the syllabus. - *TES*, 21 June 1985

> The EEC negotiating team in Geneva last week were displaying as much concern for the North-South dialogue as for their own citizens' interests. - *Daily Telegraph*, 21 July 1986

► The term derives from the North-South report produced by the Brandt Commission. This international body of 20 members under the chairmanship of Willy Brandt (West German chancellor 1969-74 and Nobel Peace Prize winner 1971) worked from 1977 investigating the disparity of prosperity between the affluent European, North American, and Australasian nations and those more impoverished. They reported in 1980 with *North-South: A Programme for Revival* and recommended a programme of priorities. In his introduction Brandt wrote about the report: 'It discusses North-South relations as the great social challenge of our time.'
The phrase has now settled in the language as a general description of such global inequities.

Norwalk virus *noun* a virus that causes gastroenteritis in humans

> A study of 103 outbreaks of gastro-enteritis associated with contaminated oysters and clams affecting 1,017 people in New York State over eight months ... [found that] the infecting organism most frequently implicated in these cases was the Norwalk virus. - *The Times*, 19 March 1986

> The Canberra returned to Southampton yesterday ... with P-and-O confident that the virus which caused sickness and diarrhoea among 170 of its passengers had been identified and dealt with. Dr David Harper ... said yesterday that he was almost certain the bug was the virus 'Norwalk', named after a town in Ohio, which can be transmitted through water, food or from person to person. - *Daily Telegraph*, 23 July 1986

---

notting *noun, informal* the practice of not doing something, especially something which one knows ought to be done

> 'Notting' is the word coined by our advisor Dr Tony Lake. ... You know how it is, you really ought to make that difficult phone call, but suddenly ... cleaning the kitchen floor becomes the most pressing and attractive proposition you can think of. - *New Health*, June 1986

► The adverb *not* has enjoyed an astonishingly adventurous career since about 1980.

The trend was started by the very successful BBC TV programme *Not the Nine O'Clock News*, an outrageous satire in the *That Was The Week That Was* (circa 1964) tradition. Starring Rowan Atkinson, Mel Smith, Griff Rhys-Jones, and Pamela Stephenson, it was compulsive viewing for many from 1979 to 1982.
Imitations of the expression included *Not the Royal Wedding* (on the Prince of Wales' marriage in 1981) and *Not the Age of the Train*, a comment on one of British Rail's hapless advertising campaigns.
In a rather more serious use, Julian Barnes has referred to (*Flaubert's Parrot*) his *not-books*, which he might have written but has not written.

---

nuclearphobia *noun* fear of nuclear technology

> As one of West Germany's easternmost states, Lower Saxony was particularly affected by post-Chernobyl nuclearphobia. – *Economist*, 7 June 1986

---

nuclear port *noun* a port through which shipments of radioactive material are frequently transported

> The Dounreay public inquiry will today be told of deep concern at the possibility that Invergordon on Scotland's northeast coast, could become a nuclear port. – *Guardian*, 23 June 1986

---

nukemare *noun* the nightmare of a disaster caused by nuclear materials

> Would you survive a nukemare? The shock waves of the Russian nuclear disaster are being felt all over the world. Everywhere frightened people are asking: Could the nuclear nightmare become a reality for Britain? – *News of the World*, 4 May 1986

---

number-fudging *noun* manipulation or selective presentation of statistical data to give a desired result

> Official calculations of public radiation exposures – including those of 'critical groups' – have always been based on the 'mean' value. ... However, connoisseurs of the Government's number-fudging activities may have noticed that in the last couple of years official and industrial publications have ceased to include the range of individual sets of monitoring data. We never had the full figures: now we only get the derived 'mean'. – *Guardian*, 1 March 1986

NUTS *noun* nuclear utilization targeting strategy: the strategy of actually fighting a nuclear war based on the assumption that new sophisticated nuclear weapons systems will be targeted on military installations rather than cities, so that the concept of mutually assured destruction (MAD) is no longer a deterrent

> The USA is changing its nuclear policy from nuclear

deterrence based on mutually assured destruction (MAD) to nuclear warfighting - a policy called nuclear utilization targeting strategy (NUTS). - *Guardian*, 22 Aug. 1986

---

n-way design *noun* MULTIPROCESSOR

> The story IBM is signalling to this market now is that it will provide these mips through systems in which a number of processors are coupled together (multiprocessing or 'n-way design'). - *Financial Times*, 6 May 1986

---

octopush *noun* a game played underwater between two teams of six players each, equipped with masks, fins, and snorkels, who attempt to propel a leaden puck into a goal with the aid of a small spatulate wooden or plastic implement

► Several novel minority sports have emerged in recent years. In 1985 Birmingham hosted a so-called World Games which excluded all well-known sports and devoted itself to such relatively esoteric pursuits as roller hockey, petanque, and fin swimming.
Octopush, sometimes known as 'underwater hockey', sounds the most bizarre of all. But despite its jokey name it is played seriously, and on an organized basis, in several countries. The European octopush championships were held in London in 1985, when Britain won both the men's and women's events.

ODC *noun, Irish* Ordinary Decent Criminal: a criminal whose acts have no alleged political motivation

> The ultimate failure of the Guinness abduction may discourage further attempts of the kind by what the Irish call ODCs. ... The Irish Republican Army and its dark offshoots may not be so easily put off. - *Economist*, 19 April 1986

---

odour fingerprint *noun* PONGPRINT

> Before we can think of taking such an odour 'fingerprint', we need to eliminate extraneous odours from toiletries and air pollution. Unless we can overcome this problem ... generous applications of aftershave or perfume might in future deflect the arm of the law. - *New Scientist*, 10 July 1986

---

oenin *noun* a flavour substance present in red wine that is held to be responsible for the quality, as distinct from the regional characteristics, of that wine

> A 36-year-old biochemist and part-time wine-maker in California claims to have isolated and chemically identified the single most important flavour substance in red wine. The ingredient was discovered just over a decade ago, but it has since been a much-debated chemical mystery, lacking even a name. Dr Leo McCloskey, whose PhD is in plant biochemistry gives it the Greek-derived name 'oenin'.
> – *Guardian*, 11 April 1986

---

off-the-wall *adjective, chiefly US informal* absurdly or amusingly eccentric or irrational; crazy

> Some DEC OEMs have said goodbye to the days of blowing a software demonstration for a client because the client's off-the-wall hardware configuration won't support the software.
> – *Hardcopy*, April 1986

> Even more baffling are publicity and 'Radio Times' references to 'off-the-wall humour' (does that mean scraped off?).
> – *Daily Telegraph*, 28 May 1986

► The precise meaning of the phrase is not significant. It follows a tradition of wide-ranging and imaginative concoctions on similar lines; *off-the-rails, off his/her rocker, off his/her trolley, out to lunch.* Shortly after his appointment as Labour Party leader, Neil Kinnock caused widespread semantic speculation when he described a leading statesman as *out of his pram.*

---

oickspeak *noun* see -SPEAK

Oort cloud *noun* a vast cloud of small bodies that orbits the sun at a distance of between 20 000 and 1 000 000 astronomical units (about 3.0×10^{12} and 1.5×10^{14} kilometres) and from which comets are pulled by the gravitational forces of passing stars, into our solar system

► There are about 1,000 million of these comets (if such a general estimate means anything at all). Their general habitat is well beyond Pluto's orbit but now and again some creep into our solar system. The name relates to the Dutch astro-physicist, Dr Jan Hendrik Oort (born 1900), who proposed the cloud's existence in 1950.

---

open station *noun* a railway station where access to and from the platforms is free and uncontrolled

► At such stations there are no barrier staff to check or collect passengers' tickets. These operations are carried out on the trains.
Open stations have ticket-issuing facilities, however, and all passengers are supposed to be in possession of a ticket before boarding the train. Open stations should not be confused with *unstaffed* or *unmanned stations,* which do not have any staff at all.

The open station system was pioneered in the north of Scotland in November 1981, but has now become common in most parts of the British Rail network.

---

open systems interconnection *noun* (*abbreviation* **OSI**) a set of internationally agreed standards intended to enable communication between computers regardless of manufacturer, size, etc

> Open Systems Interconnection (OSI) will be discussed at a four-day conference at the Tara Hotel in London ... organised by Online International. Unusually, the first day is a pre-conference tutorial in which the much mentioned but little understood seven layer reference model of the International Standards Organisation and associated matters will be explained. - *Financial Times*, 24 Feb. 1986

---

optoelectronic *adjective* of, concerning, or using OPTOELECTRONICS

---

optoelectronics *noun* a branch of electronics dealing with the study and application of the interaction and interconversion of light and electronic signals

> The Japanese know-how that would most interest American star-warriors is thought to be in the field of optoelectronics ... especially optoelectronic chips for supercomputers.
> - *Economist*, 15 March 1986

---

orbital manoeuvring vehicle *noun* any of various remotely controlled propulsion vehicles that, having been carried into space (eg aboard the Shuttle), are able to carry payloads into higher orbits, correct the position of capsules and laboratories, retrieve damaged satellites for repair, ferry materials and personnel between space stations, etc

> NASA has plans for a fleet of 'space tugs'. The tugs, officially called orbital manoeuvering [sic] vehicles, will carry out a wide range of chores in space, including cleaning up space debris and pushing satellites from one orbit to another.
> - *New Scientist*, 10 July 1986

---

organogram *noun* a diagram or chart of the structure of an organization, showing the hierarchy and relationships of departments and individual jobs within it; an organization chart

> Decision makers ... sit at meetings ... calling together experts, division heads or other leaders of units in their organisation - the people at the top of those interesting 'organogram' flow charts of who's who. - *Guardian*, 20 Aug. 1986

► Derived from *organ*isation + *-gram*, from Greek *gramma* = something written.
It is no more and no less than an organization chart. It is arranged exactly like a genealogical table, although indirect reporting relationships are sometimes shown by a dotted line.

There is nothing particularly significant or timely about the fashion for this pompous and pretentious term, although in times of staff cutbacks organizations are scrutinized more minutely. Thus organograms are examined more frequently, and sometimes they are drawn up where none existed before.

OSI *noun* OPEN SYSTEMS INTERCONNECTION

> The common belief is that ... any two machines conforming to the OSI standards should be able to communicate with each other. Smaller companies at last will be able to compete againt Big Blue. Business consumers will be able to purchase in an open market without being welded to one manufacturer. Company takeovers will have an easier time of it since different computers will be able to talk. – *Which Computer*, July 1986

---

outgoer *noun* a farmer who accepts financial inducements (eg a SET-ASIDE scheme) to abandon traditional agriculture and to find an alternative, and more profitable, use for his/her land (eg forestry, caravan sites, or HORSECULTURE)

> They fear that an enforced cut in quotas – resulting in disaster for numerous hard-pressed farmers already struggling to stay in business – will be imposed because the outgoers compensation of 18p a litre falls well short of providing a viable incentive for producers to leave the dairy industry. – *Cardigan & Tivy-Side Advertiser*, 29 Aug. 1986

> Battle lines are being drawn between landlords and tenants on the right to take part in the forthcoming EEC outgoers' scheme. – *Farmers Weekly*, 29 Nov. 1985

► Encouragement of innovative thinking has worked in parallel with political pressure to develop new uses of agricultural land. The term developed by the Ministry of Agriculture and the Agriculture Training Board indicates the importance of this, particularly in view of EEC surpluses.
A competition sponsored by the National Farmers Union and the National Westminster Bank produced some intriguing proposals: harvesting coppice willow for basketmaking, growing blueberries, growing herbs in heated polythene tunnels, and devising new cheeses from sheep's milk.
Various sources of advice have been set up to respond to the challenge, such as Branch Out (farm, woodlands, and conservation advisers) in east central Scotland.
The concept is not limited to the United Kingdom. There have been many public statements following this line of thinking from prominent agricultural administrators thoughout the EEC. For example Frans Andriessen, EEC Farming Commissioner, opening the Royal Show in July 1986: 'We must look at the prospects for wood, industrial crops and bio-ethanol. We must look at the role of farming in the countryside, not only as a producer of food but as a guardian of the rural landscape.' However, the idea

- discussed in the EEC in mid-July - of pensioning-off farmers at the age of 55 was described by John Selwyn Gummer (the British junior Minister of Agriculture) as 'manifestly barmy'.

---

outline processor *noun* software that facilitates the ordering of ideas or information into a logical hierarchical structure of sections, subsections, etc

> The idea of an outline processor sounds almost mystical in conception, driven by up-front, fast-talking marketing into promising what seems little short of a microcosmic re-run of the Creation. - *Guardian*, 6 March 1986

> Outline processors, also known rather more grandly as thought or ideas processors, aspire to be the sixth generic software category after spreadsheets, word processors, databases, graphics and comms. - *Practical Computing*, March 1986

---

outro *noun, informal* the ending of a song or musical number; opposite of intro

> 'Watching The World' with its grinding heavy metal guitar outro and the limp 'Other Side Of The World' sound like they've been taken from a dodgy rock opera while most of the other tracks meander along fairly aimlessly. - *City Limits*, 14 Aug. 1986

---

overbedding *noun* the state of having too many hospital beds for the number of patients

> Charges have been pushed up to cover high overheads as a result of low utilisation. ... 'There is a degree of "overbedding"' said Mr John Randall, of the Association of Independent Hospitals. - *Financial Times*, 22 Jan. 1986

---

pacer *noun* a lightweight rail vehicle with a bus-type body mounted on a railway carriage underframe

> The modern Sprinters and the smaller Pacer trains are replacing worn-out diesels. ... British Rail sees them as the salvation of many routes on its provincial network. - *Daily Telegraph*, 2 June 1986

► Pacers are companions to SPRINTERS. They are intended for use on light-traffic country branch lines and urban areas.

---

packet *noun* a unit of data of fixed maximum size and well-defined format (eg comprising address, control and data signals) that is sent as part of a message from one user to another through a PACKET SWITCHING NETWORK

---

packeteer *noun* one who uses a PACKET RADIO

> In the UK packet radio has got off to something of a slow start. ... Now UK packeteers have agreed on using AX.25 and the hobby has grown rapidly over the past year. - *Guardian*, 3 July 1986

---

packet radio *noun* a PACKET SWITCHING NETWORK with radio links so that a PACKET may be received by more than one station

> The system being proposed is called packet radio. Like most such trends it started in the US where some enthusiasts thought it might be a good idea to combine knowledge of amateur radio with their microcomputing. - *Guardian*, 3 July 1986

---

packet switching network *noun* a digital communications system in which PACKETS of data forming a message are sent through a circuit and intercepted by users as required

---

pager *noun* a small portable electronic device for carrying in the pocket, attaching to clothing, etc, that alerts the carrier (eg by emitting an audible tone) to the fact that he/she is required

> The technology of pagers, however, has advanced rapidly, and as well as simple tone pagers (and even these can provide more than just a single alert) there are message pagers that can bring quite lengthy messages to your attention. - *Financial Times*, 6 May 1986

---

pageturner *noun, informal* a book which holds the reader's interest enough to keep him/her reading page after page

> We are not talking about deathless prose - this is simply a question of producing what publishers delight in calling 'a pageturner'. - *The Times*, 8 Feb. 1986

---

palaeoethnobotany *noun* the study of the evolutionary relationships between man and plants as revealed by their fossil records

> Throughout the book Heiser emphasises the archaeological aspects of plants and man, a study some like to refer to as 'palaeoethnobotany'. The study of the role of plants in the cultural evolution of human society is certainly revealing, both

in terms of the plants and the people. - *New Scientist*, 19 Sept. 1985

---

palaeotopomorphologist *noun* one who studies the configuration (topography) of land surfaces as a means of detecting and locating settlements, artefacts, or other traces of primitive man

> Mr Perie, who describes himself as a 'palaeotopomorphologist' - one who uses the raw material of the landscape to unearth traces of primitive man - believes the expedition will discover hundreds of archaeologic sites that form a corridor across central Brazil. - *Guardian*, 16 July 1985

---

palette *noun* the range of colours a computer is able to produce on a visual display unit

> Using the switches you can ... set different colour palettes suitable for use with IBM and Apple computers. - *Personal Computer World*, Feb. 1986

► This is a simple analogy based on the painter's palette.
The palette provides and limits the number of colours available for use on the graphics displays. This will range from three or four shades of grey to 64 (or more) colours. At this sort of range, the limiting factor is the user's power of discrimination rather than the capability of the equipment.

Paninaro (*plural* **Paninari**), *feminine* **Paninara** (*plural* **Paninare**) *noun* a (male) member of the Italian youth cult which is centred around burger bars, whose members present a tough, violent image and have a distinctive style of dress which typically includes flying jackets, belts with large buckles, and wrap-around sunglasses

> The Paninari image is one of young machismo - all breast-beating, fake tans and hard stares behind the shades. ... The Paninari now even have their own magazines ... comic book A5 manuals that are full of violent Wham!-like escapades and sexual innuendo. - *i-D*, Aug. 1986

---

parallel processing *noun* the processing by a computer of a number of items of data simultaneously

> The new game in town is called parallel processing. This means devising computers which will perform several operations simultaneously. One American firm has just unveiled a computer with more than 65,000 processors in it. All linked together by a web of switches in a machine the size of a wardrobe, they allow a problem to be approached from several directions at once. - *Listener*, 12 June 1986

---

parallel processor *noun* a computer capable of PARALLEL PROCESSING

> The deal is to develop a new parallel processor. ... Conventional computers work sequentially - producing their results in single, traffic-jam sequences, like people peeling off an

escalator. Parallel processors use an army of microchips working in parallel, and therefore can deliver the 'people' by the lift-load. - *Guardian*, 6 Sept. 1986

---

particle-beam weapon *noun* any of a group of DIRECTED-ENERGY WEAPONS that use high-energy beams of subatomic particles (e g neutrons) to destroy their targets

> The Pentagon's Strategic Defence Initiative Organisation (SDIO), which is carrying out Star Wars research, has virtually excluded the use of lasers, X-rays and particle-beam weapons, at least for the first generation of space-based missiles that the Administration may build. - *Guardian*, 13 May 1985

► This is a theoretical capability whereby DIRECTED-ENERGY WEAPONS accelerate atomic particles to speeds approaching that of light. The damage effect would be caused by the kinetic energy (mass × velocity) of the particles. A great number of substantial problems of manufacture and use will have to be overcome before effective weapons can be developed in this way.

---

passive management *noun* management of an INDEX FUND, in which the component shares of an investment portfolio are not changed according to their individual performances

> 'Passive management' ... does mean that investors forfeit upside to protect their downside, but it does work. ... Passive managers have no need to buy or sell stocks because market movements leave portfolios under or over weight. - *Daily Telegraph*, 17 July 1986

---

passive manager *noun* a person or company practising PASSIVE MANAGEMENT

---

passive smoker *noun* someone who involuntarily inhales the tobacco smoke produced by others

---

passive smoking *noun* the involuntary inhalation of tobacco smoke from cigarettes, pipes, or cigars which other people are smoking

> Pregnant women may also be at risk from passive smoking, says a recent report from Southampton University. Cotinine, one of the by-products of cigarette smoke, has been found in the amniotic fluid of non-smokers who have smoking husbands. - *Cosmopolitan*, March 1986

► It has been found that damage to health can be done by inhaling other people's smoke on public transport, on social occasions, and at meetings. The term is not wholly new - having been used in two formal reports in 1983 - but is extremely fashionable, as was demonstrated by the cartoon caption in the *Spectator* (26 April 1986) showing a non-smoking guest at a party asking a smoking man 'Mind if I passive smoke?' However, it is not generally or seriously used in the verb form (as yet).

---

pasta war *noun* SPAGHETTI WAR

---

peanut butter *noun, US slang* BLACK TAR

---

pedalathon *noun* see -ATHON

---

penetration aid *noun* a device in a missile system which serves to confuse enemy radar detection systems or as a decoy to divert enemy air defences away from the warhead

► This is generally in the context of electronic warfare. It may be used to protect an aircraft or any other weapon platform.
The device is the highly sophisticated successor of the kind of simple decoy used during the D-Day landings of 1944 whereby masses of metal strips were dropped in the Pas de Calais to simulate aircraft movement on German radar at the time when the Allies were landing on the Normandy beaches.

---

penne *noun* macaroni-like pasta that is cut diagonally at the ends to form quill-shaped pieces

► Italian, literally 'quills' (plural of *penna* = feather, quill, pen)

PEP *noun* PERSONAL EQUITY PLAN

---

perchery *noun* (the EEC term for) the system of producing BARN EGGS

---

performance medicine *noun* treatment of the medical problems affecting musicians as a result of physical stresses or infections caused by playing their instruments over a long period of time

> American doctors are mining a lucrative new seam in specialist health care: 'performance medicine'. ... The list of potentially profitable conditions is impressive: violinist's neck, trumpeter's lip, flautist's chin (spots from the build-up of spittle below the lip), guitarist's nipple (from the instrument rubbing the chest), pianist's finger and even bag-piper's lung (infections from fungal organisms gathering in the watertight bag). – *Daily Telegraph*, 8 Sept. 1986

Personal Equity Plan *noun* (*abbreviation* **PEP**) a scheme announced by the British government in 1986 whereby individuals are permitted to invest up to £2400 a year in UK shares without paying tax on capital gains or dividend income

► This scheme is intended to encourage share-owning, as part of the thrust towards POPULAR CAPITALISM. Most commentators think it will have little effect.

---

petrocurrency *noun* the currency of a nation whose economy depends largely or partly on exports of petroleum

> Foreign-exchange dealers have decided that sterling is a petrocurrency after all. Until last week it had shrugged off a drop in the price of oil from $28 a barrel to $10. But when the price went below $10, the pound's trade-weighted value fell 3%. – *Economist*, 19 July 1986

> Financial analysts could almost be heard licking their lips at the prospect of dearer oil. Britain's status as a petrocurrency nation was firmly underlined. – *Daily Telegraph*, 6 Aug. 1986

► The compound *petro*l + *currency* has attracted a lot of general attention in the course of the fall in oil prices during 1986. The currencies of Arabian Gulf countries have had a particularly problematic year in this respect.
Despite aggressively confident comments one way or the other, there remains uncertainty as to whether sterling is a petrocurrency. Its status as such provides a convenient excuse for those who wish to keep the United Kingdom out of the exchange rate mechanism of the European Monetary System.

---

pH balanced *adjective, of shampoo, soap, etc* having a balance between acidity and alkalinity that is specially formulated for a specific purpose

> Faith Products make vegetable soaps, cleansers, moisturisers, shampoos and conditioners which are vegetarian, pH balanced, biodegradable and manufactured without cruelty to animals. – *Best of Health*, May 1986

---

photo-opportunity *noun* an event staged primarily to give newspaper and magazine photographers a chance to get good pictures and thus provide favourable press publicity for the subject; a photocall

> Heseltine visits ... tend to be one long photo-opportunity. He might be firing machine guns at model aircraft targets ... or sharing his enthusiasm for birdwatching with four helicopter loads of officials and journalists in a Falklands penguin colony. Whatever the occasion you could be sure it would produce pictures and copy. – *Listener*, 16 Jan. 1986

> Whether by accident or design, the legend of her toughness was bolstered yesterday morning when cameras got a fleeting glimpse, in the course of a photo opportunity, of her notepad. – *Financial Times*, 6 May 1986

---

phytolith *noun* a mineral particle (e g of silica) that is deposited by plants, especially grasses, within their cells

> Archaeology and paleoecology have a new speciality. This is

> the study of phytoliths. ... The phytoliths of maize have a particularly distinctive three-dimensional cross shape. They and phytoliths from other plants are adding to knowledge about the use and domestication of plants in the prehistoric and historic past, and about how forest and grassland have been modified by agriculture and climate. – *New Scientist*, 17 Oct. 1985

---

phytotherapist *noun* a person who treats body disorders (eg arthritis and skin conditions) using creams, oils, etc containing plant extracts

---

pico-wave *verb* to treat food by IRRADIATION

> Food industry lobbies are pushing for euphemistic labelling for the treated food. Instead of the straightforward 'Irradiated' ... it has been put forward that 'pico-waved' ... be used. – *Business*, July 1986

► From the international scientific prefix *pico-*, meaning 'one million millionth part' and derived from the Spanish *pico* = beak or small bit. The term may have been deliberately chosen because of its confusing similarity to the accepted word *microwave.*

Pinyin *noun* a system of writing the Chinese language in the Roman alphabet which has been the official transcription system of the People's Republic of China since 1958 and is increasingly used in the West

> There are so few sounds in the Chinese language that the Pinyin system cannot distinguish between homophones with different meanings. – *Guardian*, 9 Jan. 1986

► This is easier to write than orthodox Chinese scripts. In a country as vast, heavily populated, and culturally diverse as China, it is seen as a means of promoting unified simple communication. The attitude is similar to that of Noah Webster in the United States, who saw his (American) version of English as 'a band of national union' to weld together the various races of the young USA.
It also represents an attempt to make China, whose culture is puzzling to many Western minds, more acceptable to Europe and North America. During June 1986 Hu-Yaobang made a tour of western Europe with the same aim in view.
As it has developed since the revolution of 1949, Pinyin has attracted a certain amount of adverse comment from conservatives in China. This mostly has a political reactionary basis.
Pinyin should not affect the content or style of what is written.
As it is easy to write, it does not create much of a problem for Westerners to learn, but is irritating to those who are fluent with the conventional Chinese characters. The changed form of some Chinese proper names (*Mao Tse-tung* is now *Mao Zedong*, and *Peking* is *Beijing*) has caused a little confusion.

---

pipelining *noun* a technique, used especially in powerful computers such as SUPERCOMPUTERS, for speeding up operations, in which serial programming allows simultaneous operations on instructions (e g one instruction is fetched, one is decoded, while yet another is being executed)

> In the past two years, however, there have been new and distinct trends in the market for very powerful computers. Cray and CDC achieved power through brute force and advanced software techniques such as 'pipelining' where computer instructions are handled in several steps. When the first step of a process is completed the results are passed to the second step using separate hardware. The hardware used for the first step is therefore free to begin processing new data. - *Financial Times*, 10 April 1986

> One answer, called pipelining, is to imitate a car assembly line. Each step along the line, eg, installing the engine, bolting on the wheels (adding A to B, storing the results at C), is performed at the same time - but each on a different vehicle (or piece of data). This can reduce computing 100-fold or more. - *Economist*, 11 August 1984

---

pixel *noun* any of the small separate elements that together form an image on a television or VDU screen

► Derived from *pic*ture *el*ement.
A typical monochrome VDU screen contains over 200,000 pixels.

---

pluro-communism *noun* a political system combining communism and pluralism, i e by allowing a diversity of attitudes within a centralist government

> Mr Deng's groping after some form of pluro-communism is brave. But ... the road to a more democratic form of communism will probably in the end seem too dangerous ... to be pursued with the zest it deserves. - *Economist*, 30 Aug. 1986

---

pocketphone *noun* a small portable telephone

> By the year 2000, small 'pocketphones' will be as common as Walkman cassette players. - *Daily Telegraph*, 19 May 1986

---

poison pill *noun* any of various strategies employed by a company to make a takeover bid an unattractive or impracticable proposition to a prospective purchaser, e g by incurring debts, by merging with another company in order to raise the joint company's value beyond reach, or particularly by giving its shareholders preferential rights (see BACK-IN, FLIP-IN, FLIP-OVER)

> Argyll argued that the underwiring agreement - which will

involve Distillers in costs of at least £14m - is an unwelcome introduction to the UK of US-style poison pill tactics. - *Financial Times*, 30 Jan. 1986

---

poll *verb* to examine (eg a number of computer interfaces or terminals) in sequence, to find out which has any data on it for use or messages to be transmitted

> Every five minutes the computer automatically selected a subset of the most important readings from the sensors, compiled a telex message and loaded it into a buffer memory. ... The telexes were then sent by marine radio to Portishead, which polled (picked up) all unread telexes every hour. - *New Scientist*, 22 Aug. 1985

---

polymyositis *noun* a chronic or acute disease which causes inflammation of striated muscle

> But the life of activity and hard physical work which Mollie loved was abruptly curtailed four years ago. Hospital tests revealed that she had polymyositis, a progressive, degenerative disease which attacks nerves and muscles and can be eventually fatal. - *She*, March 1986

► This is a very serious condition involving a 50% risk of death. However, for those who survive there is a probability of complete recovery. Much progress has been made in recent years with corticosteroid and immunosuppressive drugs.
Dermatomyositis is a related collagen disorder, characterized by polymyositis in association with skin changes.

---

pongprint *noun, humorous* a sample of a person's body odour, used as a means of identification - see also SMELLOMETER

> Take a 'pongprint' from the suspect and compare it with samples of air taken at the scene of whatever villainy is being investigated. - *North Herts Mirror on Sunday*, 20 July 1986

---

pop promo *noun* a video made to promote a pop group or a record

> The promotional value of the music video pop promo ... is incalculable. ... No self-respecting band would think of leaving their recording company's office without one. - *Cosmopolitan*, May 1986

---

popular capitalism *noun* capitalism extended to a wide range of the population through an increase in small businesses, private enterprise, ownership of shares by individual investors, and co-ownership and profit-sharing schemes

> That ingenious combination [of tax cuts and allowances in the Budget] was greeted with delight. So was a series of measures intended to promote 'popular capitalism'. ... Mr Lawson

> hopes that the personal equity plan (PEP) will make Mrs Thatcher's nation of home-owners a nation of share-owners too. – *Economist*, 22 March 1986
>
> Popular capitalism is coming of age. You might not hear the expression too much in your local, but it has been sighted in the heavier newspapers and can now be heard on political platforms. It's a term that has been invented to bring together three different thrusts of the British government's crusade. – *Listener*, 26 June 1986

---

pop-up *adjective* of or being a computer facility (eg a menu) that can be accessed during the running of a program, especially on business and personal computers, and comes up onto the screen to provide the user with a set of options, instructions, etc – compare PULL-DOWN

> More and more business micro users are finding a wall built across their computerised world – a wall barring them from the sunlit uplands and bigger and better software packages, friendlier user interfaces, pop-up utilities and faster file access. – *Guardian*, 3 July 1986

---

porno-hypnosis *noun* hypnotism used to induce a subject to commit sexual acts as part of a stage show

> The federation [of Ethical Stage Hypnotists] is to seek legal restrictions to halt the spread of 'porno-hypnosis,' which, it says, is on the increase. – *Daily Telegraph*, 19 May 1986

► This line of entertainment, which has almost limitless potential, is a subject of understandable anxiety to the Federation of Ethical Stage Hypnotists. They have called for the Home Office to set up a central licensing scheme for stage hypnotists, so that improper ones can be outlawed.

It flourishes in the USA and has only recently been imported into this country. Among spectacles which have been witnessed are two naked men chasing each other around a working-men's club in South Wales. Other permutations involve a life-sized inflatable doll.

---

positive marketing *noun* advertising a product by stressing its positive or appealing features in order to deflect attention from its unappealing or negative features

> A classic in 'positive marketing' is the latest packet of Silver Spoon white sugar. ... Flashed on the front is the claim, 'Only 16 calories per average teaspoon.' On the back we are told sugar is 'wholesome ... because it is naturally present in plants' and 'it contains no additives and no artificial ingredients of any kind'. Of course white sugar ... has always had 16 calories per teaspoon. And whoever thought it contained additives? – *Guardian*, 4 July 1986

---

post-bang *adjective* of or being the period following BIG BANG

> The Bank of England is worried that dealing in stocks and shares could become too dispersed after the Big Bang. ... There is a particular danger of this with the new post-bang gilts market. - *Sunday Times*, 1 June 1986

► It is certain that the BIG BANG will be more momentous than any City event in the months following it.
However, it is probable that while the acquisition of shares by the small purchaser will become easier, disposal of them on reasonable terms may be less easy.
An interesting side effect of BIG BANG on upper-class life was discussed in a feature in *Harpers & Queen* in August 1986. Under the title *Rich Caroline, Poor Caroline* it was suggested that 'Life will not be the same again now that the new City money is splitting the family'. The enormous sums which some City men are attracting (see GOLDEN HANDCUFFS, GOLDEN HELLO, GOLDEN PARACHUTE) may so change their standards of living as to distance, and alienate, them from their friends and siblings.

---

post-feminism *noun* the period or ethos following a time of vigorous feminist activity and of social changes affecting women's status and self-image

> Had you heard that 'feminism' is over? the word 'post-feminism' is creeping into (mis)use in certain areas of publishing. Funnily enough, no-one I have heard use it much wants to be quoted - on the record that is. - *Guardian*, 21 Jan. 1986

> The new romanticism is also the world of 'post-feminism' where feminism's angry euphoria has dissipated in a sea of uncertainty. - *New Statesman*, 9 May 1986

---

post-feminist *adjective* of or being POST-FEMINISM

► The expression is attributed to Carol Rumens and is found in the introduction to her wide-ranging anthology (covering 56 women poets) *Making for the Open*: *The Chatto Book of Post-Feminist Poetry* 1964-84. She edited this in 1985 and saw it as a collection representative of the post-1960s female renaissance.
She wrote: 'This anthology is different from its predecessors in that the poems proclaim only themselves. That women have a voice, and the right to be heard goes without saying', and added 'In this sense, then, the volume is "post-feminist."'
Realistically and more cautiously, she pointed out that 'the once-oppressed' had not attained any land of milk and honey, but that important social benefits had been achieved. She cited improved levels of female education and fashions in contraceptive practice and abortion as examples of this.

---

post-polio syndrome *noun* a condition affecting polio patients, that is marked by tiredness, muscle weakness, joint and muscular pain, difficulty in breathing, and a greater susceptibility to cold, that is held to be caused by exercise- or stress-induced damage to regenerated nerves

> Richard Bunro, director of the psychophysiology laboratory at Felician College in New Jersey ... believes that the post-polio syndrome, as researchers call this new phenomenon, has more to do with the after effects of the original bout of polio. He says that 'there is no evidence of mental illness, of new viral activity', or of a new and different disease. - *New Scientist*, 5 June 1986

---

potatogram *noun* a message concealed in a potato

> The 330 workers who seized control of a huge natural-gas platform off north-west Australia after 14 drillers had been dismissed revealed yesterday that they used potatoes to get messages to relatives on the mainland. The dismissed workers ... said they hurled potatoes with messages hidden inside to a support barge where colleagues radioed the messages to ... the nearest coastal town.
> Company officials found out about the 'potatograms,' as the men called them, and moved the support barge further away. But the best cricketers among the workers continued to throw the potatoes across the gap. - *Daily Telegraph*, 20 Aug. 1986

---

power breakfast *noun* a high-level business meeting conducted over breakfast

> New York hotelier Preston Robert Tisch ... is known as the man who coined the term power breakfast, in which the heavyweights of politics, business and the media get together for early morning coffee and rashers. Despite claims ... that such events have been going on for many years in the capital, Mr. Tisch insisted this was the First Official New York Power Breakfast in Washington. - *New York Times*, 20 May 1986

---

power tea *noun* a high-level business meeting conducted over afternoon tea

> Tea-time ... is becoming the new battlefield of Big Business. ... The latest fad has arrived here, from New York and Chicago. ... Sir Patrick Sergeant, chairman of the Euromoney magazine empire ... knows well the power of the pot. 'Though I like my tea weak', says Sir Patrick, 'I'm a great believer in Power Teas. I get people along to my office at 4 p.m. for tea and fruit cake.' - *Daily Telegraph*, 14 July 1986

---

pre-embryo *noun* the first stage in the development of a human foetus, from conception to 14 days

> The term pre-embryo has become the copyright of the proponents of research on the human embryo, or rather pre-embryo. A pro-research campaign launched last week, called

Progress, says that 'what has popularly been called 'embryo' research is not really that at all. It is research using 'pre-embryos' (conceptuses) well before the 14th to 16th day after fertilisation when the embryo itself begins to form.' - *New Scientist*, 21 Nov. 1985

---

pre-lib *adjective* before the existence of the women's liberation movement

It was all simpler in pre-lib days when there was an informal code of behaviour to reduce friction between the sexes. - *Working Woman*, May 1986

---

prequel *noun* a play, film, or literary work that portrays the events leading up to those described in an existing work

The admirable documentary Before Stonewall ... might be seen as a prequel to last year's The Times of Harvey Milk, since the title alludes to the Stonewall riots in New York in 1969 which have come to be seen as a key moment in the rise of gay liberation in America. - *Guardian*, 23 Jan. 1986

► For years, as basic stories emerged in their full form, authors have felt the need to explain earlier events in more detail.
John Milton's *Paradise Lost* (1667) is an early example.
More recently, pecuniary rather than purely explanatory motives have produced another reason for this kind of writing. Sir Arthur Conan Doyle's *White Company* (1890) was followed by the chronologically earlier *Sir Nigel* (1906).
Film-making, which now has budgets frequently into 8 figures of sterling, exacerbates this need. A successful and profitable theme can be as readily extended backwards as forwards. The 1963 production of *Zulu* covering the battle of Rorke's Drift was followed by *Zulu Dawn* on the earlier battle of Isandhlwana.
The word is formed by analogy to *sequel*, although the second syllable has no meaning of its own. Its general acceptance merely notes the fact the technique is here for the foreseeable future.

---

processorrhoea *noun* verbosity and overelaborateness in writing, caused by the use of a word processor offering irresistible temptations to revise and enlarge the text continually

Their sentences, once as small and clean as workhouse plates, turned into great Proustian boa constrictors. The focus of their writing, once so unflinching, became blurred with muttered authorial opinions. All these are symptoms of advanced processorrhoea. - *New Scientist*, 14 Aug. 1986

► From *processor* + dia*rrhoea.*
This is possibly nonce, but is significant in that word processors give rise to two contrary malaises. One, as shown here, is the addition of almost limitless subordinate clauses producing ungainly sentences which are unreadable when they are disgorged from the word processor. The other is

a disinclination to appreciate the full capability and flexibility of the machines, so that standard letters are presented in the same rigid impersonal form in which they would have been uttered by conventional means.

---

pro-life *adjective* supporting restrictions on the availability of legal abortions and a ban on laboratory experiments on human embryos

> Deep divisions have emerged within the all-party pro-life group of MPs about the tactics the group should use to bring about changes in the law on abortion and a ban on embryo experiments. - *Guardian*, 4 March 1986

> A new attempt to outlaw the use of human embryos for laboratory experiments was announced by a group of pro-life MPs at Westminster yesterday. - *Daily Telegraph*, 17 Jan. 1986

► A formation in the *pro-* and *anti-* routine. The list of *anti-* combinations is long, including *anticoagulant*, *antihero*, *antimacassar*, *antipersonnel*, and dozens more. The *pro-* option has been unusual in formal writing. However, there is now not only *pro-life* but also *pro-roads*.
The expression has an important political dimension. There is a pro-life group of MPs and at elections there are pro-life candidates.
The pro-life movement is a response to two separate socio-medical phenomena. The first is liberalized abortion as a result of the Abortion Act 1967. The second is what is seen as a generally more neutral attitude to embryos in the womb.
Unsuccessful attempts were made to modify and restrict the scope of the Abortion Act in the ill-fated Corrie Bill in 1980. An investigation for the DHSS into the ethics of embryology was carried out under the chairmanship of Dame Mary (now Baroness) Warnock, who reported in July 1984. The moral aspect of embryology turns on whether the embryo can be considered to be a life before quickening or whether it may be considered disposable before that time.
The pro-life lobby has a number of articulate protagonists, notably the pressure group L.I.F.E. It draws much support from the Roman and Anglo-Catholic persuasions who, in turn, are influenced by the Pope's uncompromising position on the subject.

---

pro-lifer *noun* someone who is PRO-LIFE

> There is great progress to be made in the control of diseases like cystic fibrosis or haemophilia, if research using pre-embryos can continue. Those who oppose all such research sometimes do so on the principle that all human life, at whatever stage, is equally sacred. These are the radical Pro-Lifers. They would oppose research even though they were convinced that the outcome would be beneficial. - *Today*, 17 March 1986

---

propfan *noun* **1 propfan engine** *or* **propfan** a jet engine in which thrust is provided by counter-rotating rear-mounted propellers driven by gas turbines **2** an aircraft powered by propfan engines

> The 7J7 will be the first airliner to have a propfan engine. ... At first sight, the propfan looks like a return to the days of the turboprop, a jet engine that drives a propeller. In fact, the propfan is a development of today's most advanced jet engines. ... The propfan has fewer blades, unprotected by a casing. General Electric has put them at the back of its engine, looking rather like 'pusher' propellers. Boeing says the design is aerodynamically more efficient than a conventional turbofan. - *New Scientist*, 13 March 1986

> It is the propfan engine that shows most promise of opening a new chapter in short- to medium-range air transport. - *Daily Telegraph*, 1 Sept. 1986

---

proximity talk *noun* a diplomatic conference at which the participants are in separate rooms, with all discussion between them taking place through an intermediary

> The U.N.-sponsored talks, known as 'proximity talks' ... have reached a critical stage. - *Newsweek*, 19 May 1986

---

psoralen *noun* a chemical compound, $C_{11}H_6O_3$, that occurs in certain plants, is used medicinally to treat some skin disorders, and can also cause genetic mutations

> The Chemical Industries Association continues to put out statements ... that ... cleverly divert attention from the harmful effects of certain additives by calling food in general into question. Potatoes and tomatoes, they claim, contain poisons which affect the gastro-intestinal tract and nervous system; psoralens found in parsnips, peas, celery and parsley can cause genetic mutations. - *Listener*, 13 March 1986

---

psychographic *adjective* of or using PSYCHOGRAPHICS

> See quotation at BELONGER

---

psychographics *noun* the quantitative study of the personalities and attitudes of people, used as a marketing tool to establish profiles of potential customers

> An increase in consumer-type demographics - or 'psychographics' as it is known - that SRI confirms is the 'emulators' category. - *Guardian*, 21 May 1985
> The result of this use of 'psychographics' to target impressionable young people is that Marlboro has gone from being a failing brand to become the country's best-selling cigarette. - *Economist*, 26 July 1986

---

psychoneuroimmunology *noun* a branch of immunology that deals with the way in which the mind (eg one's emotional state) or brain can affect the body's immunity and resistance to disease

> According to Janice Kiecolt-Glaser, a psychologist from Ohio State University ... having the wrong partner can also have a harmful effect on your immune system. During the past five years, Kiecolt-Glaser and her husband Ronald Glaser, who is an immunologist, have been investigating aspects of psychoneuroimmunology. - *New Scientist*, 24 April 1986

---

pull-down *adjective* of or being a computer menu that can be accessed during the running of a program, especially on business and personal computers, and comes down over the screen to provide the user with a set of options, instructions, etc — compare POP-UP

> The old control panel allowed you to configure desk-top design, speaker volume ... key repeat rate, key sensitivity and the rate at which a selected item from the pull-down menu flashes. - *Personal Computer World*, Feb. 1986

---

qualy *or* **QALY** *noun* quality-adjusted life year: a unit of the length and quality of life given to a patient by medical treatment, used in assessing the cost-effectiveness of treatment

> Professor Alan Maynard, director of the Centre for Health Economics at York University, says ...: 'For example, if you've got a budget of £20,000, you could probably generate one qualy by spending it all on renal (kidney) dialysis. Or you could spend that £20,000 on hips, and generate perhaps 25 qualies. So one procedure offers you 25 years of full quality of life, the other offers one year for the same budget.' - *Listener*, 7 Aug. 1986

> A kidney transplant costs £3,500 per QALY, a heart by-pass operation £2,000, a heart pacemaker £1,000 and a hip replacement £750. - *Daily Telegraph*, 3 Sept. 1986

► This relates to the controversial issue of decisions about whether or not a patient (especially an elderly one) should receive treatment when NHS resources are stretched.
A recent cause célèbre concerned a patient in an extreme state of alcoholism and deteriorated standard of living, whose treatment was not considered economically worthwhile. Although there may possibly be cases at each end of the scale in which the decisions are obvious to some, there can

be no certain agreement about such matters. This kind of judgment raises appalling and inhuman calculations.
An earlier but equally sensitive type of problem in this vein was posed by Bernard Shaw in *The Doctor's Dilemma.*

---

quasicrystal *noun* any of several materials (eg rapidly cooled metal alloys) that have a structure intermediate between crystalline and amorphous

> Materials structured around this new kind of order seem to forge a link between conventional crystals and the materials called metallic glasses, which are solids formed when molten metals are frozen so rapidly that their constituent atoms have no time to form a crystalline lattice. The new materials have therefore been called quasicrystals. – *Scientific American*, Aug. 1986

---

quesadilla *noun* a filled tortilla which is fried and topped with cheese

---

Radfemspeak *noun* see -SPEAK

---

radioglaciology *noun* the study by radar of the formation, structure, and features of glaciers and ice accumulations

> The full development of what has become the discipline of radioglaciology was carried out at the University of Cambridge by Stanley Evans, Gordon de Q. Robin (the U.K. members of the IAGP's coordinating council) and David J. Drewry. As part of the IAGP the British group and the American, Russian and Australian expeditions have employed airborne radar to map the surface and bedrock elevations of a large part of Antarctica. – *Scientific American*, Aug. 1985

---

radurization *or* **radurisation** *noun, South African* IRRADIATION

> In South Africa, where irradiated foods ... already sell briskly in supermarkets, they have coined the term 'radurisation'. – *Financial Times*, 25 March 1986

---

rail gun *noun* a KINETIC-ENERGY WEAPON consisting of a device that uses electromagnets to accelerate a projectile along a rail to thousands of kilometres an hour

> They include lasers, particle beams, electromagnetic rail guns

and nonexplosive 'kinetic kill' vehicles. - *Scientific American*, Dec. 1985

---

rail trailer *noun* a railway freight vehicle which can be towed on roads

The EEC has given a grant of £82000 to pay for the building of three new freight vehicles ... known as rail trailers ... developed by Dorian Baker, a former engineer with British Rail. - *New Scientist*, 16 Jan. 1986

---

rainbow *adjective* of or representing a wide spectrum of opinions

The Alliance's best chance ... is in Liverpool where they hope to gain minority control by forming a 'rainbow' coalition with Labour opponents of council deputy leader Derek Hatton. - *Today*, 6 May 1986

► The formation of the SDP-Liberal Alliance has suggested a trend towards more permanent radical realignment of traditional political groupings than has been indicated by the temporary coalitions of earlier in the century.
The rainbow metaphor relates to a range of colours of rosettes and posters in political campaigning.
The term appeared in European Community politics immediately after the 1984 EEC elections. An alliance was formed from the 7 West German Greens who had been returned and 13 other like-minded MPs from Belgium, Denmark, Italy, and the Netherlands. This grouping was called the *Arc-en-Ciel* (French = rainbow). Curiously, this small gathering is co-ordinated by no fewer than four co-chairmen.

Ramboesque *adjective* insensitively aggressive and confrontational

One of the bluntest views ... came from the chairman of a large holding company. 'In the highly competitive sphere in which we trade, time is not available for formal management training. Managers are paid to successfully manage, and if that cannot be achieved, then they must be replaced.' During the survey ... Mangham and Silver found many examples of such Ramboesque management. - *Sunday Times*, 1 June 1986

Ramboism *noun* warlike aggression carried out in an ignorant and gung-ho fashion

As the Libyan death toll rose yesterday and details of the engagement grew woolly the doctrine of 'proportionate response' looked thinner by the hour. ... Never a John Wayne fan, Jesse Jackson called it Rambo-ism. - *Guardian*, 26 March 1986

► The film *Rambo, First Blood Part II* generated several items of terminology at the time of its release in the United Kingdom in 1985. It continues to do so and some of it shows signs of being durable. *Ramboism* and *Ramboesque* may last for some time.

Puns of the more ephemeral kind include *Rambotha*, as in the *New Statesman* article heading 'Black Unions Escalate Fight against Rambotha' covering the opposition to President PW Botha of South Africa; and *Ramboer*, applied to President Botha in a heading in the *Economist*.
Although the type of military aggression normally implied by the term is seen as mindless, John Rambo (played by Sylvester Stallone in the film) was amply equipped with academic and linguistic qualifications. His improbable adventures called for superhuman physical attainments because of the absurd odds against which he frequently operated.
The context of his endeavours has been revived through continued pressure by the kinspeople of servicemen still missing in Vietnam. Rambo's task had been to confirm that no Americans were still held prisoner there. He both exceeded the letter and contradicted the spirit of his inquiry. On 19 July 1986, President Reagan promised to leave no stone unturned in an attempt to settle the matter once and for all.

---

razor wire *noun* fencing wire armed at intervals with sharp-edged rectangular metal projections resembling razor blades

> What we got was the instant dismissal of 6,000 people and an overnight retreat to a fortress surrounded by barbed razor wire where Murdoch could reign absolutely. - *Guardian*, 7 Jan. 1986

> It is ... natural that in present-day Britain, the stones [of Stonehenge] should be surrounded by razor-wire, like most other things. - *Listener*, 26 June 1986

---

reactive armour *noun* armour (eg on a vehicle) that bears explosive devices which detonate when struck by an incoming projectile and break it up or deflect it

> Israel's tanks boast a variety of things Syria's do not possess, such as reactive armour. - *Economist*, 12 April 1986

---

readathon *noun* see -ATHON

Reagan ulcer *noun, humorous* a rodent ulcer; a skin cancer that appears as an ulcer, especially on the face, and spreads slowly outwards, destroying other tissue as it grows

> The sore place under the chin was a Rodent ulcer, familiarly known these days as Reagan ulcer. This is the commonest of the three most usual types of skin cancer, and fortunately one that does not spread to other parts of the body. - *Guardian*, 24 June 1986

► The term is humorous, but the affliction is not. It is so named as President Reagan was recently found to be suffering from one. It was found that it was benign, as rodent ulcers normally are, and was removed without further complications.

---

rebirth *verb* to (cause to) undergo REBIRTHING

---

rebirther *noun* a practitioner of REBIRTHING

---

rebirthing *noun* a technique practised by psychotherapists whereby patients are made to re-experience the moment of their birth and hence rid themselves of any related mental or emotional difficulties

> Dr Lichy ... has been particularly impressed by the work of the American 'rebirther' William Emmerson. ... 'William Emmerson told me about the work he was doing with very young children. When he rebirthed a three-year old who had asthma from birth, the child re-experienced the suffocation of the pressure of the birth canal on his chest ... filling him with panic. Emmerson repeated the rebirthing process several times, enabling the child to relive and discharge his distress. The child's asthma gradually cleared.' – *Best of Health*, May 1986

---

recession velocity *noun* the speed at which a distant galaxy appears to be receding from the centre of the universe

> Red shifts in the light from distant galaxies seem to favour certain values, at intervals corresponding to a spacing of 72 kilometres per second, if the red shifts are interpreted as indicating the recession velocities of the galaxies. According to the latest evidence, this provides a yardstick against which we can measure the absolute motion of the Sun through space. – *New Scientist*, 20 June 1985

► This is hardly a new term, any more than the recession itself. However, it has come lately to the layman's notice through increased interest in things astronomical, possibly as a result of the passage of Halley's comet at the turn of 1985–86.
The galaxies beyond those (relatively) near the earth are drifting outwards at a speed roughly proportional to their distance from the earth. Thus the universe as a whole is apparently expanding. This concept fits in comfortably with the big bang theory of the beginning of the universe (to which allusion is made under the entry on the financial BIG BANG).

---

record locking *noun* a mechanism for controlling access to a MULTI-USER database that prevents corruption of files or records by allowing only one user to input or amend data at any one time

> A multi-user database management package ... has within it a specially written code which makes sure that when one person adds new data to the database, all the other users are aware of the change and that when one alters some information, no one else can get at it until he has finished. This is called 'record locking' and is most important. – *Guardian*, 14 April 1986

---

reduced instruction set computer *noun* (*abbreviation* **RISC** *or* **risc**) a computer whose instruction set (complete set of instructions the computer is capable of performing) has been reduced to the minimum, resulting in a machine that can process data more quickly and is cheaper to manufacture than a conventional one (complex instruction set computer)

> The new architecture is based on a concept known as the Reduced Instruction Set Computer (RISC), which enables data to be processed much faster by designing computers which need fewer and simpler instructions to perform a set of tasks. – *Financial Times*, 26 Feb. 1986

---

refuse-derived fuel *noun* fuel that is produced from domestic refuse and can be used as a supplement to coal or on its own

---

relativistic bomb *noun* any of various objects or devices travelling in space that are held, because of their great speed, to be able to destroy anything in their path

> If an alien spaceship was ever observed to be approaching the earth at high speed, it should be regarded as an enemy and, if possible, ruthlessly destroyed, a scientist argued yesterday. For even if its occupants proclaimed peaceful intentions, these messages might be tape-recorded fakes, and the ship itself might be a relativistic bomb, a device thousands of times more destructive than the most powerful hydrogen bomb that has ever been imagined. – *Daily Telegraph*, 30 May 1986

---

renewable energy *noun* any of several forms of energy (eg solar energy) by natural processes whose supply is continuously renewed

> Out on the windy steppes of Inner Mongolia the tent communities of some 12000 nomadic herders are now equipped with solar panels or wind turbines, giving them electricity for the first time. In Lhasa, the first solar-powered communal bath house in Tibet has been opened. In these remote spots, and in the rest of energy-hungry China, US companies involved in renewable energy see a vast market for their products. – *New Scientist*, 25 July 1985

► This has become an extremely important area of interest to compensate for the now foreseeable end of fossil fuels. See, for example, HOT ROCKS and REFUSE-DERIVED FUEL.

---

rent boy *noun, British slang* a young male homosexual prostitute

> Abraham Jacob ... a self-confessed homosexual, cared for the elderly in the north London borough during the day but by night prowled Piccadilly, picking up a percentage of the earnings of 'rent boys' hired for sex. – *Daily Telegraph*, 15 May 1986

> A group of poorly-educated rent boys gathers at his flat in

> Fulham for a session of this self-improving entertainment.
> - *Private Eye*, 19 Sept. 1986

► The problem of boys forced into prostitution by poverty, loneliness, unhappiness, or as the indirect result of a misguided sense of adventure, arises in periodic waves in all major cities, but particularly London. It was rife in the early 1970s when many boys were picked up by pimps at Euston and other major railway termini. The Metropolitan Police carried out a series of purges which did something to keep the malaise under control. The various offences involved are covered by the Sexual Offences Act 1956, the Indecency with Children Act 1960, and other bits of legislation. Nothing in the reforms of the Sexual Offences Act 1967, which permits homosexual activity between consenting adults in private, eases restrictions on this kind of trade.

The use of boys for sexual purposes is as old as recorded history, and it has not always been discouraged. In ancient Greece and Rome it was frequently seen as more pleasurable and more laudable than intercourse with women. The great explorers almost all reported this kind of practice from Africa and the Indian sub-continent. In all these societies both castrated and non-castrated boys were offered. It seems that generally the latter commanded a higher price. Sir Richard Burton, in his characteristically frank style, explained that this was because the testicles could be used as a bridle 'to guide the animal'.

In Britain, disapproval first became general in the late eighteenth and early nineteenth centuries. Around 1720, some 20 homosexual brothels were to be found in London. Particularly celebrated was that run by Mother Clap who 'ran a sodomitical house'.

---

resonance fluorescence *noun* fluorescence (eg that recorded spectroscopically from a comet) in which light from an excited molecule is emitted at the same frequency as the exciting radiation

---

retrovirus *noun* any of a family (Retroviridae) of RNA-containing viruses that possess reverse transcriptase (enzyme that allows the synthesis of DNA on an RNA template; most cells synthesize RNA from DNA), many of which induce cancer and one of which causes AIDS

> The figure shows the points at which drugs could possibly intervene in this sequence of events. The most therapeutically promising stage is that involving reverse transcriptase, as this enzyme is unique to retroviruses, and has no mammalian equivalent. - *New Scientist*, 2 Jan. 1986

► AIDS came to attention in 1980 when a number of cases were diagnosed in the USA, particulary among the gay community and intravenous drug-users, although it had been present but unrecognized in other parts of the world, notably central Africa. The first cases in the UK were recorded in 1981. The virus HIV was proved to be the causative agent in 1983. The term *retrovirus* was coined in 1976 by virologists to describe the former genus *Leukovirus.*

Rett's syndrome *noun* a condition of mental deficiency that affects girl children from about two years of age, and is characterized by the regression of certain faculties and skills (eg speech and walking)

> It is estimated that one girl in 12,000 is born with Rett's Syndrome and about 20 cases have recently been identified in Scotland. ... A defect lurking in the genes of apparently normal, healthy girls, waits to strike around the second year of life. - *Glasgow Herald*, 29 April 1986

---

reverse engineer *verb* to manufacture goods by REVERSE ENGINEERING

---

reverse engineering *noun* the unauthorized manufacture by one company of another's product, using measurements or a mould taken from an original; *also* the unauthorized reproduction of a computer program

> If the case is successful, it will outlaw the practice of reverse engineering by which programmers try to reproduce the behaviour of a program using a different code. - *New Scientist*, 19 Dec. 1985

> The making of what has been called colloquially a 'Chinese copy' is an infringement of the copyright of the original designer. So the production of an article by 'reverse engineering' ... is an infringement. - *Guardian*, 18 April 1986

Reye's syndrome *noun* a rare often fatal childhood disease marked by vomiting followed by delirium, convulsions, and coma caused by swelling of the brain and fatty degeneration of the liver

> Chemists were told yesterday to take all junior aspirin preparations off their shelves after warnings from the Committee on Safety of Medicines that it can trigger the rare and fatal disease, Reye's Syndrome. - *Daily Telegraph*, 11 June 1986

> Canadian scientists have made a major advance in unravelling the mechanism of Reye's syndrome, the often fatal childhood illness which is believed to be provoked in some cases by aspirin. - *New Scientist*, 26 June 1986

► Named after R. D. G. Reye (1912–78), the Australian paediatrician who described the condition in 1963.

RISC *or* **risc** *noun* REDUCED INSTRUCTION SET COMPUTER

> The fashionable word in computing this year will be the acronym Risc. ... Wonderful things are claimed for Risc. It enables a substantial reduction in the circuitry used in the processor. This in turn has splendid consequences: manufacturing is cheaper and hence retail prices are lower, and with fewer components the reliability is much improved. - *Daily Telegraph*, 3 March 1986

---

robot-speak *noun* see -SPEAK

---

rock *noun, US slang* CRACK

> Chips of rock are ... smoked on an improvised pipe, sometimes just a flattened beer-can with a few pinholes over which the crack is burned with a lighted match. - *Listener*, 18 Sept. 1986

Royal Love *noun* a cocktail consisting of apricot nectar, crème de cassis, mandarine Napoléon, orange juice, and champagne

> The American Bar in London's Savoy Hotel, which has a reputation for inventing cocktails to commemorate national events, now has its latest concoction on offer. Known as *Royal Love*, it was created by head barman Peter Dorelli to celebrate the wedding of Prince Andrew to Sarah Ferguson. - *Business*, July 1986

---

rubbish *verb* to criticize severely, especially by condemning as worthless

> Denis Healey said Mrs Thatcher had rubbished the EEC summit; Canon Eric James spoke of those who rubbished the Faith in the City report; a leader in The Times asserted that Pope Leo XIII had rubbished Anglican orders, of all things, in 1896. - *The Times*, 21 Jan. 1986

► Part of the current fashion for negative - sometimes mindless - criticism.

It is used of a wide variety of topics great and small: matters of public interest, domestic affairs, personal performance, and so on. The *Daily Telegraph* (13 May 1986) reported that a British Medical Association report 'rubbishes alternative medicine'. (See IRIDOLOGY and REBIRTHING.) The *New Statesman* (4 July 1986) described advance leaks about the Peacock Report (on BBC finance) as having 'all the hallmarks of a proper government 'rubbishing job' in advance'.

Use of the word in British English is widely disliked by the conservative and it is often cited by prescriptive commentators as the most displeasing word of 1986. Some dislike the conversion of the noun *rubbish* into a verb, although this is one of the most frequent and natural processes in the English language; others apparently despise the word because of its Australian origins.

---

rubble-ize *or* **rubble-ise** *verb* to destroy completely; reduce to rubble

> There are indications that the Pentagon has contingency plans to preempt fresh Libyan attacks on US targets, if necessary by what is being called 'rubble-izing' his oil refineries. - *Guardian*, 26 Aug. 1986

> A Libyan official is said to have been given a warning that the United States was prepared to 'rubble-ise' the Libyan

> economy by striking at oil terminals and other economic targets. - *Daily Telegraph*, 26 Aug. 1986

Rumpie *noun* Rural Upwardly-Mobile Professional: a relatively affluent and basically conservative young person living in a rural area and engaged in a professional career

> In this neck of the woods, rumpies ... are for real, says Norman Gambill, a cultural historian of South Dakota State University. Spurred by the attention paid to yuppies ... Gambill looked at their rural counterparts and found some decided differences. - *Today*, 28 April 1986

► The times achieved by high speed trains (for example, Paddington to Swindon in 52 minutes or to Bath in 1 hour 11 minutes) and the opportunities offered by motorways such as the M4 have made it easy and possible for professional people to work in London, but live in remoter counties outside traditional suburbia. Others will spend each weekend in a country home.
Wiltshire, Gloucestershire, and Norfolk are among counties previously considered outside sensible commuting distance, but now available for this kind of domestic adventure.
The barrister John Strickland in Piers Paul Read's *A Married Man* could possibly be seen as a fairly early example of the species. Much of his married life seems to have been spent in frustrating travel to and from rural accommodation.

---

rupture disc *noun* a pressure-release device installed within the vault of a nuclear reactor

> According to the Soviet technical literature, the RBMK reactors are designed to cope with overpressures of this kind. The reactor vault contains 'rupture discs' which are designed to fail if the pressure becomes too high. - *New Scientist*, 15 May 1986

Savage baby *noun* a baby delivered through natural childbirth under the direct or indirect supervision of Mrs Wendy Savage

► Mrs Savage is a consultant obstetrician at the London Hospital, Whitechapel. She advocates natural childbirth methods as a result of her 20 years' experience.
She was accused of professional incompetence early in 1985 over five cases, two of which had involved a death. These charges caused widespread public protest. The resulting demonstrations included many

young children displaying the motto 'I am a Savage baby'.
A disciplinary inquiry which delivered its findings on 10 July 1986 cleared her of all charges, but added the rider that she had failed to attain the highest possible standards of care. After 15 months' suspension, she was reinstated in her job. However, difficult relationships with her colleagues led her to defer her return to work beyond the agreed date of 15 Sept. 1986. Her own account of the affair is published under the title *A Savage Enquiry*.

SAWES *noun* SMALL ARMS WEAPONS SIMULATOR

---

scanning proton microprobe *noun* an instrument that maps chemical elements by analysing the wavelengths of X rays emitted by atoms of the elements after a sample has been scanned with a finely focussed beam of energetic protons

> One of Britain's most exciting scientific leads is in jeopardy. The physicists who built Oxford University's scanning proton microprobe are furious at the Science and Engineering Research Council's refusal to tell them why ... it turned down an application for a grant. Without the money, the team at Oxford says, groups overseas will take the lead in techniques of mapping elements in materials, down to a sensitivity of parts per million. – *New Scientist*, 5 June 1986

---

scanning tunnelling microscope *noun* a device for examining and quantifying surface complexities of materials (e g the surface of a silicon chip), that directs a flow of electrons (the TUNNELLING CURRENT) onto a sample via a needle-like probe, the tip of which is maintained at a constant height above the surface of the sample and follows its contours. The motion of the tip is read and processed by a computer which produces a 3-dimensional image at magnifications of up to 100 million, so that precise measurements of the vertical positions of single atoms can be made.

> At the IBM Zurich Research Laboratory we have developed a device that makes it possible to characterize in a quantitative way such surface complexities: the scanning tunneling microscope. ... Such a tool has important implications, for example, in the microelectronic industry. As the silicon chip, which is the key element in computer architecture, decreases in size its surface area increases sharply in relation to its volume. Therefore the surface becomes increasingly important in the chip's operation and in its interactions with other logic elements. – *Scientific American*, Aug. 1985

---

scramjet *noun* a ramjet (jet engine in which the air used for combustion is compressed by the forward movement of the engine itself) in which combustion takes place in air moving at supersonic speed

> Keyworth presented his answer to the US Government in the form of a proposal for a scramjet machine that could be built

now, serve the military, and perhaps also lead the way to hypersonic civil flight at five times the speed of Concorde.
- *Guardian*, 30 Jan. 1986

► Formed from *s*upersonic *c*ombustion *ramjet.*

---

scribacious *adjective* given to excessive writing

In his 82 years he [A.L. Rowse] has certainly enjoyed himself, gone into numerous churches if only to 'stay his eye' on the stained glass, but, if anything increasingly scribacious, he has never been known to shut up. - *Daily Telegraph*, 13 June 1986

► This may not be strictly new, but is unusual and useful. The *Oxford English Dictionary* has only one record of it - from Isaac Barrow, in 1677 - and no modern dictionary lists it. It plugs a long-felt gap in one's vocabulary, for there is no single word - apart perhaps from *voluminous* - with a similar meaning.

---

scrub *noun* a skin cream containing tiny abrasive grains which remove dead skin cells and improve the complexion

You can also polish your skin with some of the new cosmetic scrubs on the market. - *Woman's Own*, 15 March 1986

---

scrunch-drying *noun* a technique of hair-drying consisting of crumpling a handful of hair at a time while aiming a hairdryer at the roots of the hair

Either dry your hair as normal or, for a lot more fullness, try scrunch-drying. - *Woman's World*, Sept. 1986

Scubaphone *trademark* - used for an underwater radio for divers

A small company in Vancouver says it has developed the most powerful underwater radio for divers. The system, called Scubaphone, enables divers to talk to each other over distances up to 1200 metres and to a depth of 80 metres.
- *New Scientist*, 26 June 1986

SDR *noun* Special Discretion Required: a warning symbol used in Britain by Channel 4 to mark cinema films shown on TV which contain material that viewers might find offensive

The white triangle with a red border symbolising SDR ... will first be seen at the top left of the screen on September 19th when the bizarre French comedy Themroc - about a worker made redundant who bricks himself up in a flat with a girl - is shown. - *Guardian*, 22 Aug. 1986

---

sea daisy *noun* any of a species (*Xyloplax medusiformis* of the class Concentricycloidea) of invertebrate animals related to the starfish, sea urchins, etc, that have small disc-shaped bodies fringed with spines

Three antipodean taxonomists recently found in sunken

driftwood, not just a new species, but one so peculiar that they have had to invent an entirely new class to contain it (*Nature*, vol 321, p862). *Xyloplax medusiformis*, informally known as the sea daisy, is a tiny round and flat echinoderm. - *New Scientist*, 3 July 1986

SEAQ *noun* Stock Exchange Automated Quotations: a computerized system of displaying share prices and recording transactions that is the heart of London Stock Exchange dealings after BIG BANG

In a year or so, the Exchange plans to introduce a system that will automatically fill small orders - 1,000 shares - at the best price in the market. Details of trades will be logged into SEAQ to provide a record of trading. - *Investors Chronicle*, 13 June 1986

Securities and Investments Board *noun* (*abbreviation* **SIB**) the quasi-official body, with powers delegated to it by the Trade Secretary, which is to take responsibility, from 1987, for policing all investment business in the City of London - compare SELF-REGULATORY ORGANIZATION

The Securities and Investments Board (SIB) produced a draft this week of many of the rules for investment firms to obey once London's securities markets are deregulated on October 27th. Incomplete and flawed as they are, the rules contain a clear message: the SIB is prepared to get tough and get detailed. - *Economist*, 1 March 1986

---

securitization *or* **securitisation** *noun* the practice of making debts marketable, i e raising money through an issue of securities rather than through a bank loan. See DISINTERMEDIATION

At the core of their concern is the way in which the process of securitisation ... has shifted risk away from the published balance sheet to a position where it is less easy to gauge. - *Financial Times*, 17 March 1986

---

securitize *or* **securitise** *verb* to raise money by SECURITIZATION

Behind the deal lies an attempt to securitise the underlying backstop credit which the borrower needs to back up sales of short-term notes. - *Financial Times*, 10 Feb. 1986

---

securitizer *or* **securitiser** *noun* a person or organization practising SECURITIZATION

Self-Regulatory Organization *noun* (*abbreviation* **SRO**) any of various bodies (eg the Stock Exchange) working under the SECURITIES AND INVESTMENTS BOARD to act as a watchdog on financial activity in the City of London

---

semi-intensive egg *noun* (the EEC term for) an egg produced by hens which are kept at a density of not more than 1600 to the acre and are allowed continuous daytime access to open-air runs – compare BARN EGG, DEEP LITTER EGG

> Would you rather buy a semi-intensive egg or a barn egg? A barn egg ... conjures up pictures of little brown hens scuttling over bales of straw in a half-timbered barn. 'Semi-intensive' sounds more like a half-hearted version of the battery shed. Wrong! – *New Health*, Sept. 1986

Sendust *noun* an alloy of iron, aluminium, and silicon that is used for recording heads

> A new alloy called Sendust has twice the capacity for magnetism that ferrite has. ... Recording engineers make the heads by compressing dust into the precise shape required. Sendust is brittle and tends to rust, but if it is mixed with chrome to prevent corrosion, its magnetic characteristics spoil. – *New Scientist*, 24 April 1986

► Named after the Sendai region in northern Japan.

---

sensitivity consultant *noun* a person employed to teach others to respect people's feelings, for example to teach men how not to offend women by displaying overt sexist attitudes

> New York dustmen are not exactly famous for their levels of social refinement, their appreciation of the niceties of normal social discourse, and most important of all their chivalry towards women. So the city has decided to hire a 'sensitivity consultant' to teach the dustmen the best way to behave when their ranks are swelled by women later this year. – *Daily Telegraph*, 13 Jan. 1986

► The job title *consultant* has come to be the automatic appellation for anyone who gives any advice, however brief or banal. The field of sensitivity (sexual, racial, or age-related) is a growth area for the appointments of arbitrators and umpires of all kinds.
A typical example of this type of work is a Midlands examination group which deleted *Christmas* in referring to *Christmas lighting*, so that it could be replaced by *festival* (lighting). There must come a point at which this kind of coyness leads to serious inaccuracy and, thus, confusion.
Regrettably a story carried by *Private Eye* (13 June 1986) that a London borough councillor had demanded that the *bottle bank* be re-named the *bottle rehabilitation centre* was later claimed (by the council concerned) to have been based on an April Fool. It was alleged that the term *bank* was too reminiscent of immoral profits, President Reagan, and other things which might be considered offensive to sensitive bottle depositors.

---

set-aside *adjective* of or being an agricultural policy whereby farmers are paid to take some of their land out of production (eg by leaving land fallow or by turning to forestry), thus reducing agricultural surpluses

> A licensed set-aside type quota system is being put forward by the NFU to control surplus cereal production. – *Farmers Weekly*, 29 Nov. 1985

> Much of the marginal land that would be affected by a set-aside policy is soil on which no grower would scatter seed unless he were subsidised to do so. – *Economist*, 3 May 1986

► Such a policy is now under consideration by the EEC. It has been implemented in the USA on past occasions. See comment at OUTGOER.

SETI *noun* search for extraterrestrial intelligence: any of various programmes which search for intelligent life elsewhere in the universe, especially by detecting electromagnetic radiations

> NASA is developing equipment to allow radiotelescopes to look for microwaves that might be deliberately aimed in our direction from space. ... The advocates of SETI favoured microwaves because they are transmitted by human activities and because molecules that are important to life on Earth show up as lines in the microwave spectrum. – *New Scientist*, 5 June 1986

---

shaking table *noun* a large flat surface which simulates the earth movement caused by an earthquake and upon which model constructions can be built for experiments by architects, civil engineers, etc

> Britain is to get its first 'shaking table' for simulating the effect of earthquakes. ... The simulator will have a table three metres square and will be able to take models weighing up to 15 tonnes. – *New Scientist*, 7 Nov. 1985

---

share economy *noun* an economic system in which part of an employee's pay consists of a share of his/her company's profits – compare WAGE ECONOMY

> The profit-sharing scheme advocated by the chancellor of the exchequer, Mr Nigel Lawson, in last week's budget draws on the thinking of an American economist, Professor Martin Weitzman. ... He argues that a 'share economy' ... would have two big advantages over a 'wage economy'. – *Economist*, 29 March 1986

---

share shop *noun* an establishment where securities can be bought and sold by the public quickly, with the minimum of formality, and without investment advice

> The mini-investor with a few thousand pounds to spare can bypass traditional brokers altogether and go to a share shop, which sells shares and gilts over the counter like cabbages and carrots. – *Economist*, 13 Sept. 1986

Sharon *noun, British slang* a lower-class girl of rather tarty appearance

> The third formers of Godolphin and Latymer school of London's Hammersmith spelt out the urban anti-chic rules for me. ... No hip schoolgirl wants to be labelled as ... a Sharon: mini skirts with lots of make-up and high heels. - *Daily Mail*, 13 Jan. 1986

► This derogatory term is an invention of the upper and upper-middle classes. Frequently heard in conversation, it is now making a few appearances in writing.
The term indicates poor taste and attempts at excessively sexy dress. The relevant character is sometimes ironically associated with a disagreeable, self-satisfied manner and immoderate sensitivity to criticism.
The name Sharon is of biblical origin, not as a personal name, but meaning *the plain* (yashar). It referred particularly to a fertile plain between Joppa and Mount Carmel, well-stocked with cattle and sheep (1 Chronicles 5.16 and 27.29). The rose of Sharon was a beautiful shepherdess (Song of Songs 2.1). By the time of Isaiah, there are indications that God's vengeance might turn the plain of Sharon into a wilderness (Isaiah 33.9).
The name was favoured by seventeenth-century puritans. It has enjoyed a revival in Britain since 1945; although it had been popular in the United States earlier. The eminence of Sharon Tate, model and actress (subsequently brutally murdered) around 1970, gave additional popularity to the name.
There are variations of the spelling: Sharron, Sharone, and many others.

Sharon fruit *noun* a large tomato-like persimmon with a tough bright-orange skin, no seeds, and sweet pulpy orange flesh

> They take a delight ... in saying that academics now believe it was the Sharon fruit which Eve used to tempt Adam. - *Guardian*, 14 March 1986

► Enthusiasts for this seedless fruit claim that it is particularly versatile and simple to prepare. It can be used in fruit salads, flans, tarts, or cheesecakes and can be embodied in ice creams and sorbets.
Its present putative popularity is the result of Israeli marketing campaigns. These are a reaction to anxiety about the 1986 entry of fruit-producing Spain and Portugal into the European Community. The campaigns highlight bizarre and novel fruits, while emphasizing quality as opposed to quantity.
The suggestion that Eve used the Sharon fruit to tempt Adam presumably impresses only Fundamentalists. This seems rather a limited market share. It is a style of advertising in the same vein as that used in the early 1970s by the producers of Emva Cream sherry, associating it with the Queen of Sheba's vineyards on Cyprus (itself a rather tenuous claim of ownership).
The etymology is a straightforward connection with the prosperity and agricultural plenty of the plain of SHARON.

---

shelf talker *noun* BARKER CARD

---

sherpa *noun, informal* an aide to a head of government participating in a summit conference, concerned especially with drafting communiqués

> In the events unfolding in Tokyo the 'sherpas' are key figures, as on Everest, in the Summit being conquered. - *Daily Telegraph*, 6 May 1986

> Mr Nakasone thought he could safely sign the rather general draft statement against terrorism presented by the bureaucratic 'sherpas' who prepare summits. - *Economist*, 10 May 1986
> The civil-servant sherpas ... as usual are preparing the leaders' communiqué well before they meet. - *Economist*, 26 April 1986

► The word came to prominence in Britain during the seven-nation economic summit meeting at Tokyo in May 1986. It has been used in diplomatic circles for several years. Indeed, the term *Sherpa guide* in such a context is recorded as long ago as 1955, referring to a summit meeting between the heads of state of USA, USSR, UK, and France. However, it has hitherto been unknown outside that highly introverted working environment. Their duties can extend into important roles beyond drafting communiqués. They prepare reports for internal use and carry out significant unattributable negotiating functions behind the scenes.
The term's origins relate to another kind of summit. Sherpas (a native word) are the people who live in the south Himalayas and act as mountain guides. The first Sherpa to come to public notice was Sherpa Tensing, Sir Edmund Hilary's aide on his successful ascent of Everest in 1953. Tensing died in 1986.

---

shooting gallery *noun, slang* a secret place where drug addicts congregate to inject themselves with drugs

> The toll of the present system is clearly seen in Edinburgh, where more than half of the city's several hundred addicts have been infected, principally because of the use of 'shooting galleries'. - *The Times*, 26 Feb. 1986

---

short-lifer *noun* someone who lives in short-life housing (temporary housing in properties which would otherwise be empty)

> Camden was already committed to rehousing former short-life families and 'vulnerable groups', but it had to join in a co-ordinated effort to help other former short-lifers, with better control of empty council properties, for instance.
> - *Hampstead and Highgate Express*, 1 Aug. 1986

---

short-termism *noun* the tendency (of politicians, investment managers, and others) to concentrate to a large extent on short-term projects in order to gain fast returns, thereby neglecting long-term projects

> There probably is a case for saying that it [the government] should spend more on the sort of research that is politically least attractive, i.e. long term and blue sky. Short-termism is

infectious, it's insidious and Downing Street hasn't escaped it. – *Listener*, 20 Feb. 1986

SIB *noun* SECURITIES AND INVESTMENTS BOARD

---

sick building syndrome *noun* a condition affecting office workers in buildings with sealed windows and humidification systems, characterized by headache, eye irritation, flu-like symptoms, and lethargy

> Headache? Skin dry, eyes smarting? General feeling of torpor, lethargy? ... It could be the very latest complaint for the office worker, the mysterious and sinister-sounding 'Sick Building Syndrome'. The old joke about being allergic to work is no longer quite so amusing. – *Daily Telegraph*, 13 May 1986

---

sievert *noun* (*symbol* **Sv**) a unit of ionizing radiation equal to the dose equivalent of 1 joule per kilogram

> See quotation at BECQUEREL

► Like the GRAY, this is used for measurements on the body. One sievert equals 100 *rems*, and there is still a tendency to make such measurements in rems, at least for the time being.
Rolf Maximilian Sievert (1896–1966), after whom it was named, was a Swedish physicist remembered particularly for his work on occupational radiation protection. He is also commemorated by an ion chamber named after him.

---

single capacity *noun* the demarcated role of a stockbroker or a stockjobber on the London Stock Exchange before BIG BANG – compare DUAL CAPACITY

> In city jargon, single capacity describes the system where jobbers take positions in securities (making money from the spread between their buying and selling prices) and brokers buy and sell securities from the jobbers for their clients (making money from commissions). – *Economist*, 2 Aug. 1986

---

single-issue *adjective* concerned with a single specific issue (especially in politics), rather than with a range of issues or a general strategy

> Thanks to new rules for budget debate, it may be hard for critics to derail the committee's new plan. ... The greatest threat to it in Congress does not come from those who will attack it as a package. The real danger is from single-issue meddlers who will try to adorn it with concessions to the special interests they represent. – *Economist*, 29 March 1986

> It [the defeat of the Shops Bill] was Britain's most notable example of successful single-issue politics. ... Its success will encourage other single-issue groups, particularly those concerned with moral issues, to try similar tactics.
> – *Economist*, 19 April 1986

---

single-lining *or* **singling** *noun* the practice of closing one line on a double-track railway line

> BR are 'single-lining' the double tracked line between Wrexham and Chester - a move which some see as a prelude to closing it down altogether. ... The effect of singling a line is that trains have to wait at one end until any trains coming in the opposite direction have come out. - *New Statesman*, 31 Jan. 1986

► A single-line railway is strictly known in railway terminology as a *single-track railway*. When a track's capacity is reduced in this way, because of a decrease in traffic, it is described as being *singled*. *Single-lining* is a layman's term rather than a railwayman's.

---

single use *adjective* designed to be used once and then thrown away; disposable

> Portex Limited are world leaders in the single use medical and surgical devices field with a major proportion of sales being overseas. - *Daily Telegraph*, 22 April 1986

Sinner *noun* a member of the Sinn Féin, the Irish republican organization that is the political branch of the IRA

> No Sinn Feiner (or Sinners, as even Unionists now tend to call the political Provos) would admit during the campaign what many are now willing to say privately. - *New Statesman*, 31 Jan. 1986

► Thought to be unusual and pronounced *sh*inner.

---

sit-out *noun* a form of protest or demonstration involving sitting outside with some kind of display, to draw attention to an issue

> As we go to press the Galway playwright Margaretta D'Arcy ... waits hourly to see whether an injunction taken out by the landlords of the Irish Arts Council's premises in Dublin will succeed in evicting her from a daily 'sit-out' before the building talking to passers-by. - *New Statesman*, 9 May 1986

---

sixth-generation *adjective* of or being a stage in the development of computers in which biological components (eg structures which mimic the nervous systems of living organisms) are incorporated to improve the power and sophistication of the handling and processing of data, especially sensory data - see also BIOCOMPUTER

> Ogata-san smiled and sipped green tea. 'We'd like to make a brain,' he said. ... The end point ... is a sixth generation computer that thinks for itself. - *Guardian*, 7 March 1986

► The expression reflects the view that generations can be detected in the history of computers; as centuries are a convenient division of social history. As with history, however, the categorization is purely a

convenience and with computers there is even greater vagueness at the borders of the periods.
Nevertheless, the first generation is clear: the kind of enormous machine which occupied several rooms and of which it was predicted that each country might need two. Some of the other generations provide clear examples. The third generation, which includes the IBM-360, was commonplace about 1965. The fifth generation is represented by the new Japanese technology of the mid-1980s capable of parallel processing (performing several functions in parallel). This sixth generation may use biological organisms and tissue to perform the 0-1 function essential to the computer's logic.

---

skat *adjective, informal* up to the minute; fashionable

> If you think of yourself as being 'trendy' ... you most certainly aren't, according to the arbiters of style in smart Soho cafe society. Even priding yourself on your 'street cred' doesn't say much for your current awareness, they claim. Both words for a person who is right on top of the times are now declared 'out'. 'In' is 'skat' which means the same as 'street cred' but is a lot shorter to pronounce. – *Hitchin Express*, 3 July 1986

---

sketch-phone *noun* a telephone with an attached VDU and electronic sketchpad, such that anything drawn on the sketchpad during a call will be displayed on the screen of the person at the other end of the line

> The sketch-phone has proved the biggest flop. Most people would rather talk than draw – except, of course, the deaf. For them, the sketch-phone is as exciting an innovation as the conventional phone was to those with hearing. – *Economist*, 19 April 1986

► This product, developed by Nippon Telegraph and Telephone, is currently being tested by a sample of subscribers in Tokyo. It is unlikely to become widely available for several years.

---

slasher film *or* **slasher movie** *noun* a film featuring scenes of violence and mutilation with knives, saws, or other cutting implements

> Amy Jones ... even goes so far as to claim her Slumber Party Massacre is the first 'feminist slasher' movie. – *Guardian*, 8 May 1986

> The other bad dream is Nightmare on Elm Street. ... If Rambo is 'ripping yarn', then this nauseating slasher film is 'superior genre'. – *Listener*, 5 Sept. 1985

---

sleeping economy *noun* an accumulation of funds and investments which are not claimed by their owners, or are unknown to them, eg dormant accounts in banks and building societies, unredeemed savings certificates, and unclaimed share dividends and Premium Bond prizes

> A 'sleeping economy' ... worth more than £1 billion, is being

> built up in Britain. ... Occasionally the sleeping economy stirs. This year, negotiations with both China and the Soviet Union have raised the possibility that millions of pounds owed to United Kingdom holders of pre-revolutionary bonds might be paid. – *The Times*, 11 Aug. 1986

► It is believed that nearly 47 million Post Office savings accounts have been untouched for at least five years. The Department of National Savings considers that over £160 million is resting in inactive accounts. £3½ million Premium Bond prizes are thought to be unclaimed.

Slim *noun, East African* Acquired Immune Deficiency Syndrome; AIDS

> Originally, the outbreak of 'Slim' in Rakai was blamed on the witchcraft of smugglers from over the border in nearby Tanzania, or on the truck drivers who travelled from Kenya to Uganda through neighbouring East and Central African countries. – *Listener*, 5 June 1986

► Named from its wasting effects.
The condition AIDS has lurked in the East African countries since 1982, but only recently has it attained serious proportions. It is now rife throughout Uganda and Kenya, with some effects in their neighbouring countries.
Two factors exacerbate the problem. Many of the societies involved are polygamous and as shame attaches to an AIDS/Slim death, the family disperses on the demise of a victim. This ensures that the disease is distributed widely. Further risks attach to prostitutes, particularly in Nairobi. The *Listener* estimated that 50% of them were affected. As they entertain, in some cases, 50 or 60 clients per week and many refuse contraception, the distribution of Slim is rapid and generous.

---

slopperati *plural noun* young people who come from a well-off background but dress in a deliberately casual and untidy manner

> It is the world's most famous carriage driver, HRH the Duke of Edinburgh; whereupon, hacks hover nervously, royalty gawpers gawp, and the sloppily dressed offspring of the slightly rich, The Slopperati, feign gross disinterest. – *Sunday Times*, 17 Aug. 1986

---

small arms weapons simulator *noun* (*abbreviation* **SAWES**) a simulator used by the army for training and practice

> It is Centronics which has developed the group's best known product, the small arms weapons simulators – SAWES – used by armies as a realistic but inexpensive war games/training tool. – *Financial Times*, 30 Jan. 1986

► The Ministry of Defence has recognized the value of simulators for some time. For example, in the well-established tradition of training

simulators for aircraft pilots, tank-driving simulators were introduced into training establishments in the mid-1970s.
Simulators are usually cheaper (eg in ammunition and in use of training areas, which may involve large compensation payments), less dangerous, and capable of being used in all weathers. This last characteristic is particularly important with recruit training cycles which run in winter as much as in summer and for troops stationed in Germany where the winters are sometimes very severe.

---

smart rock *noun* a KINETIC-ENERGY WEAPON that is designed to home in on the heat produced by the warhead of a missile under attack

> Whatever complex technology is eventually used in SDI, its ultimate goal is simple, the detection and destruction of incoming ballistic missiles with advanced weapons systems using lasers, particle beams and so called smart rocks.
> – *Guardian*, 13 Dec. 1985

---

smellometer *noun, humorous* a device which could be used by detectives to match samples of air taken from the scene of a crime to the body odour (PONGPRINT) of the criminal or criminals responsible

> Now there's news that researchers at Leeds University are working on a smellometer, which would be capable of identifying an individual's scent. The idea comes from a forensic pathologist who sees its most obvious application as another means of identifying and eliminating those suspected of crime. *North Herts Mirror on Sunday*, 20 July 1986

---

smoke hood *noun* a transparent bag of fireproof plastic with an airtight neckband for protection against poisonous fumes, as in an air crash

> Air passengers are set to be equipped with tight-fitting smoke hoods from next summer. This follows official backing for the controversial hoods from the Ministry of Transport crash investigators working on the holiday jet disaster at Manchester airport which killed 55 people a year ago this week. – *Observer*, 17 Aug. 1986

► The smoke hood allows normal breathing but keeps out poisonous fumes emitted by burning seats and other parts of an aeroplane.
A Department of Transport investigating team felt that most of the 55 who died in the crash of a British aircraft en route to Corfu in August 1985 could have been saved if they had been wearing such hoods. They recommended the hoods for use in future on commercial airline flights.

---

smokeism *noun* discrimination against smokers

> I [Keith Waterhouse] detest 'smokeism': the term I coined in the *Mirror* column for the righteous persecution of smokers. Nevertheless, it is eight years now since the weed passed my lips. – *Listener*, 3 April 1986

► Government health warnings have been carried on cigarette packets since pressure from certain medical lobbies became irresistible. In 1984

London Transport Underground forbade smoking on their trains. Since then, more local disciplines have become the norm. Establishments such as motorway service stations have no-smoking areas. Some people have returned to the Victorian convention of allowing smoking only in certain rooms of their houses (or not at all). Others are gratuitously rude to smokers in public places.
See also PASSIVE SMOKING.

---

snuff-dipper *noun* someone who indulges in SNUFF-DIPPING

> Levels of nitrosamines - known to disrupt DNA, the genetic material - encountered by a snuff-dipper are similar to the doses that produce cancer in laboratory animals. - *Guardian*, 22 April 1986

---

snuff-dipping *noun* the practice of chewing a TOBACCO TEABAG

> The growing practice of 'snuff-dipping' is much more likely to cause cancer than smoking cigarettes, according to a leading ear, nose and throat specialist. Professor Donald Harrison, of the Institute of Laryngology, said yesterday that in southern American states ... 60 per cent of snuff-dippers developed some cancer or pre-cancerous symptoms in 20 years. - *Daily Telegraph*, 22 Aug. 1986

Soarfly *trademark* - used for a remotely controlled observation and attack robot air vehicle that is designed to carry out spy missions behind enemy lines, using highly advanced electronics and computer systems and, if necessary, to make suicide attacks on enemy targets

> An insect-like creature from the realms of science fiction which could revolutionise battlefield operations goes on display at the Army equipment exhibition at Aldershot this weekend. A Milton Keynes company, Scicon, has named its invention Soarfly. - *Daily Telegraph*, 19 June 1986

> Soarfly will be launched from a tube, and fly at a low altitude with its wings fixed in an X position. Its small size (around 1 metre long) and silent electric motor, driven by lithium batteries, will allow it to remain undetected on its mission. Cameras and infrared sensors will collect data and send them to base in one short signal. This is the only time that the Soarfly gives away its position by transmitting signals. - *New Scientist*, 3 July 1986

---

soca *noun* a style of popular music, associated particularly with Trinidad, blending elements of soul and calypso

> [David] Rudder, like Marley, obviously wants his music to be popular outside the Caribbean, but he says he won't water it down to get approval, the way he says many exponents of calypso and soca ... have been doing. - *Guardian*, 26 Aug. 1986

► Soul and calypso are two black-based styles of music from the western hemisphere. Soul is essentially serious in motivation and sound. Calypso is more lightweight and jocular.
Soul emerged from the period of the rise of black culture in the early 1950s. The motto 'black is beautiful' typified the movement's thinking. Inevitably much of its energy was frustrated and its aspirations were reduced to expressions of escapism. However, it expressed itself visibly in the Black Muslim religious sect and in the Black Power political enterprise. Essentially ghetto-based, it encouraged North American blacks to interest themselves in the wider aspects of black ethnology. Later this took the specific form of the TV series 'Roots' (ABC Network, 1977) and 'Roots: The New Generation' (1979).
Calypso appeared on the international scene in the 1950s. In 1957 Columbia and RCA record companies made conscious attempts to compete through calypso music with rock'n'roll, which had dominated popular music since the previous year. Various performers emerged during the period, such as the Easy Riders and the Tarries. Predominant was the anodyne Harry Belafonte. Although Belafonte's connections with Jamaica were ancestral rather than personal, many of his records attained unprecedented sales.
Soca attempts to combine these two sentiments. It complements the reggae and jazz-Latin styles.

---

socialist commodity economy *noun* the type of economy proposed for China under Deng Xiaoping, combining central control of supply and prices with free-market forces (i e allowing market prices to be determined by supply and demand)

> China's decision to invent a so-called 'socialist commodity economy' was easy. Putting it into effect is proving difficult. ... Younger leaders like Mr Hu Qili ... have already dropped the euphemism 'socialist commodity economy' and talk freely of a 'market-oriented economy' without coy qualifications.
> – *Economist*, 26 July 1986

---

social mountaineer *noun* an extreme or inveterate social climber

> And the fact that Princess Michael ... is here, inevitably attracts those social mountaineers for whom the pleasure of name-dropping is priceless. – *Daily Express*, 13 Jan. 1986

► This is a comic superlative of *social climbing*, which does not diminish as an ambition as barriers of social class become less significant. The formation is an obvious product of the vogue for hyperbole and exaggeration.

---

social ownership *noun* ownership and control of a business or industry by national government

> He [Nigel Lawson] said Labour knew nationalization was unpopular which is why it had produced the phrase 'social

> ownership' but that would fool no one. – *The Times*, 19 July 1986
>
> The 'militants' shall get most of their own way, though in a manner disguised by semantics, e.g. the substitution of phrases like 'social ownership' for nasty, brutal words like 'nationalisation'. – *Daily Telegraph*, 25 Aug. 1986

► The Labour party's riposte to POPULAR CAPITALISM.

---

soft proofing *noun* the viewing and checking of an image (eg during printing processes) on a monitor or visual display unit, before the final stage of its production

> 'Soft' proofing on a high-resolution colour monitor is a cheap way to view the final result after initial scanning, but before the film is produced. – *New Scientist*, 26 Sep. 1985

---

somatostatin *noun* a neuropeptide that transmits impulses between nerve cells in the brain and that inhibits the release of various hormones (eg growth hormones)

> The neurotransmitter to come under suspicion most recently, and thought to be an intrinsic cortical transmitter, is somatostatin. It is one of the peptide neurotransmitters, the class that includes the morphine-like enkephalins. – *New Scientist*, 22 Aug. 1985

---

song

– **on song** in good form or condition; *also* in peak working order

> Once the turbo [of a Saab Turbo] is 'on song', the power comes in with a blood-tingling rush and catapult acceleration. – *Daily Telegraph*, 2 April 1986

► This ornithological metaphor has become a cliché of sports commentators and reporters, and may well spread to other fields.

---

sonochemistry *noun* a branch of chemistry that deals with the use of ultrasonics

> The development of sonochemistry came from a chance observation in the laboratory that chemical reactions could be triggered by ultrasonic agitation of liquids. But it remained a textbook curiosity. It works when a probe is placed in the liquid, emitting soundwaves of a higher than audible frequency, creating cavities which are in effect tiny bubbles but under immense pressures. When the bubbles burst, the energy released triggers chemical reactions. – *The Times*, 14 April 1986

Sordan grass *noun* a cereal grain plant that is a hybrid of sorghum and Sudan grass, developed for its ability to grow in otherwise uncultivable soils containing high concentrations of sodium salts

In many arid regions there is not enough rain to wash out of the soil the sodium salts released from minerals by weathering. The sodium makes the soil dense and impermeable to air and water, rendering it uncultivable. A group of workers from the U.S. Agricultural Research Service has discovered a remedy for the problem. It is Sordan grass. - *Scientific American*, Aug. 1985

---

south-easternization *or* **south-easternisation** *noun* the conversion (of England) to the relative prosperity and bourgeois attitudes considered typical of the south-eastern region of the country

Moving to the altogether more agreeable topic of Manchester, Alf Morris [MP, speaking in the House of Commons] denounced what he memorably called 'the creeping South Easternisation of this country'. - *Daily Telegraph*, 13 May 1986

► Since the election of a monetarist Conservative government in 1979, it has been a cliché of Opposition commentary that the country is divided clearly and dramatically into the (impoverished) North and the (prosperous) South. Obviously this is an oversimplification contradicted by pockets of opposite conditions, such as poverty in the Medway Towns and Cornwall. This polarization has a certain crude appeal to those who are dissatisfied with the government's philosophy.
South-easternization restricts it further to what is seen as the most affluent and self-satisfied corner of the more comfortable half. This localization stems partly from the conventional view of suburban Surrey, and also from the belt of relatively high employment (often based on computer and retail trades) running down the M4 Motorway and the main Paddington to West Country railway line through Slough and Reading as far as Swindon.
The extent to which the values and standards of this region pervade other parts of the nation (beyond pure governmental control) is uncertain. Many areas regrettably lack the necessary resources to imitate such tastes and habits. In principle it is similar to the process which Karl Marx called *bourgeoisification.*

---

space mine *noun* a satellite equipped with an explosive device that can be made to detonate on command or on being disturbed (eg when under attack)

One example is the space mine, a satellite carrying an explosive charge, conventional or nuclear, that can be detonated on command. It could also be salvage-fused, in order to detonate when attacked or disturbed. - *New Statesman*, 1 Nov. 1985

---

space plane *or* **spaceplane** *noun* a reusable aircraft-like vehicle (eg the Space Shuttle, Hermes, or HOTOL) designed to travel at HYPERSONIC speeds and to carry satellites and other payloads into space

Europe's space plane, Hermes, will carry a set of booster

rockets to give the crew a chance of jettisoning from an aborted take off. - *New Scientist*, 10 July 1986

---

space tug *noun* ORBITAL MANOEUVRING VEHICLE

---

spaghetti war *or* **pasta war** *noun* the trade dispute between the USA and EEC in 1985–6 which led to a series of retaliatory tariff increases imposed on food imports (eg on EEC pasta exported to the USA, and on US lemons and walnuts exported to the EEC)

> The EEC and the United States have reached agreement on ending a trade dispute which threatened major international trade negotiations being held next month. ... Dubbed the 'spaghetti war', the dispute centred on the US claim that the Common Market is discriminating against US exports of citrus fruit through the series of preferential trade arrangements between Europe and a number of Mediterranean countries. - *Guardian*, 11 Aug. 1986

> America and the EEC moved towards ending their longtanding 'pasta war'. - *Economist*, 16 Aug. 1986

-speak *suffix* language peculiar to or characteristic of (a specified person, group, subject, or place), especially when considered to be equivocal or obscurantist; jargon

► One of the most popular suffixes of the decade. Possibly the most specific if not the most intriguing has been *Haigspeak*, referring to the convoluted and vacuous sayings of General Alexander Haig, President Reagan's first Secretary of State.
The ending has even been coupled with dates, as in: 'Sir Alan Walters, one time political adviser for Mrs Thatcher, did stick with 1979-*speak* (*New Statesman*, 5 Sept. 1986), referring to the political logic of the first Thatcher election.
Oick is a strangely antiquated word to spawn a new compound. It was (independent) schoolboy slang in the inter-war years for a common boy. It derives from *oickman* (= a labourer). Both the word and its origins are derogatory. *Oick* no longer survives except in the dialogue of overdrawn TV plays about public schools.
Some of the compounds refer to quite well-established vocabularies, such as *Marinespeak*. This imitation of naval language is nothing new, although it has been given boosts of publicity from occurrences such as the Falklands war or Prince Edward's marine service.

> **catalogue-speak** the language typical of catalogues

> It's no good changing the catalogue-speak if the works themselves are still entangled in vacuous, modern self-consciousness. - *New Statesman*, 25 April 1986

> **computerspeak** information recorded in a form usable by a computer; machine language

> The drawings were digitised ... with information about

distances and size converted into computerspeak. - *Sunday Times*, 1 June 1986

Hand in glove with fibre optics is ... digital transmission - sending spoken or picture messages coded as the ones and zeros of computerspeak. - *Economist*, 23 Aug. 1986

dp-speak the jargon of computer users

A prototype suggests that what we've got is a pre-production model of the real thing. In dp-speak, a 'prototype' is the real thing. It is a real solution, giving real productivity. - *Datalink*, 2 June 1986

econospeak the jargon of economists

This stickiness in wages - 'hysteresis' in econospeak - baffles and disappoints Mrs Thatcher's government. - *Economist*, 9 Aug. 1986

educationspeak the jargon of educationalists

Like the dialect of some mountain tribe cut off from the plains, 'educationspeak' seems to be becoming ever more remote from the speech of ordinary people. - *Daily Telegraph*, 15 Feb. 1986

Marinespeak the jargon of the Royal Marines

One more thing the Prince [Edward] will need to know is Marinespeak. Food will be 'scran' and a night out in a local pub will be a 'run ashore'. - *Daily Telegraph*, 9 Aug. 1986

oickspeak the language of uncouth and ill-educated people

Sloppiness is, indeed, everywhere: in mispronunciation ... in dubious grammar ... and in the oickspeak of much advertising and many tabloid newspapers. - *Economist*, 24 May 1986

Radfemspeak the jargon of radical feminists

The American Radfemspeak is not so current here, but it wouldn't be impossible to hear that 'you can tell a woman centred woman by her friendship network'. - *Guardian*, 20 May 1986

robot-speak automatic and insensitive language

The government's economic policy had failed, but they were 'too callous or too blinkered' to admit it, Mr Rodney Bickerstaffe ... told Congress [the TUC]. He said: ... 'Their distortion and propaganda comes out in "robot-speak"'. - *Daily Telegraph*, 4 Sept. 1986

techspeak the jargon of scientists

The steady spread through the English language of 'techspeak'... has been charted to starting effect by Edward Tenner in a new book. ... 'Tech-speak brings rigorous functional-structural description to the terrifyingly complex set of phenomena we call everyday life', says Tenner.

telespeak the jargon of people who make television programmes

For those unversed in media jargon, 'OB' is standard telespeak for an outside broadcast - British telespeak, that is. When you hear the disembodied drawl yell: 'OK guys, we'll cut the anchor here and take a stand-up before the bumper', you quickly realise that Yankee telespeak is another language altogether. - *Listener*, 31 July 1986

twitchspeak the jargon of TWITCHERS

Twitchspeak is a very curious language. Telescopes become 'scopes', binoculars 'bins', and you don't see a bird - you 'have' it or 'twitch' it. - *Listener*, 4 July 1985

---

specialogue *noun* a catalogue advertising goods aimed at a specific specialized market

'Targetting' and 'precision marketing' are the current buzzwords. But if the new look 'specialogues' with the feel of the finest fashion magazines and enticing titles are bringing in the young smart money 90 per cent of sales still come from the reinforced D-cup corselette brigade who like to try things on in the privacy of their own home. - *Daily Mail*, 7 July 1986

---

specism *noun* prejudice or discrimination on the grounds of species

Specism is the word for it; the way human beings suppose that their fellow mammals are that much brighter than the birds. It is not clear why cuddly looks and suckling young ones should make it all right to look down on beakiness and laying eggs. - *New Scientist*, 10 Oct. 1985

► A shorter form of the established term *speciesism*, which originated in the mid-1970s. Opponents of specism appear throughout the political spectrum. They note that victimizing other people is almost universally frowned on and consider that animals have rights similar to human beings. Some believe that violence is justified to attain their ends.
An example of anti-specist activity is the campaign by the International Fund for Animal Welfare against the eating of dogs and cats.

---

specist *noun* someone who displays the characteristics of SPECISM

---

speckle interferometry *noun* a technique for observing distant or faint stars or those whose images are distorted by the Earth's atmosphere, in which a number of very short (0.1–0.001 second) exposures are taken in rapid succession to produce images that are made up of spots or speckles which, after processing and computer analysis, reveal the true structural details

> A study [has been made] by Dr. David J. Tholen of the Institute of Astronomy in Hawaii of the latest, most detailed observations of the Pluto-Charon systems by astronomers. ... Tholen bases his calculations on observations using 'speckle interferometry' (a way of making use of every single photon received) made in France, Germany and the United States. - *Guardian*, 22 Nov. 1985

► This technique deals with atmospheric turbulence as a result of the very quick succession of photographs freezing the interference. The term *speckle* derives from the speckles which make up the overall image.

---

spendaholic *noun* someone who spends money excessively or compulsively; a spendthrift

> Niceness can keep things going but those who don't do what is expected of them, or who go 'off the rails' often make more interesting companions. Gamblers and spendaholics would seem to come into this category. - *Over 21*, April 1986

► The *-aholic* ending originated with *alcoholic*, the condition of *alcoholism* being recognized in 1852 and the first reference to its sufferers as *alcoholics* dating from 1891.
In the last ten years or so the condition has been treated more sympathetically. Because of this, a series of words has been formed on the same model, some serious, such as *workaholic*, and some frivolous, such as *bookaholic*.
The trend for forming words in this way is now less usual. The behaviour of a spendaholic, however, is an important social phenomenon. It often results from a lack of security. It sometimes afflicts young people and often those who have been deserted by their spouse. It is not restricted to those two typical groups, of course.

---

spiroplasma *noun* any of a group of microorganisms that resemble the mycoplasma-like group of bacteria, are spirally shaped, and are found in plants and insects

> Various cunning cell-based brews have been conjured up, yet well over half the spiroplasmas require special diets that have not yet been identified. This barrier to cultivation is a galling frustration to those who would exploit this curious group of microbes in insect control. In particular, scientists in the US have been hoping for the past three years that it might be possible to turn a host-specific creature known as the Colorado Potato Beetle Spiroplasma (CPBS) into a new and better means of controlling the dreaded beetle. - *Guardian*, 10 Jan. 1986

Sport Aid *noun* a fund-raising campaign, centred on sponsored runs throughout the world in May 1986, the proceeds from which are to be divided between UNICEF and the Band Aid Trust for relief work in Africa

> Sponsors of the Sport Aid marathon said yesterday that they had no idea how much money would be raised - and appealed to the millions who took part in 78 countries to collect and pay in cash as quickly as possible. - *Daily Telegraph*, 28 May 1986

> More than 2,000 runners clocked in at Fairland Valley, Stevenage, to do their bit for Sport Aid, the third Band Aid project to be inspired by rock star turned charity supremo Bob Geldof. - *Hitchin Express*, 29 May 1986

► This was the sequel to *Band Aid*, a recording effort (Christmas 1984), and the massive global rock concert *Live Aid* (July 1985).
It took the form of great athletic exertion, including some by handicapped contributors. Many of those who took part continued to wear shirts with the legend 'I ran the World' many weeks after the event.
Its mentor, the Boomtown Rats lead-singer Bob Geldof, was awarded the KBE (honorary, as he is an Irish Citizen) in June 1986 for this and his earlier related charitable work. His achievements had been not only raising a vast sum of money, but also stimulating consciousness and awareness of the plight of the starving regions of Africa. His funds have been carefully stewarded with the intention of achieving long-term agricultural development of the relevant areas; rather than just emotive gifts for immediate needs.
Many smaller-scale fund-raising activities took place in Britain during the year. For example, the Institute of Professional Civil Servants launched *Mandarin Aid*, with the aim of raising £250,000 within five years; the Royal Academy hosted *Academy Aid* by exhibiting and selling Peter Blake's collages for the Band Aid record; and Sue Cunliffe-Lister, Lord Whitelaw's daughter, organized *Sheep Aid* to raise money through agricultural events in Yorkshire.
The *Guardian* (16 Aug.) even reported a unique *Crook Aid* scheme: burglars who robbed the London flat of a figure with underworld connections were threatened with reprisals unless they donated the proceeds of their haul to charity.

---

sprinter *noun* a new class of diesel train introduced by British Rail as a companion to PACERS

> British Rail is to restore many long-distance cross-country train services which may have been abandoned in cost-cutting measures since the 1939–45 war. A 'souped' version of the Sprinter diesel train, which is revitalising local urban and rural lines, will be used. - *Daily Telegraph*, 2 June 1986

► A sprinter is one of British Rail's new generation of fast diesel trains for provincial services. They are usually 2-car trains with underfloor power equipment and they can be driven from either end. Sprinters may be coupled together to form longer trains. The first sprinters came into service

in 1985. It is intended that, together with PACERS, they will entirely displace the old diesel multiple units (known as DMUs) during the next few years.
The name sprinter was originally applied to the fast, cross-country electrical multiple unit trains of Dutch Railways. As the term is thus borrowed from Dutch, it may be noted that several European railway companies have borrowed the term *Inter-City* from British Rail's introduction of it in the mid-1960s.

---

spritzer *noun* a drink consisting of white wine and soda water

> So, as we sip our spritzers at the Groucho, let's not be too hasty in drinking to the demise of the profession for gentlemen. - *Publishing News*, 7 June 1985

> Nowadays Chancellors prefer colourless gin-and-tonics but Lawson is said to favour 'spritzer'. ... This year though in order to present a sober, patriotic image, I understand Lawson tippled British Ashbourne Water as Mrs Thatcher is wont to do. - *Daily Telegraph*, 19 March 1986

► It derives from the German *spritzen* = (to) squirt, splash.
It is fashionable with yuppies and other like-minded groups. It has dual advantages of flexibility both in that it can reasonably be drunk at any time of day and in that the wine and the soda can be mixed in any proportions according to taste. It is particularly refreshing in hot weather. Although it is popular now and the term is new, the drink is not. It was Lord Byron's favourite cure for hangovers:
I say the future is a serious matter
And so, for God's sake, hock and soda water!
It was also favoured by Oscar Wilde, and his taste has been recorded by Sir John Betjeman in several separate lines of his 'The Arrest of Oscar Wilde at the Cadogan Hotel':
He sipped at a weak hock and seltzer
As he gazed at the London skies
....
I want some more hock in my seltzer
And Robbie, please give me your hand -
....
More hock, Robbie - where is the seltzer?
Dear boy, pull again at the bell!

SQL *noun* structured query language: a computer query language (the section of a database management system which provides facilities for the interrogation of the database) that enables applications to be written for use with a number of related databases

> Digital Equipment is following in the footsteps of mainframe database vendors, and is hiring a small US software development company to provide a Structured Query Language (SQL) interface for its recently announced

> relational database management system Rdb. IBM's SQL has already become a de facto standard query language, and is soon to be endorsed by the American National Standards Institute. - *Datalink*, 26 May 1986

---

squid *noun* a leaden puck used in the game of OCTOPUSH

SRO *noun* SELF-REGULATORY ORGANIZATION

---

stag-hunter *noun, informal* someone in a banking or broking concern who sifts applications for allotments of shares in a new issue in order to identify and reject improper applications from stags (speculators who buy newly issued shares with the intention of reselling them for quick profit)

> Four families evidently living in a single house in Swindon and sharing the same signature ... will be hurt to know that their applications went straight into the waste paper basket. More intriguing for the stag-hunters - bankers Robert Fleming - were the applications from 75 women who all had first names beginning with G and also shared a single address. - *Financial Times*, 10 Feb. 1986

► *Stag* is an extension of the Stock Exchange menagerie of bulls and bears. It is not yet in such common use, however. As privatization issues (eg TSB and British Gas are oversubscribed many times, some stags apply under pseudonyms to increase their holdings or their chances of getting any shares at all.

---

star fruit *noun* CARAMBOLA

> Prickly pear and star fruit both look rather like a cactus, but neither taste particularly exciting. - *Daily Telegraph*, 2 March 1986

---

state terrorism *noun* terrorism sponsored by a national government either inside or outside its own borders

> It is no accident that this charge of 'state terrorism' has become the latest buzzword in the US lexicon. It fits the crude theory that 'crazy states' are the reason for terrorism. But governments that use violence to muffle critics and stifle democracy haven't just dropped from the sky. These states use terrorism for one purpose: to shore up their own power. And more often than not they are directly supported or maintained by the Soviets or the Americans. - *New Internationalist*, July 1986

► It is not new for a country to sponsor and supervise subversive military activity on a neighbour's terrain for its own political ends or for the

extension of a particular political philosophy. The Chinese in Malaya and the Egyptians in Aden are illustrations.
However, it has been given a topicality by the activities of Colonel Gadaffi of Libya and the support given by the Reagan administration, albeit haltingly, to the Contra rebels in Nicaragua.
The term thrown up in this way also extends to violent techniques used by governments to silence opposition within the government's own country. The murder of Benigno Aquino in the Philippines by the Marcos regime, the methods used by the South African government during the 1986 emergency, and the domestic policies of several Latin American governments are recent examples. These procedures are not new but are possibly more brazen than formerly and are now given greater publicity by the media.

Stendhal syndrome *noun* a condition of stress and disorientation affecting tourists who are over-stimulated by visiting art galleries and other depositories of culture

> After three years study, doctors there [in Florence] have identified a new illness afflicting tourists, particularly single, middle-aged women who have lived monotonous lives. ... The ailment could be called cultural indigestion but the Florentine doctors have a fancier name for it: Stendhal Syndrome.
> - *Daily Telegraph*, 5 June 1986

► The condition is accompanied by breathlessness and a buzzing in the ears. Akin to it is the kind of disorientation which is endured by businessmen who travel to many parts of the world in quick succession, staying in international-chain hotels which are very similar in design and engaging in tense commercial discussions which are themselves very stressful.
Its name originates in the visit by Stendhal (Henri Beyle, 1783-1842) to Santa Croce, Florence on 22 January 1817 after taking in many more of the splendours of that city during the same morning. He wrote (in *Rome, Naples and Florence*): 'As I emerged from the porch of *Santa Croce*, I was seized with a fierce palpitation of the heart (the same symptom which, in Berlin, is referred to as an *attack of nerves*); the well-spring of life was dried up within me, and I walked in constant fear of falling to the ground'.

Stockholm syndrome *noun* the development by a hostage of a sympathetic and cooperative relationship with his/her captor

> In spite of the endeavours of government psychiatrists to persuade him that he is a victim of the 'Stockholm syndrome' ... Father McCloughlin remains unequivocal: if a terrorist holds innocent lives to ransom to change the policy of a democratically elected government, 'I say more power to him, if the policy is corrupt!' - *Listener*, 5 Sept. 1985

► The phenomenon was first recognized in 1973 but has only recently become widely discussed. It owes its name to a friendship which grew up between some hostages in a Swedish bank and their captors.

Another early application was the 1974 capture of the heiress Patty Hearst by Californian radicals. She took one as her lover and helped the gang in subsequent robberies.
The phenomenon was recently represented in the TV series 'The Price' in which a rich young married woman captured by the IRA formed an ambivalent relationship towards the young man who was her gaoler.
A number of hostages taken by Arab groups have indicated sympathy with their captors, for example in Beirut. However, there is difficulty, in such a sensitive situation, in determining whether these declarations suggest genuine sympathy or are the result of anxiety on behalf of those still left in captivity.

---

street hockey *noun* a game resembling ice hockey, played with a hollow plastic ball by two teams of six players on roller skates, originally taking place outdoors on a scratch basis but now increasingly as an organized indoor sport

> Kitting up for street hockey, once the initial enthusiasm is past, doesn't come cheap. The style is urban astronaut out of ice hockey and American football, white plastic helmets and visors, heavy padding. - *Listener*, 5 June 1986

► It has been played for some time in North America, but has more recently been seen in Britain. Although originally informal and impromptu, it is now becoming more formalized on both sides of the Atlantic.
The similarity to ice (as opposed to field) hockey is the result of the larger kind of stick and the wearing of padding.

---

street-proofing *noun* the skills (eg a knowledge of self-defence) which give protection against attack or molestation on the streets

> Since its founding, SAFE has counselled and taught thousands of children and their parents the fundamentals of street-proofing and has won state-wide acclaim. - *Glasgow Herald*, 4 April 1986

---

sulphoxidizer *or* **sulphoxidiser** *noun* one who can break down sulphur compounds in the body into harmless excretory products

> Some people cannot break down certain sulphur compounds, and these therefore pass unaltered into the urine. This girl was one of these so called poor sulphoxidisers but she was unable to excrete sulphur containing breakdown products of garlic. - *The Times*, 6 March 1986

---

sunblock *noun* a substance, such as a cream, which is applied to the skin to protect it from harmful ultraviolet rays

> It is not, of course, news that we should use a sunblock every day, but Kligman is alarmed that despite this knowledge we ignore the advice. - *Observer*, 4 May 1986

---

super- *prefix* higher in quantity, quality, or degree than the norm; surpassing all or most others of its kind

► This prefix's heyday was in the late 1970s when it was boosted by advertising and public relations hyperbole, such as the description of Olivia Newton John as a *superstar* for her performance in the film musical *Grease* (Paramount, 1978), an ephemeral box-office success.
To some extent it has been replaced as a superlative by MEGA-, but its overuse remains evident enough to prompt a parody by a writer in the *New Scientist* who reported that 'the supercost of supercomputers spells out superbusiness and this is heralded by misleading superhypes'. Now there are signs that *giga-* is emerging to outdo both *super-* and *mega-*.
A selection of self-explanatory SUPER- compounds appears below; more important terms have their own entries in alphabetical order.

> **superagent** A row is brewing over the International Air Transport Association's plan to offer bigger commissions ... to 'superagents' who invest heavily in automation and marketing and so take more of the travel-selling load off the airlines themselves. - *Economist*, 5 July 1986

> **supercentre** The decision by the Science and Engineering Research Council last week to move the Royal Greenwich Observatory to Cambridge University will create a 'supercentre' for astronomy that will be unrivalled in Britain. - *New Scientist*, 26 June 1986

> **supercop** Telly supercops Dempsey and Makepeace have blown away their smash-hit show - by asking for king-sized pay rises. - *News of the World*, 4 May 1986

> **super-fixer** Disembarking from every international flight landing at Johannesburg's Jan Smuts Airport ... are an increasing number of middle-men, crisply-dressed, keen-eyed super-fixers looking for any opportunity to profit from any form of sanctions that may be imposed on South Africa. - *Daily Telegraph*, 14 July 1986

> **supergran** Supergran Hazel Woodman ... who fostered more than 100 children, has suffered a mild stroke. But she still hopes to visit London to pick up a magazine's £500 Supergran prize. - *Daily Express*, 30 Jan. 1986

> **supergrass** Steve Long and Marion Bingham, of the biological sciences department at Essex University ... have identified 200 species of grass which photosynthesise as efficiently as tropical species, yet can withstand severe winters. ... Long's group is now testing the supergrasses in pilot trials at four sites during the next three years. - *New Scientist*, 21 Aug. 1986

> **superhod** Superhod Maxi Quarterman has told his children the secret of his £1 million will - they will not get a penny. ... Grafter Maxi 44, who earned his title from his king-sized hod

and wage-packet, is determined that Lee, 22, Angeline, 21, and Emma 16, will not become spoilt, super-rich layabouts. - *Sun*, 22 Jan. 1986

superpill Scientists at the Chemical Defence Establishment, at Porton Down, Wilts., are working on a 'superpill' ... which would allow troops to fight through a normally lethal nerve gas attack largely unaffected by the deadly chemicals. - *Daily Telegraph*, 11 June 1986

super-retailer Successful retailers ... are saying that what goods are sold, and how, matters at least as much as where they are sold. ... More contentiously, they are also saying that retailing skills are transferable - that a successful seller of Walkmen is likely to prove as good at selling books or furniture or suits. This cult of the super-retailer has gone furthest in Britain, the nation of shopkeepers. - *Economist*, 28 June 1986

super-rich see SUPERHOD

superthug The Popplewell report ... hits at the 'superthug' who avoids alcohol in order to keep a clear head for violence. - *Daily Express*, 17 Jan. 1986

superwalker [caption] The long march: superwalker Bruce Kent sets a furious pace. - *The Times*, 11 July 1986

superweapon The 'Stinger' anti-aircraft missile supplied to Afghan and Angolan rebels ... is too complicated for many guerrillas to use. ... The shoulder-fired missile 'superweapon' is 'unnecessarily difficult' to handle even for many fully-trained American soldiers, says a study by the army's research institute. - *Daily Telegraph*, 25 Aug. 1986

superyob A sinister new breed of thug is menacing Britain's football terraces - the Superyob. ... Once they have sneaked past police into the gounds, the superyobs have just one aim - to beat the hell out of rival supporters. - *Sun*, 17 Jan. 1986

---

superbug *noun* any of various microorganisms whose biochemistry and metabolism enable them to survive harsh or adverse environments: eg **a** a species of bacterium that is resistant to one or more antibiotics **b** a species of bacterium that lives in hot sulphuric acid springs

The medics had contributed to the development of resistant strains by over-prescribing of antibiotics anyway. The hapless nursing sister charged with eradicating this superbug from the hospital had to go about her work with the stealth of a stalker and the tact of a priest. - *Guardian*, 4 Feb. 1986

Horikoshi's team is scouring very hot, salty or alkaline places all over the world for other 'superbugs'. These are defined as having new abilities, like halophilicity, which are of potential use to industry. One possible application is in biocomputing because the bacterium can remain active in the presence of high salinity, whereas a normal cell would be too fragile for such an environment. - *New Scientist*, 31 July 1986

---

super-chip *noun* a very powerful chip containing many integrated circuits

Sir Clive Sinclair is again trying to launch his super-chip for computers. ... The first chip is to be a 'memory device for business computers'. The device is 'wafer-scale integration' which uses dozens of chips on a single slice of silicon. - *Daily Telegraph*, 8 July 1986

---

supercomputer *noun* any of a class of very powerful computers that are capable of performing at a rate of several million FLOPS and are used for repeated calculation cycles on vast amounts of data (e g for weather forecasting or predicting how a nuclear bomb will explode)

Supercomputers are a rare breed of machine. They have the same relationship to conventional commercial computers that Formula One racing cars have to the humble family saloon. - *Financial Times*, 10 April 1986

---

supercomputing *noun* the action, process, or use of SUPERCOMPUTERS

What network of processors was best for supercomputing? Connecting every processor to every other processor is an obvious solution but the costs rule it out - even in the rarified atmosphere of supercomputing. - *Financial Times*, 10 April 1986

---

superfit *noun* someone who is bursting with health and vitality and who works hard at maintaining his/her fitness, eg by eating natural foods and taking regular exercise

DMG&B warned its clients that a full 17 per cent of the population, described as the opinion-forming Superfits, had now taken up the gospel [of FOODISM]. - *Guardian*, 4 July 1986

---

superovulate *verb* to produce several mature eggs in the ovary simultaneously, usually as a result of drug therapy during treatment for infertility

---

superovulation *noun* the act, process, or result of SUPEROVULATING

The idea behind this 'superovulation' is that the more eggs that are available for fertilisation in the laboratory and

> transfer to the womb, the better the chances of ending up with a baby. - *New Scientist*, 3 July 1986

---

supersheep *noun* a sheep which is immunized against SOMATOSTATIN, its growth-inhibiting substance, in order to make it grow faster and become larger

> Some St Kilda lambs at Langford have put on weight nearly twice as quickly as usual and grown larger too. These 'supersheep' develop longer bones, and this in turn means that they have more of the muscle protein which we consumers recognize as meat. - *Guardian*, 31 Jan. 1986

---

supertitle *noun* SURTITLE

---

suramin *noun* a drug that inhibits the activity of the enzyme reverse transcriptase, and that has therefore been used against the RETROVIRUS that causes AIDS

> Bayer, a German pharmaceutical company, developed suramin (Germanin) in the 1920s as a treatment for trypanosomiasis (sleeping sickness) in Africa. In 1979, scientists noticed that, in the laboratory, suramin could block reverse transcriptase in retroviruses that attack animals. Because people have taken suramin for decades. and because we know a great deal about its spectrum of toxicity, the drug was an excellent candidate for treating AIDS. - *New Scientist*, 2 Jan. 1986

---

surface mounting *noun* a technique for connecting processor chips, memory chips, or other components, in which all necessary wires are contained in a ceramic substrate and connections are made with solder through a specially pierced coating of quartz on the chips

> Surface mounting is commonly used these days, especially by the Japanese, but IBM was a pioneer. Conventionally, processor and memory chips are connected to the outside world by fine gold wires. ... IBM has done away with all that. - *Financial Times*, 6 May 1986

---

surtitle *or* **supertitle** *noun* a translation of the dialogue of an opera or play which is projected onto a screen above the stage

> The Royal Opera House is to risk offending purists among its clientele next season by screening English 'Surtitles' to some of its opera productions which it performs in the original language. - *Daily Telegraph*, 23 June 1986

---

swap *noun* a financial transaction in which two borrowers exchange their debt payments (either interest or principal) in such a way that both can gain from having their debts in a different currency or a different structure

> Internationalisation has underpinned the fastest growing

> financial business of the moment - swaps. ... Estimates suggest that its volume grew to around $150 billion in 1985 from $50 billion in 1984 and only $5 billion in 1983. - *Economist*, 7 June 1986

Swimathon *noun* see -ATHON

---

taco *noun* a tortilla which is filled (eg with meat), then rolled or folded and fried

► Thc dish - a slight misnomer in view of its informal service - originates in Mexico. There it seems to have both the simplicity of preparation and the role of a pasty in Cornwall. It is a close relation of the BURRITO. In Mexico there are two kinds; *tacos suaves*, which are just rolled up and eaten, and *tacos dorados*, which are pinned together and fried. As with the BURRITO, the range of fillings is virtually limitless. Among the most common are chilli, pepper and onion (*tacos de rajas*), and chicken (*tacos de pollo*).

Tae Kwon Do *or* **taekwondo** *noun* an Oriental system of self-defence, developed in Korea, that features kicking and punching and resembles karate

---

Taffy *noun* Technologically-advanced Family: a relatively affluent and well-educated family, owning a home computer and other electronic devices

> American word-coiners ... have come up with a new one: 'Taffies' - Technologically-advanced families. The neologism is offered by Prof. William Oates of the journalism department at the University of North Carolina. - *Daily Telegraph*, 19 April 1986

---

tangor *noun* a cross between an orange and a tangerine

> Topaz Jaffarines or Tangors, as the larger ones are known, are a cross between an orange and a tangerine. They're easy peelers and have a distinctive aromatic flavour. - *Living*, Sept. 1986

---

tanky *noun, British slang* a member of the British Communist Party who supports official Soviet policy

> The long-running row between the Euro-Communists who control the British Communist Party and the pro-Moscow 'tankies' continues. - *Daily Telegraph*, 7 June 1986

► Possibly so-called because they support the movement of Soviet tanks into Czechoslovakia, Afghanistan, and elsewhere?

---

tartrazine *noun* a yellow dye, $C_{16}H_9N_4Na_3O_9S_2$, used in foods and drugs

> Tartrazine, the yellow colouring that has for years coloured bread crumbs on fishfingers, made ice-cream yellow and fizzy drinks orange, is being removed by various manufacturers because it is believed to be responsible for hyperactivity in children and other allergic reactions. - *Daily Telegraph*, 5 June 1986

Taurus *noun* a computerized system for transferring and registering shares, without the need for share certificates, on the London Stock Exchange

> The 'dematerialisation' of share certificates is now scheduled for early 1989, using a new system called Taurus which is under development at an expected cost of £6 million. - *Guardian*, 22 May 1986

► The word is an acronym of *T*ransfer and *Au*tomated *R*egistration of *U*ncertificated *S*tock.
The system replaces certificates and produces electronic entries on companies' registers of members. It simplifies transfer of stocks, reduces costs, and removes security problems for safe storage of certificates.

Taxicard *noun* a scheme allowing disabled people in London to use taxis at a reduced rate

---

T dress *noun* a long T-shirt worn as a dress

> Everyone is into T dresses this season, from designers to chain stores. Betty Jackson and Katharine Hamnett style form-fitting T shirt Dresses that fit like a glove. - *Daily Telegraph*, 8 May 1986

T dressing *noun* the wearing of T DRESSES

> What is needed is a look that bridges the awkward fashion gap between the indifferent now and (hopefully) long, hot summer. T dressing is the answer: that most basic of weekend wear, the T shirt, taken to extreme lengths and turned into a smart dress. - *Daily Telegraph*, 8 May 1986

---

teaser *noun* an advertisement designed to stimulate interest while usually withholding some information, eg a very short TV commercial which is part of or related to a longer commercial which will be shown in a later advertisement break

> Cadbury could now spend heavily on advertising with complete confidence, and spend they did at a national equivalent of £6 million. The launch comprised of [sic] 10 second teaser commercials followed by three 40 second TV commercials and a massive poster campaign. - *Financial Times*, 11 March 1986

---

technical office protocol *noun* (*abbreviation* **TOP**) a scheme to standardize the manufacture of computer systems concerned with the coordination of functions carried out by design and engineering offices

> The demonstration includes two standard systems: MAP for shop floor link-ups and the Technical Office Protocol (TOP) which is concerned with communications between backroom computer systems used to monitor and manage production and produce design drawings. - *New Scientist*, 7 Nov. 1985

► The development of Technical Office Protocol is led by Boeing Computer Services. Just as General Motors' MANUFACTURING AUTOMATION PROTOCOL (MAP) brings tools and processes together, so TOP will coordinate word processing, diaries, drawing boards, and so on.

---

technobattle *noun* a conflict involving technology; *specifically* competition between rival technological systems to gain acceptance as the standard

> Europe and Japan are waging a technobattle over how best to provide the public with top-quality television pictures in the 1990s. - *Economist*, 26 July 1986

---

technofear *noun* fear or distrust of technology, especially of computers

> Many people shun electronic mail due to 'technofear'. - *Guardian*, 15 May 1986

---

technofreak *noun, informal* someone with an enthusiastic interest in technology, especially in computers

> Steve Braidwood reports on the latest haunt of technofreaks: the zany world of computer bulletin boards. - *Observer*, 4 May 1986

---

technophobe *noun* someone afflicted with TECHNOFEAR

> Terrorists now see a potential reservoir of support among the more extreme 'technophobes' who have been attracted to the Green Party. - *New Scientist*, 17 July 1986

---

technophobia *noun* TECHNOFEAR

> 'Technophobia has disappeared' says Mr Stanley - people are

no longer frightened of computers. – *Daily Telegraph*, 15 Sept. 1986

---

technopole *noun* a place which is a centre for industries and businesses manufacturing and dealing in high-technology equipment

► This seems to be a buzzword in high-tech business circles. Two recent publications bear the resounding titles *Science Parks Technopoles and Innovation Centres* and *France and her Technopoles.* The word is an anglicization of the earlier *technopolis*, whose main sense is 'a society dominated by and dependent upon technology'.

---

techno-politics *noun* the use of computers to help organize and monitor a political campaign, e g by storing lists of party members or calculating expenses

> All of the major parties have become involved with 'techno-politics'. ... In computer politics, the Conservative Party has been in the lead for a number of years. Their ICL ME29 mainframe ... serves the central office in a number of increasingly sophisticated office, finance and database functions. – *Guardian*, 8 May 1986

---

technostress *noun* stress brought about by too much involvement with technology, especially with computers

> One possible justifiable reason for not recruiting over-35s is the possibility of what was once termed programmer burn-out – technostress. ... It can be cured by greater involvement with people and less involvement with computers. – *Datalink*, 26 May 1986

---

techspeak *noun* see -SPEAK

---

teddy bear syndrome *noun* the tendency to enter into marriage or a similar relationship for the emotional comfort of having someone to hold and cuddle, thus curing one's loneliness, rather than for deeper, more meaningful reasons

> The Teddy Bear Syndrome was cited as a reason yesterday for the break-up of four in ten of Britain's second marriages. Mrs Audrey Baker, a marriage guidance counsellor, said people whose first marriage failed often used their new partners as a child used a teddy bear. – *Daily Telegraph*, 6 June 1986

---

tekky *noun, informal* a TECHNOFREAK

> The electronic mail service needs, it seems, carriage returns every 60 characters or so, or else it cuts stuff off mid-flow. ... Now any 'tekky' would have known that. But why should the ordinary user have to have that problem? – *Listener*, 20 March 1986

---

telebanking *noun* a financial service which enables the client to manage his/her banking electronically, via a television or home computer

> Telebanking is the financial service on Prestel which is of the widest appeal - and is also probably the least satisfactory. - *Investors Chronicle*, 13 June 1986

---

telecommute *verb* to work from home, using electronic mail to communicate with clients and a central office

> The office tower-blocks of the city centres will be deserted as the workers 'tele-commute' out in the suburbs. There is even a theory that this way we will compete with the Japanese. - *Guardian*, 13 March 1986

---

teledrivel *noun* the product of TELEVISIONIZING

---

telemarketing *noun* the practice of telephoning companies or individuals to try to sell them something; telephone selling

> In the operations room of BT's tele-marketing service in Victoria, London, a team of young people spend their days dialling thousands of subscribers and pumping out a smooth line in immaculately-scripted sales talk. - *Daily Telegraph*, 10 June 1986

---

teleport *noun* an area (eg in a house) designed to be a place where a computer is kept and used for TELEWORKING.

---

teleshopping *noun* **1** a service whereby customers can make an order by telephone for goods to be delivered **2** a service whereby customers can order goods chosen from product information screened on a VDU

> Stores and mail order companies taking space in the magazine ... will provide a tele-shopping number, and a courier service to deliver goods - purchased by credit card - either the same or following day. - *Guardian*, 11 June 1986

> A pioneering teleshopping experiment in Gateshead, Tyne and Wear, is to be replicated, initially at one town in the south of England. ... At 10 focal points around Gateshead those who have difficulty in getting to shops ... can make up a list from screened information and place their orders. These are then delivered to the centres at no extra charge. - *The Times*, 11 April 1986

---

telespeak *noun* see -SPEAK

---

teletrivance *or* **teletriviance** *noun* the act of TELEVISIONIZING

---

teletrive *verb* TELEVISIONIZE

> John Naughton ... proposed the word 'televisionize' to describe what television does to its subject matter. ... His coinage appears, in fact, to be critically neutral. ... I [Alan Roberts] will risk a counter-suggestion and offer 'teletrive'; from 'contrive' and perhaps suggesting 'trivialise'. ... The worst results of teletrivance (or teletriviance) could then be described, via a small mutation, as 'teledrivel'. – *Listener*, 14 Aug. 1986

---

televisionize *or* **televisionise** *verb* to adapt an event or activity in order to make it suitable for television coverage

> There ought to be a word for what television does to its subject-matter. 'Televise' clearly won't do; I therefore propose 'televisionise'. ... Televisionising involves simplification and vulgarisation of the more subtle points of a game. It involves perverting the natural schedule of sporting events in order to fit them into programme slots. It requires that leading performers in the sport become actors and clowns, with the result that their activities off the field of play become at least as newsworthy as their progress on it. – *Listener*, 7 Aug. 1986

---

teleworking *noun* TELECOMMUTING

> 'Teleworking' is the coming thing, and in California they are building homes with 'teleports' where there used to be a study. – *Daily Mail*, 10 Sept. 1986

---

theme park *noun* an amusement park in which the structures and settings are all based on a specific theme (e g space travel)

> Scotland's premier year-round resort, combining five hotels with a near-olympic-sized swimming pool, a huge ice rink ... and a theme park with various rides and activities for children. – *Daily Telegraph*, 8 Feb. 1986

► The concept is seen in one of its most successful and pronounced forms in Disneyland and Disneyworld in the USA. The theme is obvious and is consistently followed.

Theoretically the enterprise concerned provides a wide range of facilities in amplification of the stated theme and all are covered by a single comprehensive entry fee. For example, Pleasurewood Hills in Suffolk follows an American theme and Camelot, strangely in Lancashire, follows an Arthurian theme somewhat generously interpreted.

Other establishments have borrowed the term *theme park* and – although they frequently provide admirable entertainment – the theme is often obscured or lost.

---

third generation *adjective* of or being a range of nuclear weapons that includes KINETIC ENERGY WEAPONS (e g hypervelocity guns) and DIRECTED ENERGY WEAPONS (e g lasers, radio-frequency devices, and PARTICLE BEAM WEAPONS)

> Although President Reagan has repeatedly referred to Star

> Wars as 'non-nuclear', large sums have been set aside in the Department of Energy budget for testing so-called 'third generation' nuclear weapons in addition to tests on first and second generation atom and hydrogen devices. These third generation systems include X-ray lasers, hyper-velocity pellets, microwaves, particle beams and optical lasers. - *Guardian*, 22 April 1986

---

third market *or* **third tier market** *noun* a market on the London Stock Exchange, opening in 1986, run by dealers in shares (eg those qualifying for the Business Expansion Scheme) that are not dealt in on either the main market or the Unlisted Securities Market (USM)

> Look at the boom in management buyouts, in business start-ups, in the Unlisted Securities Market, in the new 'third market' to be started later this year by the Stock Exchange. - *Guardian*, 24 June 1986

> The latest initiative from The Stock Exchange to create a third tier market is perhaps the most important development in the raising of equity capital for high risk new ventures since the introduction of Business Expansion Scheme relief three years ago. - *Business Success*, July/Aug. 1986

---

thought processor *noun* OUTLINE PROCESSOR

Tientsin pear *noun* a firm thin-skinned pale yellow pear from China, having a crisp texture and much juice

---

titanium nickelide *noun* an alloy of titanium and nickel that is used orthopaedically in splints to treat curvature of the spine, mend fractures, etc, and also in bras that return to their original shape when worn.

> Physicists at Tomsk State University's Siberian Physical Technical Institute have developed uses for titanium nickelide alloys which are dramatically changing the face of orthopaedic surgery in the Soviet Union. These alloys have the peculiar characteristic of straightening out at temperatures between 35 and 40°C - the temperature of the human body. - *New Scientist*, 12 June 1986

---

tobacco teabag *noun, informal* a sachet containing tobacco for chewing

> Maureen Cramb, from the health service union Cohse, told delegates the 'tobacco teabags' could cause mouth cancer and called for a campaign to ban them. - *Glasgow Herald*, 23 April 1986

---

toe-divider *noun* a device for keeping the toes apart, especially to prevent smudging of nail varnish applied to the toenails, that typically consists of a piece of foam rubber shaped like the head of a rake

> The star [George Hamilton], when sunbathing like a lizard in

the Californian sun, wears 'toe-dividers' in order to ensure that the white bits are toasted to the same brown as his torso. - *Star*, 13 Jan. 1986

---

tombstone *noun* a one-off payment made by a soon-to-be-abolished council to a favoured project or institution

The Westminster council, fronting for other aggrieved London boroughs, has challenged the Greater London Council tombstones. It lost the first round, won the second and the case is now with the House of Lords. - *Listener*, 3 April 1986

In a lightning court action the LRB [London Residuary Body] managed to retrieve £45 million directed to GLC housing renovation by Livingstone's 'tombstone funding' techniques, designed to commit the authority's funds after formal abolition. - *Illustrated London News*, Sept. 1986

---

tootsie roll *noun, US slang* BLACK TAR

TOP *noun* TECHNICAL OFFICE PROTOCOL

Tortilla Curtain *noun* the fence along parts of the US–Mexico border, designed to keep out illegal Mexican immigrants

There [at El Paso] the Americans erected ... seven miles of the indestructible Tortilla Curtain. 'But our indestructible fence has been destroyed,' said my guide, and so it had, with steel cutters and welding torches. - *Guardian*, 26 Aug. 1986

---

total quality management *noun* (*abbreviation* **TQM**) a technique in business management that seeks to involve staff at all levels in improving the quality and competitiveness of their products or services

How is 'total quality management' different from any of the buzz-word techniques ... which over the past decade have been introduced into many companies on both sides of the Atlantic with varying degrees of success? ... Every individual in a company has a role to play in improving quality on the job, and the programme is initiated from the executive level, where specific objectives are identified and filtered down. ... A typical TQM programme requires approximately 18 months in operation before its benefits will be realised. - *Financial Times*, 1 Aug. 1986

---

touchpad *noun* an electronic device comprising a small pad on which are keys, buttons, etc for remotely controlling a piece of equipment

A revolutionary computer-controlled household burglar alarm was unveiled in London yesterday. ... According to the designers: 'The householder controls the whole system from a small portable touchpad, which can be operated from anywhere within the house.' – *The Times*, 26 Feb. 1986

TQM *noun* TOTAL QUALITY MANAGEMENT

---

trainman *noun* someone who drives and/or carries out guard's duties on a train

The final productivity improvement is the so-called 'trainman' concept, with which BR will seek to abolish demarcation lines between drivers and guards. No attempt is to be made to introduce it until all other productivity issues have been resolved. – *Daily Telegraph*, 20 May 1986

---

transportable *adjective or noun* (of or being) a self-contained mains-powered microcomputer designed to be carried from place to place

Although the hard-disc Compaq Plus transportable has been around for some time, Olivetti delayed the launch of its hard-disc M-21 until it was satisfied that the delicate mechanics were sufficiently protected against the rigours of being treated like an item of luggage at Heathrow. – *Practical Computing*, March 1986

---

transputer *noun* a powerful microprocessor chip developed as the building block for SUPERCOMPUTERS, that comprises a 32-bit microprocessor containing the equivalent of 200000 transistors condensed onto a piece of silicon 9 millimetres square and capable of handling 10 MIPS

Computers no bigger than a suitcase yet powerful enough to model a nuclear explosion or to plot Voyager's path to Neptune – not a dream, but something that is possible with existing technology. Indeed, prototypes for such machines exist. Based on a new type of microprocessor chip, known as a transputer, these prototypes cost a fraction of the price of a supercomputer. – *New Scientist*, 20 March 1986

The term 'transputer' reflects this new device's ability to be used as a system building block. The word is derived from 'transistor' and 'computer', since the transputer is both a computer on a chip and a silicon component like a transistor. – *Transputer Architecture* (*Inmos Pamphlet*), Sept. 1985

---

trans-racial fostering *noun* the adoption of black children by white foster parents

The lexicon of social work has acquired a new term: trans-racial fostering. ... And you're going to be hearing more of it because there's growing controversy about the banning of such adoptions by a number of local authorities acting under pressure from radical black social workers. – *Listener*, 12 June 1986

---

triple glazing *noun* a system of glazing in which three panes of glass are separated by air spaces providing heat and sound insulation

> In Scandinavia and West Germany triple glazing is commonplace and the best glass includes a protective film to retain heat inside a garden room. - *Financial Times*, 26 Feb. 1986

---

triple-witching *adjective* of or happening at TRIPLE-WITCHING HOUR

> Chicago Board Options Exchange spokesman Robert A. Bassi says that investors can actually cash in on the triple-witching frenzy. - *USA Today*, 21 June 1986

---

triple-witching hour *noun* the last hour of trading on the New York stock exchange on the four annual days (the third Friday of March, June, September, and December) when contracts expire simultaneously on futures, options on indexes, and options on many individual stocks

> Concern about a weak U.S. economy and Friday's 'triple-witching hour' ... had investors anxiously awaiting the final hour of trading, analysts said. - *International Herald Tribune*, 21-22 June 1986

> The triple-witching hour throws the New York Stock Exchange and the Chicago Mercantile Exchange into turmoil. Closing the contracts can mean massive trades in common-or-garden shares as well as the futures and options based upon them. - *Economist*, 28 June 1986

---

trisuit *noun* a close-fitting one-piece garment for triathlon competitors, that consists of shorts and sleeveless or short-sleeved top in a shiny stretchy material

---

trithiadiazepine *noun* any of a class of aromatic organic chemical compounds (eg BENZOTRITHIADIAZEPINE) whose structure contains a 7-membered ring comprising two carbon atoms and three sulphur atoms alternating with two nitrogen atoms

> Ever since August Kekulé coined the term in 1865, to describe the special stability of benzene and its derivatives, aromaticity has fascinated organic chemists. Now 120 years later, a new class of compounds, called trithiadiazepines, has been synthesised. Kekulé would have had difficulty recognising these compounds as aromatic, but they confirm more than 50 years of theoretical speculation about aromatic compounds. Moreover, benzotrithiadiazepine could be one of the growing band of new non-metallic conductors that currently fascinate the electronics industry. - *New Scientist*, 26 Sept. 1985

---

tunnelling current *noun* the flow of electrons produced by applying a voltage between the probe and a sample under investigation in a

SCANNING TUNNELLING MICROSCOPE, that is used to measure surface complexities of the sample

---

twin-tracking *noun, British informal* the practice of serving simultaneously as an employee of one local authority and as a councillor on another local authority

> The committee of inquiry headed by Mr David Widdicombe, QC, says senior council officials should not be allowed to become councillors on other local authorities. ... The ban on 'twin tracking' ... would generally affect local government officers earning about £12,000 a year or more. – *Daily Telegraph*, 20 June 1986

---

twitch *verb, informal* **1** to be or act as a TWITCHER **2** to observe (a bird)

► There are various theories to account for this term. One suggests that it derives from *ticker*, since the ornithologists would tick, on a list, the name of the bird observed. Another implies that the birdwatchers twitched by moving from one observation position to another.
Twitch and *twitcher* have been used within an inner circle of birdwatchers for about 30 years, but have not been known to the uninitiated until recently. Once derogatory, they are now neutral in tone.

---

twitcher *noun, informal* a fervent or obsessive bird-watcher

---

twitchspeak *noun* see -SPEAK

---

two-earner *adjective* of or being a family or household where two members are in paid employment

> The majority of two-earner households will see their combined tax allowances reduced from the equivalent of two and a half times the single allowance ... to just two single allowances. – *Daily Telegraph*, 2 Jan. 1986
> At present, a two-earner couple receives $2\frac{1}{2}$ times a single person's tax allowance. – *Economist*, 15 Feb. 1986

UDF *noun* UNDUCTED FAN ENGINE

> During 100 hours of testing on the ground ... the UDF produced more than 25,000 lb of thrust while consuming less fuel than any jet engine. – *Economist*, 30 Aug. 1986

---

ultra-orthodox *adjective* extremely orthodox; of or belonging to an extreme wing of an orthodox group, especially within the Jewish community

> Advertising posters in Israel showing a pretty girl in a swimsuit are to be withdrawn after a campaign by the ultra-orthodox community. ... The girl in the swimsuit, part of an advertising campaign, has adorned bus shelters for months. This immodesty enraged the ultra-orthodox community, which set about burning down or defacing the bus shelters, causing more than £160,000 damage in Jerusalem alone. - *The Times*, 5 June 1986

► This word was used in its general sense by Pusey in 1830, but it had only a shadowy existence in the language until recent conflict between Orthodox and secular elements in Israel gave it prominence.
One ultra-orthodox Jewish community in Jerusalem, known as Naturei Karta, does not even recognize the state of Israel. People driving cars in their quarter of the town on the Sabbath risk having their vehicles stoned.

---

ultra-tech *adjective or noun* (of or being) the most advanced technology

> Beyond high-tech in the industrial spectrum lies ultra-tech - today a mere multi-billion-dollar stripling of a business, but by the year 2000 potentially a trillion-dollar leviathan. - *Economist*, 23 Aug. 1986

---

underclass *noun* the lowest class of society, usually characterized by poverty, poor education, social instability, and a low level of personal ambition and aspiration

> In the inner cities the United States is developing an underclass perhaps 5m–7m strong in which poverty is handed on from generation to generation. - *Economist*, 15 March 1986

> The starting point for most revisionist thinking about welfare has been the belated discovery of a largely black underclass, hooked on welfare and worse. ... For the past six months this underclass has rivalled AIDS and cocaine as an object of morbid press contemplation. - *Economist*, 5 July 1986

► This sounds like a translation of a German sociological term. But its roots may go much further back: 'a government of the under classes by the upper on a principle of *let-alone* is no longer possible in England in these days' (Thomas Carlyle, *Chartism*, 1839).

---

unducted fan engine *noun* (*abbreviation* **UDF**) PROPFAN 1

---

unfriendliness *noun* the state or condition of being UNFRIENDLY

---

unfriendly *adjective, of a computer system, piece of software, etc* not user-friendly

> One problem ... was that my client had read various articles. ...

'All the journalists say Unix is not suitable for micros or for business, it's too unfriendly.' - *Guardian*, 6 Feb. 1986

► This covers everything which computers were before efforts were made to make them FRIENDLY by such means as WINDOWS.

---

ureteroscope *noun* a device for locating, observing, and treating stones in the urinary tract, that consists of a tubular structure containing optical fibres along which laser pulses are sent to shatter the stones, and a basket-like structure in which the stones are captured and their fragments removed

The patient is given either a general or a spinal anaesthetic, then the urologist inserts a device, known as a uretersocope, into the ureter. - *New Scientist*, 12 June 1986

---

user-hostile *adjective* USER-UNFRIENDLY

The typical electronic mail service is pretty user-hostile, requiring awkward and some complicated sign-on messages, and not particularly logical commands. - *Daily Telegraph*, 14 April 1986

► This rather silly over-statement could be replaced by USER-UNFRIENDLY. It is an abuse of the metaphor to suggest that the machine is going to be actually aggressive, notwithstanding various fanciful American films aimed at teenage audiences to that effect, *War Games* (MGM/UA, 1985).

---

user-unfriendly *adjective* not user-friendly

Anyone who has tugged heavy hand baggage down endless airport corridors, or waited for a delayed flight in a sterile lounge will know how user-unfriendly many airports are in design terms. - *Daily Telegraph*, 11 March 1986

---

vacusage *noun* a suction treatment applied to the skin to break down fatty tissue

On the first morning, I was confused with a Mrs Budd and given her treatment slip. ... At 8.30am, there was the mysterious word 'vacusage'. This sounded like a form of torture invented by the French Revolution. - *Guardian*, 4 July 1986

Vals *noun* a PSYCHOGRAPHIC system of classifying people in social groups according to their values and lifestyles, as revealed by their responses to a set of standard questions

> Nato strategists ... have considered using Vals research. ... A version was used during both Mr Reagan's presidential campaigns and it is currently being used by the Bush campaign for the Presidency. – *The Times*, 5 Aug. 1986

► See note at BELONGER

VAN *noun* value-added network: a communication service that uses common carrier networks for transmission and provides added data services (eg storing and forwarding messages) with separate individual equipment

> Leighfield's [Istel's chairman] computer insurance scheme is only one aspect of Istel's innovative work, which also includes automation and the private data networks known as value-added networks (Vans). – *Sunday Times*, 1 June 1986

---

vegeboom *noun, informal* the growing popularity of vegetarianism

> Whatever your reason for going vegetarian ... you are contributing to what is rapidly developing into a mass movement. The 'vegeboom', evidenced by the findings of recent opinion polls, is definitely upon us. – *Green Cuisine*, Spring 1986

---

vegelate *noun* a word coined in the European Parliament to describe British chocolate, which is at present banned on the continent because of the vegetable fats it contains, but will be able to be sold in future if it is called something other than 'chocolate'

> The report didn't actually suggest 'Vegelate' though this was one of the depressing coinages that the debate produced. – *Daily Telegraph*, 23 May 1986

---

vegucate *verb, informal* to teach about vegetarianism (eg about cooking vegetarian meals)

> To help you tackle the problem of vegucating meat eaters, we turned to the stars ... to find out how they react when faced with the question '*why* are you a vegetarian?' – *Green Cuisine*, Spring 1986

---

vegucation *noun, informal* education about vegetarianism

> Grab the opportunity while you can, and try a little 'vegucation'. You never know – one cold bean bonanza could mean one more convert to the Glorious Greens! – *Green Cuisine*, Spring 1986

---

vendozoan *noun* any of a kingdom (Vendozoa) of extinct aquatic animals with highly flattened bodies and no skeleton

> Adolf Scilacher of Tübingen believes that a set of impressions in Australian marine sandstones were made about two billion years ago by an organism so unusual it deserves to fall into a sixth animal kingdom. He calls it Vendozoa. These creatures measured a metre across, and ... were water-filled bags that looked like quilted air-mattresses. – *New Scientist*, 5 June 1986

---

videosomatography *noun* a technique used in industrial engineering to design or improve the man-machine interface, based on an analysis of video pictures which can be manipulated on a screen to create a representation of the workplace under investigation

> Videosomatography is a technique used for the analysis and design of the man-machine interface. ... [The book] shows how the method can be used to check and improve such aspects as task sequencing, positioning of machine controls, and materials layout/flow. – *Financial Times*, 10 Feb. 1986

---

villagization *or* **villagisation** *or* **villageization** *or* **villageisation** *noun* the forcible resettlement of a population in newly-built villages

> The Ethiopian government chose Harerge as the first province to undergo their new policy of 'villagisation'. (Villagisation is entirely separate from the resettlement of 1.5 million Ethiopian people from the north, where lands are suffering severe erosion, to the south of the country.) – *Geographical Magazine*, May 1986
>
> Earlier this month no fewer than 14 members of the European Parliament expressed grave concern about the so-called 'villagisation' programme being conducted with brutality by the Ethiopian government. – *Daily Telegraph*, 24 June 1986

► Neither the concept nor the word is strictly new. Villagization schemes have been practised in African countries for over 20 years – particularly in Tanzania, where over three-quarters of the population was subjected to villagization in the late 1960s. However, the word has come to new prominence, and has acquired new connotations, because of events in Ethiopia. The country's leader, Col. Mengistu, has launched a villagization programme which, according to several western commentators, seems aimed less at establishing self-sufficient communities than at confining secessionists and dissidents. The scheme has led to a massive exodus of refugees into Somalia, has transformed rural society, and has greatly altered the physical appearance of the landscape in the easternmost Ethiopian province of Harerge.

The traditional arrangement of such communities had been in a number of homesteads of about 1–5 hectares and a few mud huts. The government felt that these were uneconomical to support and to administer from educational and health standpoints. They also wished to stimulate greater

community spirit and felt that a village-based society would make this easier.
More than 3 million people (in a province of population 3.5 million) have been rehoused in this way and the homesteads have been renamed *ghost steads.*

---

violent disorder *noun* the crime of being a member of a group of three or more who uses or threatens violence in a way which would cause a person of reasonable firmness present at the scene to fear for his or her personal safety

> The [Public Order] Bill does three important things. Firstly, it gathers together and redefines the old common law offences of riot, unlawful assembly (now to be called violent disorder) and affray. - *New Statesman*, 20 June 1986

---

virustasis *noun* inhibition of the growth and replication of viruses without their destruction

> In each patient, the rate of viral replication and the activity of reverse transcriptase slowed down. However, there was no significant change in immunological parameters. This observation suggests that virustasis - inhibiting or slowing down the growth and replication of the virus - by itself may not be therapeutic at the late stage of disease. - *New Scientist*, 2 Jan. 1986

---

visor *noun* a hood for racehorses, similar to blinkers in which the cowls have holes cut in them permitting limited side or rear vision

> Greville Starkey ... won the Ladas Maiden Stakes on Tez Shikari. This colt, wearing a visor today, was ending a frustrating sequence of five seconds. - *Daily Telegraph*, 27 Aug. 1986

► Visors have become popular for use on horses which run better with some, but restricted, side vision. They were first seen in British racing in 1984 on introduction from the USA where they have been worn for a number of years. They are to be found on flat-racing and National Hunt runners.
They are covered by (Rule 147 of) the Rules of Racing. These require them to be specified to the Overnight Declarations office when declarations to run/not to run are made.
They are distinguished from a *hood* which has ear covers but no eye cowls. An *eyeshield* is different in that it has one eye completely covered by a shield.

VLSI *noun* very large scale integration: the process or technology used in the fabrication of electronic circuitry that allows a high packing density of logic elements

> The T414 is a chip made by techniques of very large scale integration (VLSI). VLSI condenses the equivalent of 200000

transistors into a space just under 9 millimetres square on the new microprocessor. - *New Scientist*, 20 March 1986

Most of the improvements [in computer hardware] result from improved technology in packing the components ever tighter on the chips with the advent of VLSI - very large scale integration. - *Daily Telegraph*, 16 June 1986

---

voluntarization *or* **voluntarisation** *noun* the transfer of control of welfare services (eg children's homes and residential centres for the handicapped) from the public sector to voluntary organizations

As publicly-provided social services are squeezed between rising need and static resources, voluntary charities mop up surplus demand. ... 'Voluntarisation' is fast becoming the acceptable face of privatisation in Britain's social services. - *Economist*, 4 Jan. 1986

---

wage economy *noun* an economic system in which all of an employee's pay consists of a fixed wage - compare SHARE ECONOMY

---

wagon and drag *noun* a tractor unit with a three-decked trailer, designed to transport cars by road

Road transport over long distances has recently become more competitive with the advent of the so-called 'wagon and drag'. - *Modern Railways*, April 1985

---

wapping *noun, Bahamian slang* the act or practice of smoking CRACK

Everyone in Nassau knows crack-users. A newspaper editor told me she had to fire her entire printing staff for smoking crack at work (oddly enough, the local slang for crack smoking is 'wapping'). - *Listener*, 18 Sept. 1986

Wappnik *noun, British informal* a journalist employed by News International who has refused to cross the print unions' picket line to work at the company's new plant in Wapping

The Wappniks are treated with respect and sympathy by other journalists. - *UK Press Gazette*, 19 May 1986

► A blend of *Wapp*ing and refuse*nik*.
Wapping is the heavily fortified plant of the News International group in East London. Production of *The Times*, *The Sunday Times*, and the group's

less cerebral newspapers was moved there early in 1986. The site has been the scene of demonstrations involving formidable picket lines and a massive police presence throughout the year (particularly on Saturday nights when *The Sunday Times* has been driven out for distribution).

---

warnography *noun* films or other material depicting war or violence in a glorifying or chauvinistic manner capable of arousing feelings of aggression or xenophobia

> Paris's well-earned reputation as Europe's most sophisticated film-going city took a knock last week when thousands queued for hours in the rain to see Rocky IV. ... The fascination with anti-Soviet 'warnography' is only the most garish display of a gradually evolving phenomenon.
> - *Guardian*, 11 Feb. 1986

> In the wake of the Soviet Union's campaign against the Anti-Soviet 'war-nography' of American films such as Rambo and Rocky IV, a major US television network is in trouble with the Reagan Administration for 'capitulation to bullying' by Moscow. - *Guardian*, 13 Jan. 1986

► Pun on *pornography*. The fashion for films glorifying (particularly American) patriotic escapades in war are seen by many as an unattractive expression of the Reagan administration's robust position in foreign affairs. As with pornography, warnography is alleged to give rise to socially undesirable practices. As *Rambo*: *First Blood Part II* toured British cinemas during the early months of 1986 many hideous stories of savage use of the crossbow were reported. (Rambo made liberal use of the crossbow amongst other weapons in his bizarre arsenal.) The RSPCA had many accounts of animals being shot with the weapon, sometimes in particularly gruesome fashion. There were several incidents of robbery supported by threats with crossbows.

---

war-porn *noun* WARNOGRAPHY

> In America ... this sort of movie is now called war-porn and some brave soul has assessed the body count in Cobra as 530. - *Hampstead and Highgate Express*, 8 Aug. 1986

---

watchpoodle *noun* a person or organization who is supposed to guard against waste, theft, or undesirable practices, but who has little power to act; a toothless watchdog

> Suspend judgment ... on the way it [the British government] has turned public monopolies into private ones at British Telecom and soon British Gas, with only watchpoodle regulators to safeguard the public. - *Economist*, 15 March 1986

► Comic and probably nonce imitation of *watchdog*.
The proliferation of (often self-appointed) monitoring bodies makes this highly relevant.

It is based on the (slightly unreasonable) caricature of a poodle as an inconsequential dog of no ferocity and limited practical value. Many redoubtable poodles have given the lie to this patronizing stereotype, such as Prince Rupert of the Rhine's Boy, killed at the battle of Marston Moor in 1644.

---

weakly interacting massive particle *noun* (*abbreviation* **WIMP**) a hypothetical elementary particle with a mass about 5 times that of a proton

> These are the particles sometimes referred to as 'cold, dark matter'; Faulkner prefers the term 'weakly interacting massive particles', or WIMPS, because they are thought to interact with other particles only through the weak nuclear interaction and gravity. ... If these ideas do stand up to closer scrutiny, and the WIMP model gains credence it will involve rewriting at least the details of our understanding of stellar structure, since every star in the Galaxy should be affected, to some degree, by a build up of WIMPS in its interior. The prospect is daunting, but suggests that many old problems in stellar astrophysics may need reworking. – *New Scientist*, 24 July 1986

> And particle physicists, struggling to piece together a unified theory of the forces of nature, were beginning to favour a theory called supersymmetry, or Susy, which requires the existence of many more 'fundamental' particles than the ones that had yet been detected in laboratories on Earth. ... He checked the calculations, and found that the 'new' Susy particles, fashionable in both particle physics and cosmology, exactly fitted their description of Wimps! – *Guardian*, 1 Aug. 1986

---

welfare shop *noun* an establishment run by a British local authority where advice is given to people receiving supplementary benefit on how they can claim grants for purchasing household items considered essential (eg bedding and cooking utensils)

> In recent months, 'welfare shops' have been set up in many areas of London and other big cities throughout Britain. ... The cost of the claims for the single payments has been shooting up from £45 million in 1981 to £308 million last year. – *Daily Telegraph*, 21 July 1986

Westlandgate *noun* the political scandal in Britain in January 1986 caused by events surrounding the sale of the Westland helicopter company

> 'Westlandgate' ... may or may not be over. But the time to start learning the lessons of the affair is now. – *Business*, March 1986

► The controversy over the ailing Westland firm centred on whether it should be sold to a European consortium, or to the USA-Italian grouping of Sikorsky-Fiat. The Defence Secretary, Michael Heseltine, supported the

Europeans; the Trade Secretary, Leon Brittan, took the opposite view. After simmering during the closing months of 1985, the row erupted on 6 January 1986 when a private letter written by the Solicitor-General, strongly critical of Heseltine, was leaked to the press by the office of the Department of Trade and Industry. On 9 January, Heseltine resigned. Fifteen days later, Brittan was forced to resign, being held responsible for a deliberate attempt to discredit Heseltine. In February shareholders of Westland voted to accept the Sikorsky-Fiat bid.
The suffix *-gate*, once so fashionable but apparently now moribund, made an interesting comeback here. After the *Watergate* scandal in the USA in 1973, almost every political scandal was dubbed *-gate*. The vogue was never as strong in Britain as in the USA, and in any case was waning in the 1980s.

---

whakapohane *noun* exhibiting one's naked buttocks as a Maori insult or gesture of protest

> Maori activists tend to perform what is known as the Whakapohane insult to royal guests. This involves the lifting of a grass skirt by men wearing no under-garments. – *Daily Telegraph*, 27 Feb. 1986

> The dropping of pants and baring of buttocks is a recognised Maori insult known as whakapohane, and has been described by one expert in local customs as: 'the ultimate culturally sanctioned Maori way of displaying opprobrium.' – *Daily Telegraph*, 24 Feb. 1986

► The Queen was subjected to a tediously large number of these protests during her visit to New Zealand in February 1986. These were the efforts of Maori rights activists who have been particularly vociferous during the year, usually in more articulate forms of expression. The events gave rise to a *Private Eye* cartoon showing a member of the Royal Household apologizing to Her Majesty for yet another 'bum scare'. The custom is ancient and widespread in Oceania. When Captain James Cook visited the island of Tanna in the New Hebrides in 1774, he reported that 'one fellow shewed us his back side in such a manner that it was not necessary to have an interpreter'. The Maori word *whakapohane* or *whakapōhanehane* means 'to act in a ridiculous or excited manner' as well as 'to expose the person' (the prefix *whaka-*, of vague meaning, is so common in Maori that most dictionaries ignore it for the purposes of alphabetization).
This offensive salutation is not unknown in the United Kingdom, where it is generally known by the name of *mooning*. In the summer of 1980 the Boomtown Rats pop group were accused of greeting a bus full of old women in this way in a north of England lay-by. Some young men from Coventry were sentenced to prison in Greece during the summer of 1986 for performing such a gesture to the Greek flag.

---

wheelie bin *or* **wheely bin** *or* **wheeley bin** *noun* a large wheeled dustbin, provided to ratepayers by some local authorities in Britain in an attempt to simplify the rubbish collection system

> The row is part of the great 'wheeley bin' controversy which

has affected large parts of Berkshire as councils try to cut back the cost of refuse collections. - *Daily Telegraph*, 5 August 1986

► Various councils have introduced them, for example Winchester District Council which covers substantial areas of rural Hampshire. In such places, where houses may be well set back from the dustcart's route, it simplifies moving rubbish to the appointed convenient collecting-place. The bin is kept at the back of the house during the week and wheeled out on the relevant day.
Convenient and economical in the main, the bins are frequently very large (5ft tall) and thus a problem to the old or infirm.

---

white knight *noun* someone who comes to the rescue of a person or organization; *especially* a person or company that finances a company to save it from an unwelcome takeover

Mr Pickens ... appeared on the scene in the unlikely role of a 'white knight' whose $800m offer was gratefully accepted by Pioneer's board. - *Financial Times*, 25 March 1986

The Country Gentleman's Association has found a White Knight to counter the unwanted bid from Mr Tony Cole's Bestwood group. - *Guardian*, 29 March 1986

► The metaphor here is a medieval one: the chivalrous pure-hearted knight galloping up to save a damsel in distress.
The phenomenon has become more significant as potential takeovers have produced inappropriate and unwelcome suitors.

---

wild card *noun* a facility for searching data held on computer files, which provides user-friendly access to all possible sources of the information required via a single character or character string

'Search and replace' enables users to change a specified word or phrase with an alternative. Some facilities are cleverer and can disregard upper and lower case, or permit the use of a 'wildcard' to permit variations of a word. - *Daily Telegraph*, 30 June 1986

► It is derived from the poker term for a particular card which may by common consent stand for any denomination convenient to its user. A blank at Scrabble has the same function, albeit permanently.

WIMP *noun* WEAKLY INTERACTING MASSIVE PARTICLE

► Neither this nor the following entry have any connection with *wimp*, the vogue term for a weak or ineffectual person.

WIMPS *or* **wimps** *noun* Windows/Icons/Mouse/Pointer *or* Pointing *or* Pull-down Menu: user-friendly devices built into computers to facilitate entry into and use of the programs

WIMPS is a portmanteau term for the new breed of 'user-friendly' displays using Windows, Icons, and Mouse-pointing.

They use graphic representations of the common tasks, 'icons', and you use a mouse to 'point' the cursor at the relevant icon. – *Daily Telegraph*, 14 April 1986

---

wind farm *or* **windmill farm** *noun* an array of windmills (wind turbines) for generating electric power

Announcement of the project coincided with the company's disclosure that it has sold a 25Mw wind farm in California to a big US institutional investor for $48m. – *Financial Times*, 17 Jan. 1986

A number of individual windmills and windmill farms or arrays of mills, are contributing to the local electric-power system in several countries. – *Scientific American*, June 1986

---

[1]**window** *noun* a rectangular area on a display screen inside which part of an image or file is displayed (e g when two or more programs are running or when a POP-UP menu is revealed). Windows can be any size up to that of the screen, and more than one window can be displayed at once.

Taxi has a maximum of two windows which cannot be resized by the user. – *Personal Computer World*, Feb. 1986

► Here is one of many attempts by the computer industry to be friendly to the user. It is a particularly important attempt. In the early days of such technology only one image could be seen at a time, thus making comparisons difficult or impossible. This development has eased things during the last year or two.

---

[2]**window** *verb* to process (stored data of a large image in a computer) so that a part can be displayed

---

wingsail *noun* a metallic sail, resembling an aircraft wing, which is computer-controlled to provide thrust and reduce fuel consumption

The first ship to be fitted with a 45ft wingsail, a British invention which may revolutionise world shipping, sailed from Southampton yesterday. – *Daily Telegraph*, 14 June 1986

► This revolutionary device was invented by John Walker, who with his wife struggled for 20 years to get it accepted. At one stage Mrs Walker even went on hunger strike to draw attention to their need for funds to continue development work. In 1986 it looked as though they had finally succeeded: a wingsail was fitted to the cargo vessel *Ashington*, and sea trials proved its fuel-saving qualities. Unfortunately this success came just too late to save Mr Walker's company from liquidation.

Witdoek (*plural* **Witdoeke**) *or* **Witdoekie** *noun* a member of a group of conservative black vigilantes in South Africa who are in conflict with the COMRADES

Residents and community workers claim that the vigilantes, known as the *Witdoeke* after the white armbands they wear, have been supported by the police in their battles against the radicals. - *Daily Telegraph*, 10 June 1986

The vigilantes are known by the Afrikaans word *witdoekies*, because of the white headbands or *doekies* which they wear as identification. - *Economist*, 31 May 1986

► From Afrikaans *wit* = white + *doek* = cloth or scarf.
In fighting between Witdoeke and Comrades in May and June 1986 at least 40 people died and 60,000 were made homeless. This was given as one of the immediate causes of the state of emergency declared in South Africa on 12 June.

---

workerist *noun, British* a hardline advocate of the rights of the proletariat

The Liverpool Militants have, hitherto, had scant support from the rest of Labour's left, many of whom regard them as neanderthal 'workerists' (Labour's latest epithet for unreconstructed class-warriors). - *Economist*, 1 March 1986

---

workfare *noun* a welfare system in which recipients of benefits are required to do unpaid work on behalf of the community

The Government is to consider introducing an American-style 'workfare' scheme in an effort to crack down on hippies living off social security benefits. - *Daily Telegraph*, 6 June 1986

A blast in the *New Republic* shoots down workfare schemes ... and concludes that 'only work works' - meaning that cash benefits should be thrown out altogether, to be replaced by low-wage jobs created by the Government. - *Economist*, 5 July 1986

► Formed by analogy with *welfare.* Workfare schemes are well-established in the USA, and the issue is becoming highly topical in Britain as people come to terms with the inevitability of high unemployment levels.
At the TUC on 2 September 1986, Neil Kinnock promised that a Labour government would create 1 million new jobs. He further stated that he would require the nationalized industries to take back 40,000 employees whose jobs had been deliberately eliminated as part of streamlining policy. The government has produced a number of schemes to create work in a similar way, such as that under the co-ordination of Richard Branson to tidy up the environment.
Nothing on the precise lines of workfare has been seen here yet, however.

---

workie *noun, informal* somone who is in work; an employed person

A colleague in the area tells me of one Middlesbrough estate where children greet the arrival of delivery men ... with the cry: 'Look out - a workie'. - *Daily Telegraph*, 22 May 1986

---

workshadowing *noun* the practice of watching somebody at work in order to gain a greater understanding of different areas of working life

> One of the advantages of work shadowing is that it offers access to occupations such as dentistry which do not lend themselves to work experience because of the skills and knowledge that are required. Work shadowing is also more economical in terms of time. - *TES*, 6 June 1986

> Workshadowing, whereby sixth-formers gain work experience by spending time alongside executives, should be broadened to include teachers, Mr John Butcher, Industry Under-Secretary, said yesterday. - *Daily Telegraph*, 7 Aug. 1986

WORM *noun* write once read many times: an optical disc designed for use with personal computers

> Meanwhile, other optical media can still challenge CD-ROM in its stronghold in the computer industry. CD-ROM is essentially a publishing medium, but 'write once / read many' (times) or WORM discs enable people to save their own data. - *Guardian*, 5 June 1986

---

write-in *noun* a method of organized lobbying or propagandizing by flooding the target with letters on a certain subject

► The formation is modelled on the *sit-ins* which were a form of protest in the late 1960s in universities and other establishments. They were startling, tiresome to the relevant administrations, and therefore quite often effective.
In the 1970s more imaginative variations were devised. There were, for example, *love-ins* and *pray-ins.*
The technique is now generally passé and not effective. Write-ins frequently take the form of orchestrated correspondence to, say, an MP or councillor. It is usually unsuccessful as MPs recognize the same formula being used on every occasion. Its organizers believe that the recipient will be impressed by the sheer weight of the letters: in the main this view is naive.
In the USA, a *write-in* is also 'a vote cast by writing in the name of a candidate'.

WYSIWYG *noun* what you see is what you get: a computer programming principle used especially for outputting data as hard copy

> Logotron has launched a word processor for very young children. ... The program works on the WYSIWYG principle. - *Guardian*, 30 Jan. 1986
> WYSIWYG (pronouced wizzywig) ... is a lie generally speaking but even so what the program will provide is useful. - *Daily Telegraph*, 30 June 1986

WYSIWYGity *noun* the quality of a WYSIWYG program

> There is a high degree of WYSIWYGity. ... This means that

the paper image matches the screen image. - *New Scientist*, 26 June 1986

X400 *noun* a standard for electronic mail and message handling that allows text transfer between different computers

Based on OSI, the X400 standard is being supported by British Telecom for message handling. - *Which Computer*, July 1986

yobbism *noun* the mode of behaviour characteristic of thugs and louts; insensitive and heavy-handed behaviour

I am appalled at the spectre of a yob society growing out of our schools. But I am equally appalled by the yobbism of the Tebbit approach to these problems, and the yobbism of solutions that seek to concentrate resources on so-called centres of excellence for a tiny minority while ignoring the needs of the majority. - *Daily Telegraph*, 10 April 1986

► The word *yob* (originally backslang for *boy*), always derogatory, has produced a good crop of abusive words over a long period, such as *yobbish*, *yobby*, *yobbery*, *yobbo* (even *Sid Yobbo*, a *Private Eye* code for a prominent and controversial journalist and broadcaster of plebeian speech and unsophisticated mien).
Yobbish behaviour is blamed for many social ills and public misconduct by those who like to see more traditional discipline in schools and families. This thinking has been supported by Norman Tebbit, Chairman of the Conservative Party. However, some observers see a contradiction in that Tebbit's own approach and appeal are largely based on a deliberately rough and forthright manner.

yobbocracy *noun* rule by louts and thugs

An undergraduate contemporary of Mr Kilroy-Silk at the London School of Economics, sees it differently; 'I don't think that people actually realise what it's like under the 'yob-bocracy' of Militant in Liverpool. You find you're dealing with people who live by abuse and by venom and by poison.' - *Daily Telegraph*, 1 Aug. 1986

Yuppie Five *noun* the five young financiers involved in YUPPIEGATE

Yuppiegate *noun* the scandal involving five young employees of New York investment banks accused in 1986 of stealing secret information and of insider dealing

> As the London Stock Exchange gears up for its deregulatory Big Bang its practitioners should pause to note that the phrase 'the Yuppie Five' has lately begun appearing in American newspaper headlines. ... In its more ominous manifestation the phrase becomes 'Yuppiegate'. ... The Securities and Exchange Commision (SEC) appears to have caught up with some lite ethics in which the yuppie tag has proved irresistible in the ever-widening insider trading scandals which have been impressing even Wall Street. - *Guardian*, 26 Aug. 1986

► The scandal concerned five young Americans aged between 27 and 23. They were all closely connected socially, three of them living in the same apartment block. They were all well-educated, well-placed in the Wall Street financial establishment, and extremely well-paid.
It was alleged that they stole information about proposed takeovers and traded it with brokers and ARBS.

---

yuppyish *adjective* like a yuppy; successful in a trendy way

> In recent months the activities of the engineering 'yuppies' ... have taught the city that there is more to engineering than metal bashing and bending. But there is nothing yuppyish about the Folkes Group. - *Financial Times*, 22 April 1986

---

zapper *noun* someone who frequently changes from channel to channel in search of an appealing television programme

> The zappers' paradise is at hand! Forget the keypad that lets you just race from one channel to another in search of instant gratification. ... The new technology now promised will give electronic codes to programme types. So set your machine to

quiz shows, news, whatever, and it will hunt them out for you. – *Guardian*, 2 Dec. 1985

---

zeranol *noun* a synthetic hormone, $C_{18}H_{26}O_5$, that causes an increase in the size and weight of skeletal muscle and is artificially implanted into livestock (eg beef cattle) to improve meat production

> The European Commission, which proposed banning all five legal hormones last autumn, admits it was responding to political pressure rather than scientific evidence. An EEC working party cleared the three natural hormones, progesterone, testosterone and oestradial, and has not yet pronounced on the other two, zeranol and trenbolone acetate. – *Financial Times*, 13 Jan. 1986

► The EEC banned the use of growth-promoting hormones on 20 December 1985; Britain's Minister of Agriculture, Michael Jopling, obtained exemption for Britain until 1989.

---

zombie food *noun, informal* decayed or contaminated food that has been made fit for human consumption through IRRADIATION

► From the voodoo name for a corpse reanimated by sorcery, which in turn derives from an African snake deity.

---

zero-grazing = limited promiscuity.